Rockingham County New Hampshire Paupers

by Pauline Johnson Oesterlin

HERITAGE BOOKS
2014

HERITAGE BOOKS

AN IMPRINT OF HERITAGE BOOKS, INC.

Books, CDs, and more—Worldwide

For our listing of thousands of titles see our website
at
www.HeritageBooks.com

Published 2014 by
HERITAGE BOOKS, INC.
Publishing Division
5810 Ruatan Street
Berwyn Heights, Md. 20740

Copyright © 1992 Pauline Johnson Oesterlin

Heritage Books by the author:

Hillsborough County, New Hampshire Court Records, 1772–1799

Hopkinton, New Hampshire Vital Records: Volumes 1 and 2

New Hampshire 1742 Estate List

New Hampshire Marriage Licenses and Intentions, 1709–1961

Rockingham County, New Hampshire Paupers

Surname Guide to Massachusetts Town Histories
Pauline J. Oesterlin and Phyllis O. Longver

International Standard Book Numbers
Paperbound: 978-1-55613-561-3
Clothbound: 978-0-7884-6808-7

Preface

These records were transcribed from Rockingham County Superior Court Records found at the New Hampshire State Archives. All of the people listed here were in a position to be supported by either the county or one of its towns. The entries are arranged alphabetically by last name. There were some instances in which no last name was given, as was the case with many Negroes; in these cases, they are alphabetized by their first names. The entries include the date and source of the support along with the document number. The reader can use this number to find other related documents filed with the Superior Court records at the Archives. These documents can include: warning out records, town records of support, affidavits explaining the reason the applicant required support, descriptions of lineages, vital records, burial records, and medical payments. The number of related documents included in the Superior Court Records for each person can vary.

The original spellings of personal and town names as written in the documents have been retained. Some names were difficult to read; those were transcribed as accurately as possible. At times, a name would appear several different ways on the same document. And some names transcribed correctly will still seem strange by today's standards.

Abbreviations in parentheses are used here when certain information was clearly indicated in the records. They are as follows: (c) child; (alias) the name given was known to be an alias; (m) married; (gc) grandchild; (s) single; (w) widow.

These records are a good source to lost or missing women. Many women had to turn to the towns for support when their husbands would become sick or unable to work or care for the family. One remarkable woman resorted to asking for support in Portsmouth when she could no longer travel. She had left New York for Nova Scotia with her three young children, and could go no further when they reached Portsmouth--they were making the journey on foot! Other interesting stories such as this are included in the Archives records.

This project began in order to provide a listing to keep on record at the Archives. It is being published so that people without convenient access to the New Hampshire Archives can still use the information. Certainly, no work of this type can ever be complete and free of error. I hope that for some of you trying to research your ancestors, this work will at least give you a place to start so that you may find that missing link.

Pauline Oesterlin
January, 1992

Introduction

When New Hampshire was separated from Massachusetts Bay in 1679, Paragraph 40 of its General Laws took notice that the poor were part of the populace:

> That if any person come into any Town within this Province, and be there received & entertained three months; if such person fal sick or lame; He shal be releeved by the Town, where he was so long entertained. But if the Constable of that Town, or any of the Select-men, have given warning to such person within the space of three months, that the Town will not admit of them; If such person shal stand in need of releef, the Town shal supply his necessity; until the President and Councel can dispose of them, as to them shal seem most just & equal." [*Laws of New Hampshire* I, (Concord, 1921), p. 36]

Chapter 6 of the provincial laws of 1686 allowed the towns to levy a tax for supplying the poor and for furnishing almshouses, and in 1687, by Chapter 39, justices of the peace were given responsibility "for the necessary reliefe and maintainance of the Poore in each Towne in such manner as by the Laws and Statutes of England is directed." Chapter 17 of the 1688 laws appears to be the first time that the phrase "overseer of the poor" was used, and it assigned that title and its duties to the selectmen who in effect already had them.

In the matter of taking care of the poor in New Hampshire, little changed for the next century. Acts of the legislature during the Revolution and under the state constitution of 1784 simply confirmed earlier acts which made towns responsible for any poor that the officers had failed to warn out of town within ninety days of the beginning of their dependence on the town. By 1807, the state allowed courts to levy a fine of between fifty and three hundred dollars as penalty for bringing a known pauper into the state.

By 1817, the five counties [Rockingham, Hillsborough, Strafford, Cheshire, and Grafton] were given some responsibility for paupers and their share of that responsibility increased with time. Two laws enacted on December 16, 1828 addressed the settlement of paupers and the maintenance of the poor, allowing the selectmen or overseers to contract out the work of the poor, including children, to assist the town in paying for their upkeep.

It must be made clear that the data that follows has been taken from records at the New Hampshire State Archives, but that this is not a comprehensive listing of all paupers that appear in records at the Archives. There is a separate collection known as "Warnings Out of Town" which is indexed by name on index cards, but those names are not included here.

Nor does this include paupers from counties other than Rocking-ham, even though many of the records for Merrimack, Hillsborough, Strafford, and Sullivan counties are now at the archives. The records for these counties are being processed, but at a very slow pace, and are not expected to be accessible for several years. For records of other counties [New Hampshire currently has ten], it is necessary to search at the county courthouse.

For records from towns not listed here, it is advised to search through the town or city clerk directly. Relatively few town records have been deposited with the Archives.

The following list is a valiant attempt by Pauline Oesterlin, a volun-teer using her own time and equipment, to make this information better known and more accessible to all researchers, particularly those who share her love of genealogy. While the Archives staff appreciates her efforts and shares her enthusiasm, it must disclaim any credit or re-sponsibility for the formulation of the following information.

Frank C. Mevers, Director & State Archivist
New Hampshire Division of Records Management & Archives
71 South Fruit Street
Concord, New Hampshire 03801
November 11, 1991

We Elvin Rand and John Philbrick Selectmen of the town of Rye certify, and depose
that it appears by the records of said town
that Joseph Hall was supported or assisted
by said town from the year 1796 to the year
1801 inclusive, the time of his death as appears
by the records aforesaid for funeral expenses—
that the widow Hall was supported or
relieved by said town in the years 1805, 1806 & 1809.
That Hannah Hall whom we always understood
was a daughter of the aforenamed Joseph Hall
was supported by the said town of Rye from
the year 1797 to the year 1839 the time of her death.
that it does not appear from said records that
Sarah Mace was ever taxed in said town.—
That Molly Saunders or Mary Saunders as
she is sometimes styled on the records has
been supported by said town of Rye from the
year 1808 to the present time, that prior
to the year 1809 as we understand the
records she was supported or assisted by
said town as "Mrs. Braggs child" in 1805 as
"John Bragg's child" in 1806 as "Braggs child" in 1807
and as "Molly Bragg in 1808 — that John
Braggs funeral charges were paid by said
the widow Bragg
and in 1816 the time of her death as appears
by charges for funeral expenses—

Elvin Rand
John Philbrick

This document is a record of support from Rye

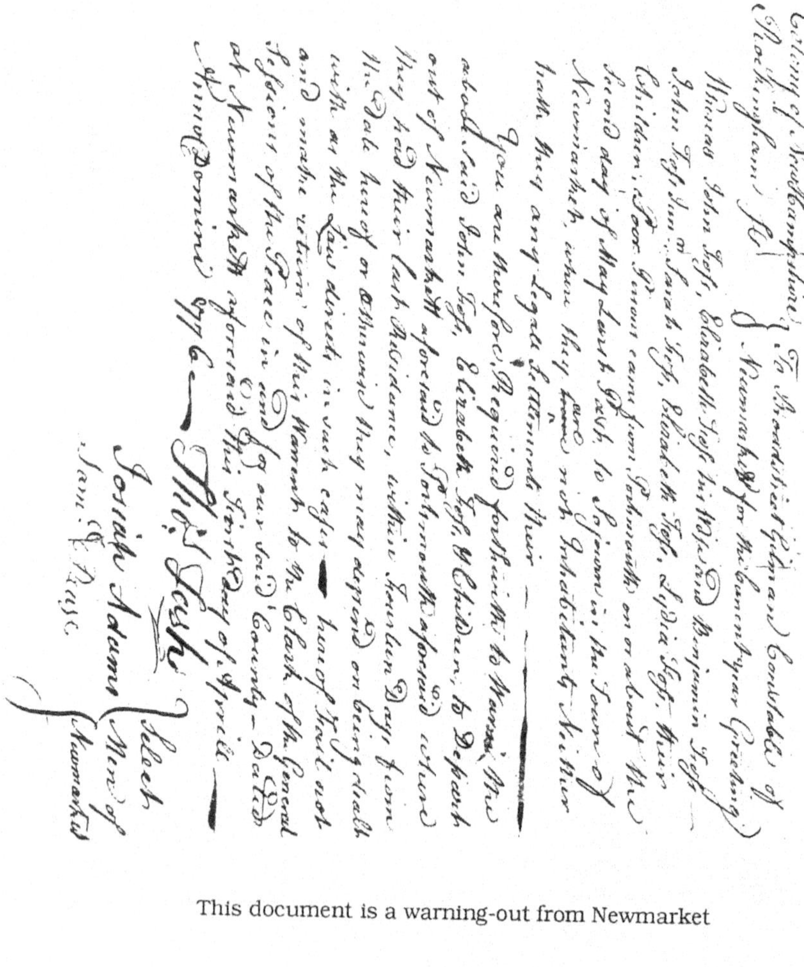

Colony of New Hampshire } To Broadstreet Gilman Constable of
Rockingham ss } Newmarkett for the Current year Greeting
Whereas John Foss, Elizabeth Foss his Wife and Benjamin Foss
John Foss Junr. Sarah Foss, Elizabeth Foss, Lydia Foss, their
Children; Poor Persons came from Portsmouth on or about the
Second day of May Last Past, to Sojourn in the Town of
Newmarket, where they ~~have~~ are not Inhabitants Neither
hath they any Legall Settlements their
You are therefore Required forthwith to Warn the
above said John Foss, Elizabeth Foss, & Children, to Depart
out of Newmarkett aforesaid to Portsmouth aforesaid where
they had their last Residance, within Fourteen Days from
the Date hereof or Otherwise they may depend on being dealt
with as the Law directs in such cases hereof Fail not
and make return of this Warrent to the Clark of the General
Sessions of the Peace in and for our said County – Dated
at Newmarkett aforesaid this Sixth day of Aprill
Anno Domini 1776
Thos. Tash
Josiah Adams } Select Men of Newmarket
Saml. Pease

This document is a warning-out from Newmarket

I, Joanna Todd of thirty one years of age, testify & say, that I was born in Halifax, Nova Scotia, my late husband Thomas Todd was born in Scotland, Europe, I was married to him in Deptford, Europe, I left England thirteen years ago & came to Halifax aforesaid, we left Halifax about four years ago & went to St. Johns New-Brunswick where we lived about two years, we then went to Ellsworth State of Maine, where I lived about 16 months, my husband being at sea, & then went to New-York to my husband, where he was drowned about eight months ago, I left New York about five weeks ago & have travelled on foot to this place with three children one ten years old, one five years & one about eight months old, intending to return to Halifax where my mother & some other connexions are living, I had no means & have been assisted by charity in my travelling to this place & having no place & being very tired & my children so much exhausted that I was taken into the Alms House in this Town. —

Witness
John Grant j

         her
Joanna ✕ Todd
        mark

State of New Hampshire,
Rockingham. Ss.   } Portsmouth June 9th. 1827

Then the above named Joanna Todd personally appeared & made solemn Oath that the foregoing affidavit by her subscribed is true. —

      Before me,   Thomas P. Brown
                          Justice Peace

This is an affidavit, describing the subject's need for support

Rockingham County Paupers

ABBOT Jenney by E Kingston 1793 Doc 13190
ABBOT Mary by Londonderry 1854 Doc 2371
ABBOTT Aaron by Concord 1809 Doc 32876
ABBOTT Aaron by Concord 1812 Doc 34232
ABBOTT Abigail by New Chester 1832 Doc 13399
ABBOTT Andrew by Londonderry 1842 Doc 20107
ABBOTT Andrew by New Chester 1832 Doc 13399
ABBOTT Ann by New Chester 1832 Doc 13399
ABBOTT Benjamin by New Chester 1832 Doc 13399
ABBOTT Benjamin by Londonderry 1828 Doc 9823
ABBOTT Benjamin by Londonderry 1842 Doc 20107
ABBOTT Betsey by Poplin 1843 Doc 20629 A
ABBOTT Charles by Londonderry 1842 Doc 20424
ABBOTT Charles by Londonderry 1842 Doc 20107
ABBOTT Charles by Londonderry 1843 Doc 21216
ABBOTT Charles by New Chester 1832 Doc 13399
ABBOTT Dolly by Loudon 1793 Doc 13587
ABBOTT George by Exeter 1840 Doc 18856
ABBOTT Horace by Londonderry 1842 Doc 20424
ABBOTT Horace by Londonderry 1846 Doc 22356
ABBOTT Horace (c) by Londonderry 1845 Doc 21835
ABBOTT James by Londonderry 1842 Doc 20107
ABBOTT James by Londonderry 1842 Doc 20424
ABBOTT James by Londonderry 1846 Doc 22356
ABBOTT James by Londonderry 1850 Doc 311
ABBOTT James by Londonderry 1851 Doc 931
ABBOTT James by Londonderry 1852 Doc 1554
ABBOTT James by Londonderry 1853 Doc 2085
ABBOTT James by Londonderry 1854 Doc 2371
ABBOTT James (c) by Londonderry 1843 Doc 21216
ABBOTT Jenny by Hampton 1791 Doc 11910
ABBOTT John by Brentwood 1800 Doc 18692
ABBOTT Joseph by Londonderry 1842 Doc 20424
ABBOTT Joseph by Londonderry 1846 Doc 22356
ABBOTT Joseph by Londonderry 1851 Doc 931
ABBOTT Joseph by Londonderry 1852 Doc 1554
ABBOTT Joseph by Londonderry 1853 Doc 2085
ABBOTT Joseph (c) by Londonderry 1843 Doc 21216
ABBOTT Joseph (c) by Londonderry 1845 Doc 21835
ABBOTT Joseph (c) by Londonderry 1850 Doc 311
ABBOTT Joseph by Poplin 1843 Doc 20629 A
ABBOTT Margaret by Londonderry 1842 Doc 20424

ABBOTT Margaret (c) by Londonderry 1843 Doc 21216
ABBOTT Mary by Londonderry 1842 Doc 20424
ABBOTT Mary by Londonderry 1843 Doc 21216
ABBOTT Mary by Londonderry 1845 Doc 21835
ABBOTT Mary by Londonderry 1850 Doc 311
ABBOTT Mary by Londonderry 1851 Doc 931
ABBOTT Mary by Londonderry 1852 Doc 1554
ABBOTT Mary by Londonderry 1853 Doc 2085
ABBOTT Mary by New Chester 1832 Doc 13399
ABBOTT Mary (c) by New Chester 1832 Doc 13399
ABBOTT Maryette (c) by Londonderry 1845 Doc 21835
ABBOTT Molly by Exeter 1792 Doc 12882
ABBOTT Molly by Loudon 1790 Doc 11611
ABBOTT Mrs George J by Exeter 1840 Doc 18856
ABBOTT Sarah Ann by Portsmouth 1836 Doc 16214
ABBOTT Sarah Ann by Portsmouth 1836 Doc 16216
ABBOTT Theresa (c) by Londonderry 1843 Doc 21216
ABBOTT William by New Chester 1832 Doc 13399
ABIT Abigail by Raymond 1792 Doc 12882
ABIT Ephraim (c) by Raymond 1792 Doc 12882
ABIT Hannah (c) by Raymond 1792 Doc 12882
ABIT Joshua by Raymond 1792 Doc 12882
ABIT Joshua (c) by Raymond 1792 Doc 12882
ABIT Polly (c) by Raymond 1792 Doc 12882
ADALINE Mary by Brentwood 1844 Doc 21216
ADAMS Ebenezer Jr by Barnstead 1827 Doc 8077
ADAMS Elizabeth (c) by Newington 1786 Doc 9466
ADAMS Ezekiel (c) by Newington 1786 Doc 9466
ADAMS Ezekiel Gill by Newington 1786 Doc 9466
ADAMS Favor by Windham 1810 Doc 33660
ADAMS John by Greenland 1773 Doc 2095
ADAMS Mary by Newington 1786 Doc 9466
ADAMS Molley (c) by Newington 1786 Doc 9466
ADAMS Nancy (c) by Newington 1786 Doc 9466
ADAMS Samuel (Negro) by Portsmouth 1843 Doc 20629
ADAMS Sarah by Portsmouth 1843 Doc 20629
ADAMS William (Negro) by Portsmouth 1843 Doc 20629
ADAMS William by Londonderry 1851 Doc 931
ADAMS William by Londonderry 1852 Doc 1554
ADAMS William (c) by Newington 1786 Doc 9466
ADJUTANT George by Rockingham County 1825 Doc 6505
ADJUTANT Mary by Boscawen 1817 Doc 44178
ADJUTANT Mary by Exeter 1817 Doc 44178
AETEN Abiel by Salem 1778 Doc 3981
AETEN Joanna by Salem 1778 Doc 3981
AIKEN Sally by Londonderry 1817 Doc 45992
AINS Polly by Portsmouth 1846 Doc 22356
AKSKINGTON Susan by Portsmouth 1853 Doc 2086
ALARD Elizabeth by Newington 1842 Doc 20107
ALDRICH Sally by Center Harbor 1817 Doc 44178
ALERD Elizabeth by Newington 1843 Doc 20629
ALEXANDER Sarah by Londonderry 1844 Doc 21503

2

ALLAN Polly Huse by Portsmouth 1817 Doc 44178
ALLARD Elizabeth by Londonderry 1842 Doc 20424
ALLEN Abiel by Deerfield 1801 Doc 19665
ALLEN Alonozo (c) by Newmarket 1835 Doc 16214
ALLEN Alonozo (c) by Newmarket 1836 Doc 16214
ALLEN Anna by Northwood 1793 Doc 13190
ALLEN Anna (c) by Northwood 1793 Doc 13190
ALLEN Deborah by Lee 1835 Doc 15557
ALLEN Elizabeth by Newmarket 1789 Doc 10911
ALLEN Elizabeth by Portsmouth 1808 Doc 29235
ALLEN Ellira by Rye 1813 Doc 36435
ALLEN Harriet (c) by Newmarket 1835 Doc 16214
ALLEN Harriet (c) by Newmarket 1836 Doc 16214
ALLEN Henry by Northwood 1793 Doc 13190
ALLEN Josiah by Deerfield 1845 Doc 21835
ALLEN Josiah by Deerfield 1846 Doc 22356
ALLEN Josiah by Deerfield 1850 Doc 311
ALLEN Josiah by Deerfield 1851 Doc 931
ALLEN Josiah by Deerfield 1852 Doc 1554
ALLEN Josiah by Epping 1846 Doc 22356
ALLEN Lyeday (c) by Portsmouth 1808 Doc 29235
ALLEN Margaret by Exeter 1836 Doc 16931
ALLEN Mary by Newmarket 1835 Doc 16214
ALLEN Mary by Newmarket 1836 Doc 16214
ALLEN Mary (c) by Newmarket 1835 Doc 16214
ALLEN Sarah by Hampton Falls 1785 Doc 8391
ALLIN Polly by Deerfield 1793 Doc 13587
ALLLEN Josiah by Deerfield 1818 Doc 45992
ANDERSON Chaney (c) by Portsmouth 1843 Doc 20629
ANDERSON John by Portsmouth 1830 Doc 12197
ANDERSON John by Portsmouth 1843 Doc 20629
ANDERSON John by Portsmouth 1846 Doc 22356
ANDERSON John by Portsmouth 1851 Doc 931
ANDERSON John (Negro) by Portsmouth 1851 Doc 311
ANDERSON John (Negro) by Portsmouth 1852 Doc 1554
ANDERSON Lydia by Portsmouth 1843 Doc 20629
ANDERSON Mary Ann by Portsmouth 1835 Doc 15900
ANDERSON Mary Ann by Portsmouth 1836 Doc 16214
ANDREW Atarah by Poplin 1843 Doc 20629
ANDREWS Elizabeth by Londonderry 1840 Doc 19510
ANDREWS Elizabeth by Londonderry 1843 Doc 21216
ANDREWS Elizabeth (c) by Londonderry 1840 Doc 18856
ANDREWS Ezra by Londonderry 1840 Doc 18856
ANDREWS Ezra by Londonderry 1840 Doc 18856
ANDREWS June by Londonderry 1840 Doc 18856
ANDREWS June by Londonderry 1840 Doc 18856
ANDREWS Lisburne by Pembroke 1796 Doc 15733
ANDREWS Lucy by Londonderry 1836 Doc 16931
ANDREWS Mary by Londonderry 1839 Doc 18267
ANDREWS Mary by Londonderry 1840 Doc 19510
ANDREWS Mary by Londonderry 1842 Doc 20424
ANDREWS Mary (c) by Londonderry 1840 Doc 18856

3

ANDREWS Nat (c) by Pembroke 1796 Doc 15733
ANDREWS Rosanna by Londonderry 1836 Doc 16931
ANDREWS Rosanna by Londonderry 1840 Doc 19510
ANDREWS Rosanna by Londonderry 1842 Doc 20424
ANDREWS Rosanna by Londonderry 1843 Doc 21216
ANDREWS Rosanna (c) by Londonderry 1840 Doc 18856
ANDREWS Rosanna (c) by Londonderry 1845 Doc 21835
ANDREWS Salley by Pembroke 1796 Doc 15733
ANDREWS Salley (c) by Pembroke 1796 Doc 15733
ANDREWS Vincent (c) by Londonderry 1840 Doc 18856
ANDROSE Edward by Portsmouth 1791 Doc 12228
ANESWORTH Almond E by Portsmouth 1836 Doc 16214
ANKLER John by Portsmouth 1812 Doc 35052
ANNIS Hannah by Windham 1775 Doc 3514
ARCHBIALD Abigail by Goffstown 1838 Doc 18543
ARCHBIALD Aurilla by Goffstown 1838 Doc 18543
ARCHIBALD Simon by Derry 1845 Doc 21835
AREWINE John by Sandown 1788 Doc 10229
AREWINE Mary by Sandown 1788 Doc 10229
ARLEN Nancy by Barrington 1842 Doc 20424
ARM Edward by Exeter 1782 Doc 4882
ARMSTRONG John by S Hampton 1851 Doc 931
ARMSTRONG John by S Hampton 1852 Doc 1554
ARMSTRONG John by S Hampton 1853 Doc 2085
ARMSTRONG John A by Rockingham County 1853 Doc 2371
ARNOLD Joseph by Portsmouth 1852 Doc 1554
ASHINGTON Susan by Portsmouth 1851 Doc 931
ASHINGTON Susan by Portsmouth 1851 Doc 932
ASHINGTON Susan by Portsmouth 1852 Doc 1554
ASHINGTON Susan by Portsmouth 1852 Doc 1555
ASHINTON Susan (Negro) by Portsmouth 1851 Doc 311
ATKINSON Rose by Stratham 1802 Doc 21391
ATKINSON Tho by Portsmouth 1840 Doc 18856
ATWOOD Sarah by Plaistow 1793 Doc 14018
AUSTIN Aaron by Concord 1809 Doc 31571
AUSTIN Reuben by Stratham 1774 Doc 2656
AUSTIN Samuel by Derry 1850 Doc 311
AVERY Darkus by Brentwood 1783 Doc 5923
AVERY Olive by Portsmouth 1832 Doc 13399
AVERY Peter by Brentwood 1783 Doc 5923
AVERY Peter (Negro) by Kingston 1784 Doc 7804
AYER Mary E by Portsmouth 1836 Doc 16214
AYER Mary E by Portsmouth 1836 Doc 16216
AYERS Hannah by Strafford 1817 Doc 44178
AYERS Ketuah by Newington 1772 Doc 731
AYERS Lydia by Newington 1772 Doc 731
AYERS Mary by Newington 1772 Doc 731
AYERS Mehitible by Hampton 1799 Doc 18299
AYERS Olive by Newington 1772 Doc 731
AYERS Olla by Newmarket 1790 Doc 11611
AYERS Polly by Portsmouth 1851 Doc 311
AYERS Polly by Portsmouth 1851 Doc 931

AYERS Polly by Portsmouth 1843 Doc 20629
AYERS Samuel by Newmarket 1790 Doc 11611
AYERS Sarah by Newington 1772 Doc 731
AYERS Thomas by Newington 1772 Doc 731
BACHELDER Betsy by Allenstown 1842 Doc 20425
BACHELDER Lucy Jane (c) by Allenstown 1842 Doc 20425
BACHELDER Moses by Portsmouth 1842 Doc 20107
BACHELOR William by E Kingston 1822 Doc 2912
BADGER Ruth by Newtown 1817 Doc 44178
BAGLEY Charles by Newton 1853 Doc 2085
BAGLEY James by Chester 1850 Doc 311
BAGLEY John by Campton 1835 Doc 15557
BAGLEY Lafayette (c) by Campton 1835 Doc 15557
BAGLEY Mary Ann by Campton 1835 Doc 15557
BAGLEY Orlando by Kingston 1795 Doc 15018
BAGLEY Polly by Kensington 1792 Doc 13190
BAGLEY Polly by Chester 1850 Doc 311
BAGLEY Sarah by Campton 1835 Doc 15557
BAGLEY Sarah by Candia 1846 Doc 22356
BAGLEY Sarah by Kensington 1793 Doc 13587
BAGLEY Sarah by Candia 1843 Doc 20928
BAGLEY Sarah (w) by Candia 1845 Doc 21835
BAGLEY Timothy by Candia 1843 Doc 20928
BAILEY Elizabeth by Salem 1779 Doc 4241
BAILEY Nathaniel by Portsmouth 1842 Doc 20107
BAILEY Olive A by Canterbury 1861 Doc 6144
BAILEY Phinchias by Salem 1779 Doc 4241
BAILEY Sewell by Canterbury 1861 Doc 6144
BAILEY William by Portsmouth 1851 Doc 931
BAILEY William by Portsmouth 1851 Doc 311
BAILEY William by Salem 1779 Doc 4241
BAKER Hannah by Poplin 1831 Doc 13399
BAKER Hannah by Sandown 1838 Doc 17575
BAKER James by Sandown 1833 Doc 14122
BAKER Jonathan by Kingston 1791 Doc 12531
BAKER Mary Ann by Portsmouth 1833 Doc 14122
BALL Betsey by Chester 1858 Doc 4985
BALLARD Jeremiah by Hampton 1773 Doc 2095
BALLARD Joseph by Deerfield 1804 Doc 22771
BALTE John by Londonderry 1850 Doc 311
BALTE Margaret by Londonderry 1850 Doc 311
BANCROFT Charles by E Kingston 1850 Doc 311
BANCROFT Ann by Rye 1840 Doc 18856
BANCROFT Ann by Windham 1836 Doc 16214
BANCROFT Anna (Negro) by Windham 1840 Doc 18856
BANCROFT Caleb by Dunbarton 1844 Doc 22592
BANCROFT Charles by E Kingston 1844 Doc 22592
BANCROFT Charles by E Kingston 1846 Doc 22592
BANCROFT Charles by E Kingston 1851 Doc 931
BANCROFT Charles by E Kingston 1853 Doc 2085
BANCROFT Charles by E Kingston 1852 Doc 1554
BANCROFT Charles by E Rochester 1853 Doc 2371

BANCROFT Charlotte by Windham 1836 Doc 16214
BANCROFT Charlotte by Windham 1836 Doc 16214
BANCROFT James by E Kingston 1846 Doc 22592
BANCROFT Jeremiah by Windham 1836 Doc 16214
BANCROFT John by Dunbarton 1844 Doc 22592
BANCROFT Lucinda by Windham 1836 Doc 16214
BANCROFT Lucinda by Windham 1836 Doc 16214
BANCROFT Olive by Londonderry 1846 Doc 22356
BANCROFT Olive by Londonderry 1842 Doc 20424
BANCROFT Olive by Londonderry 1843 Doc 21216
BANCROFT Olive by Londonderry 1836 Doc 16931
BANCROFT Olive by Londonderry 1833 Doc 14119
BANCROFT Olive by Londonderry 1840 Doc 19510
BANCROFT Olive (w) by Londonderry 1840 Doc 18856
BANCROFT Savory by Londonderry 1846 Doc 22356
BANCROFT Savory by Londonderry 1850 Doc 311
BANCROFT Savory by Londonderry 1854 Doc 2371
BANCROFT Savory by Londonderry 1833 Doc 14119
BANCROFT Savory by ? 1853 Doc 2085
BARBER Levi by Portsmouth 1832 Doc 13755
BARCKLAY Anne by Portsmouth 1851 Doc 311
BARKER Abgail (w) by Rye 1792 Doc 13587
BARKER Abigal by Greenland 1792 Doc 13190
BARKER Abigail by Nottingham 1795 Doc 14879
BARKER Alice by Exeter 1831 Doc 13399
BARKER Betsey by Exeter 1844 Doc 20629 A
BARKER Elenor by Stratham 1795 Doc 15359
BARKER Josiah G by Exeter 1844 Doc 20629 A
BARKER Levi by Portsmouth 1832 Doc 13754
BARKER Philip by N Hampton 1792 Doc 12882
BARKER Philip by N Hampton 1794 Doc 14018
BARKER Samuel by Greenland 1792 Doc 13190
BARKER Samuel by Hampton 1843 Doc 20629
BARKER Sarah by Greenland 1791 Doc 11910
BARKER Susannah by Greenland 1792 Doc 13190
BARKLEY Anne E by Portsmouth 1851 Doc 931
BARNARD Mary Ann by Exeter 1830 Doc 12682
BARNARD Andrew by Portsmouth 1836 Doc 16214
BARNARD Mary Ann by Exeter 1830 Doc 12197
BARNES Betsey by Deerfield 1852 Doc 1554
BARNET Betsey (c) by Windham 1789 Doc 17890
BARNET Isabel by Windham 1789 Doc 17890
BARNET John by Windham 1789 Doc 17890
BARNET John (c) by Windham 1789 Doc 11310
BARNET Polly Janney (c) by Windham 1789 Doc 17890
BARNET Rebecca (c) by Windham 1789 Doc 11310
BARNET Susannah (c) by Windham 1789 Doc 17890
BARNS Sarah by Epping 1778 Doc 4043
BARONON John by Portsmouth 1789 Doc 10911
BARRASS Rufus by Deerfield 1851 Doc 932
BARRETT Moses by Derry 1830 Doc 11981
BARRETT Moses by Derry 1830 Doc 20107

BARRETT Rachael by Derry 1830 Doc 20107
BARRETT Rachael by Derry 1830 Doc 11981
BARRETTE William by Portsmouth 1852 Doc 1555
BARRETTE William by Portsmouth 1852 Doc 1554
BARREY William by Raymond 1850 Doc 931
BARRY Elizabeth by Exeter 1840 Doc 19510
BARRY Margaret by Portsmouth 1846 Doc 22356
BARRY Thomas by Portsmouth 1845 Doc 22356
BARRY Thomas by Portsmouth 1842 Doc 20424
BARRY Thomas by Exeter 1840 Doc 19510
BARTER Amelia by Raymond 1788 Doc 10640
BARTLETT George by Danville 1843 Doc 20629 S
BARTLETT Mehitable by Epsom 1810 Doc 33660
BARTLETT Oliver by Newton 1826 Doc 7524
BARTLETT Perley by Hampton 1835 Doc 15557
BARTLETT Philip (c) by Pittsfield 1801 Doc 19665
BARTLETT Susanna by Epsom 1810 Doc 33660
BARTLETT Thomas by Litchfield 1831 Doc 12683
BASFORD John by Portsmouth 1841 Doc 19511
BASFORD Malinda by Portsmouth 1841 Doc 19511
BATCHELDER Annah by Pittsfield 1810 Doc 32331
BATCHELDER Betty by Deerfield 1801 Doc 20738
BATCHELDER Esquire (c) by Deerfield 1801 Doc 20738
BATCHELDER James (c) by Deerfield 1801 Doc 20738
BATCHELDER Jeremiah by Deerfield 1801 Doc 20738
BATCHELDER Josiah by Deerfield 1801 Doc 19665
BATCHELDER Josiah (c) by Deerfield 1801 Doc 20738
BATCHELDER Malcon by Salem 1827 Doc 8077
BATCHELDER Polly (c) by Deerfield 1801 Doc 20738
BATCHELDER Rhoda by Deerfield 1843 Doc 20629 S
BATCHELDER Rhoda by Deerfield 1844 Doc 21216
BATCHELDER Rhoda by Deerfield 1846 Doc 22356
BATCHELDER Rhoda by Deerfield 1845 Doc 21835
BATCHELDER Rhoda by Deerfield 1850 Doc 311
BATISBY Dorcas by Portsmouth 1835 Doc 15900
BATISBY Dorcas by Portsmouth 1836 Doc 16214
BAUETT Rhoda by Lisbon 1832 Doc 13399
BAYLEY Joseph by Windham 1794 Doc 14648
BAYLEY Joseph (c) by Windham 1794 Doc 14648
BAYLEY Joseph (c) by Windham 1794 Doc 14648
BAYLEY Polly by Windham 1794 Doc 14648
BAYLEY Polly (c) by Windham 1794 Doc 14648
BEADEE Samuel (Negro) by E Kingston 1850 Doc 311
BEADLEY Joseph by Portsmouth 1833 Doc 14119
BEAN Abigail by E Kingston 1845 Doc 21835
BEAN Abigail by Seabrook 1843 Doc 20928
BEAN Abigail by Kingston 1790 Doc 11310
BEAN Abigail by Seabrook 1793 Doc 13587
BEAN Benjamin by Kingston 1789 Doc 11310
BEAN Joanna by Windham 1842 Doc 20107
BEAN Jonathan by Kingston 1790 Doc 11310
BEAN Joseph by Poplin 1804 Doc 23419

BEAN Obediah by ? 1806 Doc 25429
BEAN Ritsey by Portsmouth 1842 Doc 20629
BEAN Robinson by Windham 1842 Doc 20107
BEAN Robinson by Windham 1843 Doc 20928
BEAN Sarah (c) by Seabrook 1793 Doc 13587
BEATTLE Joseph by Plaistow 1793 Doc 14018
BECK Peggey by Portsmouth 1843 Doc 20629
BECK Peggy by Portsmouth 1846 Doc 22356
BECK Polley by Portsmouth 1843 Doc 20629
BECK Polly by Portsmouth 1846 Doc 22356
BECKMAN Grace by Kensington 1789 Doc 10911
BEDEE Samuel by E Kingston 1855 Doc 3620
BEDEE Samuel by E Rochester 1853 Doc 2371
BEDEE Samuel by E Kingston 1844 Doc 21216
BEDEL Elizabeth by Salem 1774 Doc 3514
BEEDE Samuel by E Kingston 1843 Doc 20629 A
BEEDE Ruth by Newington 1794 Doc 14018
BEEDE Samuel by E Kingston 1852 Doc 1554
BEEDE Samuel by E Kingston 1853 Doc 2085
BEEDE Samuel by E Kingston 1846 Doc 22356
BEEDE Samuel by E Kingston 1851 Doc 931
BEEGEN John by Kingston 1851 Doc 931
BELL Jacob Jr by New Castle 1828 Doc 9201
BENNET Edward by Hampton 1835 Doc 16931
BENNET Lucy by Sandown 1795 Doc 14648
BENNET Rhoda by Sandown 1795 Doc 14648
BENNET Sally by Exeter 1794 Doc 14018
BENNET Sarah by Kensington 1789 Doc 10911
BENNETT David by Northwood 1834 Doc 14817
BENNETT Ebenezer L by Northwood 1834 Doc 14817
BENNETT Edward by Hampton Falls 1834 Doc 15899
BENNETT Edward by Hampton Falls 1829 Doc 10409
BENNETT Edward by Hampton Falls 1842 Doc 20107
BENNETT Edward by Hampton Falls 1832 Doc 14119
BENNETT Edward by Hampton Falls 1830 Doc 12197
BENNETT Edward by Hampton Falls 1840 Doc 18856
BENNETT Edward by Hampton Falls 1839 Doc 18267
BENNETT Edward by Hampton Falls 1841 Doc 19510
BENNETT Edward by Hampton 1840 Doc 18856
BENNETT Thomas by Chester 1829 Doc 12682
BENNETT Thomas by Chester 1828 Doc 10409
BENNETT Thomas by Chester 1831 Doc 13081
BENNETT Thomas by Chester 1827 Doc 9200
BENNETT Thomas by Chester 1811 Doc 32876
BENNETT Thomas by Exeter 1810 Doc 31571
BENNETT Thomas by Chester 1826 Doc 6965
BENNETT Thomas by Chester 1829 Doc 11709
BENNETT Thomas by Chester 1827 Doc 8073
BENSON Alfa by Chichester 1821 Doc 1592
BENSON Charles W by Hampton 1857 Doc 4985
BENSON Eliza M by Hampton 1857 Doc 4985
BENSON Esther by Chichester 1821 Doc 1592

BENSON Joseph by Londonderry 1852 Doc 1554
BENSON Joseph C by Londonderry 1850 Doc 311
BENSON Mary by Pembroke 1778 Doc 3797
BENSON Sally by Chichester 1821 Doc 1592
BENTLY Robert by Portsmouth 1837 Doc 16931
BENY Thomas by Rye 1850 Doc 931
BERNARD John N by Portsmouth 1836 Doc 16216
BERNARD John N by Portsmouth 1836 Doc 16216
BERNET Andrie by Nottingham 1854 Doc 2371
BERRY Mary Ann (c) by Exeter 1854 Doc 2371
BERRY Benjamin by Portsmouth 1843 Doc 20629
BERRY Ebenezer by Stratham 1853 Doc 2371
BERRY Hannah by Stratham 1852 Doc 1554
BERRY Hannah by Stratham 1853 Doc 2085
BERRY James by Portsmouth 1852 Doc 1554
BERRY John by Portsmouth 1852 Doc 1554
BERRY John by Portsmouth 1851 Doc 931
BERRY John by Portsmouth 1851 Doc 932
BERRY Jona by Greeland 1851 Doc 931
BERRY Lydia by Rye 1852 Doc 1554
BERRY Lydia by Portsmouth 1843 Doc 20629
BERRY Lydia by Rye 1850 Doc 311
BERRY Lydia by Rye 1850 Doc 931
BERRY Lydia by Rye 1843 Doc 20629 S
BERRY Lydia (c) by Farmington 1835 Doc 15557
BERRY Margaret by Portsmouth 1852 Doc 1554
BERRY Martha by Rye 1846 Doc 22356
BERRY Martha (c) by Rye 1843 Doc 20629 S
BERRY Mary by Exeter 1854 Doc 2371
BERRY Mary Ann by Exeter 1853 Doc 2371
BERRY Osgood by Stratham 1852 Doc 1554
BERRY Osgood by Stratham 1851 Doc 931
BERRY Patrick by Derry 1841 Doc 19510
BERRY Rachael by Rye 1846 Doc 22356
BERRY Solomon by Greenland 1846 Doc 22356
BERRY Solomon by Rye 1843 Doc 20629 A
BERRY Solomon by Farmington 1835 Doc 15557
BERRY Solomon by Greenland 1797 Doc 16897
BERRY Solomon by Portsmouth 1843 Doc 20629
BERRY Thomas by Rye 1850 Doc 311
BERRY Thomas (c) by Rye 1843 Doc 20629 S
BERRY Wm H (c) by Portsmouth 1852 Doc 1554
BERRY Martha Cate by Portsmouth 1843 Doc 20629
BEVERLY Molley by S Hampton 1778 Doc 4164
BEVERLY Ruth by S Hampton 1778 Doc 4164
BICKFORD Anna by Epping 1790 Doc 11310
BICKFORD Rhoda by Nottingham 1814 Doc 37727
BICKFORD Sally by Chichester 1820 Doc 1143
BICKFORD Samuel by Epping 1790 Doc 11310
BICKFORD Samuel by Pembroke 1787 Doc 9898
BILLINGS Mary by Londonderry 1842 Doc 20107
BISHOP James by Portsmouth 1846 Doc 22356

BISHOP James by Portsmouth 1851 Doc 311
BLACK James by Windham 1831 Doc 15123
BLACK Mary by Hawke 1776 Doc 3797
BLACKBORN David by Plaistow 1795 Doc 15359
BLACKBORN David Jr by Plaistow 1802 Doc 21391
BLACKBORN Elizabeth by Plaistow 1795 Doc 15359
BLACKBURN Edward by Portsmouth 1836 Doc 16214
BLACKBURN Edward by Portsmouth 1835 Doc 15900
BLAFORD Timothy by Kingston 1797 Doc 16546
BLAISDEL Abner by Hampton Falls 1845 Doc 21835
BLAISDELL Abner by ? 1850 Doc 311
BLAISDELL Abner by Hampton Falls 1853 Doc 2085
BLAISDELL Abner by Hampton Falls 1851 Doc 931
BLAISDELL Abner by Hampton Falls 1846 Doc 22356
BLAISDELL Abner by Hampton Falls 1843 Doc 20928
BLAISDELL Abner by Hampton Falls 1842 Doc 20424
BLAISDELL Carter (c) by Holderness 1827 Doc 8077
BLAISDELL Daniel by Kingston 1790 Doc 11611
BLAISDELL Elora (c) by Holderness 1827 Doc 8077
BLAISDELL Harriet (c) by Holderness 1827 Doc 8077
BLAISDELL Jeremiah by Holderness 1827 Doc 8077
BLAISDELL Lydia by Hampton Falls 1850 Doc 311
BLAISDELL Lydia by Hampton Falls 1843 Doc 20928
BLAISDELL Lydia by Hampton Falls 1842 Doc 20424
BLAISDELL Lydia by Exeter 1843 Doc 20629 A
BLAISDELL Lydia by Hampton Falls 1846 Doc 22356
BLAISDELL Lydia by Hampton Falls 1854 Doc 2371
BLAISDELL Samuel (c) by Holderness 1827 Doc 8077
BLAISDELL Susan by Holderness 1827 Doc 8077
BLAISDELL William by Hampton Falls 1842 Doc 20424
BLAKE Betty by Northwood 1787 Doc 9898
BLAKE Charles by Rockingham County 1831 Doc 13399
BLAKE Christopher by Epsom 1808 Doc 28434
BLAKE Christopher by Deerfield 1792 Doc 12531
BLAKE Christopher by Hampton 1787 Doc 10016
BLAKE Deborah by Epsom 1808 Doc 28434
BLAKE Elizabeth by Nottingham 1791 Doc 12228
BLAKE Hannah by Deerfield 1792 Doc 12882
BLAKE John (c) by Brentwood 1794 Doc 14339
BLAKE Jonathan by Brentwood 1794 Doc 14339
BLAKE Jonathan by Hawke 1789 Doc 10229
BLAKE Luce (c) by Brentwood 1794 Doc 14339
BLAKE Lucy by Hawke 1789 Doc 10229
BLAKE Mehatabel by Kensington 1792 Doc 13190
BLAKE Tabitha by Hampton 1787 Doc 10016
BLANEY Elizabeth by Kensington 1791 Doc 12228
BLASDEL Lydia by S Hampton 1780 Doc 4331
BLASDEL Micajah by Exeter 1775 Doc 3703
BLASDEL Peter by Northwood 1802 Doc 21391
BLASDEL Phebe by Northwood 1802 Doc 21391
BLASDEL Sarah by S Hampton 1780 Doc 4331
BLASDELL Henry by Pittsfield 1810 Doc 32331

10

BLASDELL Lydia by Hampton Falls 1851 Doc 931
BLASDELL Micajah by Exeter 1772 Doc 1880
BLASDELL Peter by Pittsfield 1810 Doc 32331
BLASDELL Phebe by Pittsfield 1810 Doc 32331
BLASDELL William by Pittsfield 1810 Doc 32331
BLAZO Hannah by N Hampton 1794 Doc 14018
BLOSSOM Hannah by Exeter 1844 Doc 21216
BLOSSOM Hannah by Portsmouth 1842 Doc 20107
BLOSSOM Hannah by Exeter 1843 Doc 20629 S
BLY Asa by Sandown 1814 Doc 37727
BLY Brian (c) by Epping 1840 Doc 18858
BLY Brian (c) by Epping 1840 Doc 18857
BLY Elizabeth by Sandown 1814 Doc 37727
BLY Mary by Epping 1840 Doc 18858
BLY Mary by Epping 1840 Doc 18857
BLY Robert by Epping 1840 Doc 18857
BLY Robert by Epping 1840 Doc 18858
BLY Robert (c) by Sandown 1814 Doc 37727
BOARDMAN D John H by Portsmouth 1841 Doc 19510
BOARDMAN John H by Portsmouth 1842 Doc 20107
BOATMAN Mary by Greenland 1808 Doc 29235
BOLTON John by Portsmouth 1827 Doc 8073
BOND Hannah by Gilford 1838 Doc 17575
BOND Joseph by Hampstead 1770 Doc 1612
BOND Mary by Exeter 1844 Doc 21216
BOND Mary by Exeter 1845 Doc 20629 A
BOND Mary by Exeter 1843 Doc 20629 S
BOND Mary by Exeter 1845 Doc 21835
BOND Mary by Exeter 1842 Doc 20107
BOND Mary by Exeter 1842 Doc 20107
BOND Mary by Exeter 1846 Doc 22356
BOND Molly by Exeter 1850 Doc 311
BOOKER Dorcas by Portsmouth 1836 Doc 16214
BOOKER Dorcas by Portsmouth 1837 Doc 16931
BOOKER Doveais by Portsmouth 1835 Doc 15900
BOOMER Mary by Portsmouth 1828 Doc 9200
BOROUGH Josiah by Salem 1779 Doc 4241
BOROUGH Sarah by Salem 1779 Doc 4241
BOTILL Polly by Portsmouth 1808 Doc 29235
BOTMAN Anna by Enfield 1838 Doc 18543
BOULEY Mehitable by Brentwood 1799 Doc 17750
BOULEY Sargent by Brentwood 1799 Doc 17750
BOULEY William by Newton 1852 Doc 1554
BOURROUGHS Chandler by Kensington 1795 Doc 15018
BOUTONS John by Sommersworth 1827 Doc 8073
BOWDLEAR Samuel by Portsmouth 1791 Doc 12228
BOWEN Bridget by Portsmouth 1852 Doc 1842
BOWERS Mary by Portsmouth 1832 Doc 13399
BOWERS Philip by Portsmouth 1832 Doc 13399
BOWERS Philip by Portsmouth 1832 Doc 13755
BOWERS Phillip by Portsmouth 1832 Doc 13754
BOWLEY Sergent by Stratham 1800 Doc 19247

11

BOWLEY William by Newton 1853 Doc 2085
BOYCE Edmund by Rockingham County 1831 Doc 13399
BOYLES Charles by Newton 1852 Doc 1554
BRACEY Margaret by Brentwood 1798 Doc 17408
BRACEY Peggey by Poplin 1798 Doc 17408
BRACEY Peggy by Epping 1793 Doc 13190
BRACY Jos A by Portsmouth 1840 Doc 18856
BRACY Joseph A by Portsmouth 1839 Doc 18267
BRACY Josephine by Portsmouth 1839 Doc 18856
BRADBURY William by Poplin 1796 Doc 15359
BRADLY Joseph by Hampton 1770 Doc 1612
BRAGE John Jr by Rockingham County 1825 Doc 6505
BRAGG John by Rye 1846 Doc 22356
BRAND Thomas by Portsmouth 1837 Doc 16931
BRANDON Hann W by Nottingham 1850 Doc 931
BRANSCOMB Arthur by Newmarket 1850 Doc 311
BRANSCOMB Catherine by Haverhill 1822 Doc 2912
BRASA Margaret by Nottingham 1793 Doc 14339
BRASCOMB Prudence by Kensington 1782 Doc 5186
BRAWEN Harriah W (c) by Nottingham 1851 Doc 932
BRENNAN J W by Rockingham County 1831 Doc 13399
BRENNAN W by Rockingham County 1831 Doc 13399
BREWER David by Portsmouth 1832 Doc 13755
BRIAN James by Derry 1853 Doc 2371
BRICKET Edmond (c) by Salem 1792 Doc 13190
BRICKET John by Salem 1792 Doc 13190
BRICKET John by Atkinson 1795 Doc 15018
BRICKET Joseph (c) by Atkinson 1795 Doc 15018
BRICKET Joseph (c) by Salem 1792 Doc 13190
BRICKET Mary by Salem 1792 Doc 13190
BRICKET Mary by Atkinson 1795 Doc 15018
BRICKET Moses by Newton 1842 Doc 20424
BRICKET Thomas by Atkinson 1795 Doc 15018
BRICKLEY Gidien by Pembroke 1813 Doc 36435
BRIDGE Lydia by Portsmouth 1851 Doc 931
BRIDGES Ann by Portsmouth 1851 Doc 311
BRIDGES Dide by Exeter 1787 Doc 9740
BRIDGES Lydia Ann by Portsmouth 1851 Doc 932
BRIDGET George by Portsmouth 1832 Doc 13399
BRIDGET George Duffy by Portsmouth 1832 Doc 13399
BRIDGET Olive by Portsmouth 1832 Doc 13399
BRIDGET Olive (c) by Portsmouth 1832 Doc 13754
BRIER Rachael by Epping 1790 Doc 11310
BRIGHAM Thomas C by Auburn 1851 Doc 931
BROCKENBURY Susan by Exeter 1826 Doc 6965
BROCKENBURY William by Exeter 1826 Doc 6965
BROOKS George S by Deerfield 1852 Doc 2086
BROOKS John by Greenland 1773 Doc 2472
BROOKS Rebecca by Portsmouth 1832 Doc 13754
BROOKS Rebecca by Portsmouth 1832 Doc 13755
BROOKS Samuel by Portsmouth 1832 Doc 13755
BROWN Eliphalet by Brentwood 1801 Doc 20206

BROWN Ezekiel by E Kingston 1793 Doc 13190
BROWN Miriam by E Kingston 1793 Doc 13190
BROWN Nathaniel by E Kingston 1793 Doc 13190
BROWN (alias) Michael by Portsmouth 1791 Doc 12228
BROWN Abigail by Pittsfield 1801 Doc 19665
BROWN Abigail by Poplin 1786 Doc 9631
BROWN Abigail (c) by Pittsfield 1801 Doc 19665
BROWN Ann by E Kingston 1795 Doc 15018
BROWN Ann by Portsmouth 1830 Doc 12197
BROWN Atarah by Poplin 1843 Doc 20629
BROWN Atarah by Poplin 1845 Doc 21835
BROWN Atavah by Poplin 1844 Doc 21216
BROWN Atavah by Poplin 1846 Doc 22356
BROWN Benjamin by Poplin 1843 Doc 20629 A
BROWN Benjamin by Pittsfield 1801 Doc 19665
BROWN Benjamin by Kingston 1786 Doc 9151
BROWN Benjamin Jr (c) by Pittsfield 1801 Doc 19665
BROWN Betsy by Hampstead 1833 Doc 14414
BROWN Betsy (c) by Pittsfield 1800 Doc 19247
BROWN Christopher by Derry 1828 Doc 10409
BROWN Deborah (c) by Pittsfield 1801 Doc 19665
BROWN Elizabeth by Rye 1829 Doc 12682
BROWN Ephraim by Poplin 1846 Doc 22356
BROWN Ephraim by Poplin 1796 Doc 15598
BROWN Ephraim by Poplin 1854 Doc 2371
BROWN Ephraim by Poplin 1849 Doc 311
BROWN Ephraim by Poplin 1851 Doc 931
BROWN Ephraim (c) by Pittsfield 1800 Doc 19247
BROWN Ephrain by Poplin 1852 Doc 1554
BROWN George by Portsmouth 1839 Doc 18856
BROWN George by Portsmouth 1840 Doc 18856
BROWN George by Portsmouth 1839 Doc 18542
BROWN Hannah by Nottingham 1846 Doc 22356
BROWN Hannah by Deerfield 1818 Doc 45992
BROWN Hannah by Nottingham 1842 Doc 20424
BROWN Hannah (c) by Pittsfield 1801 Doc 19665
BROWN Harriet by Poplin 1845 Doc 21835
BROWN Harriet by Poplin 1853 Doc 2085
BROWN Harriet (c) by Poplin 1846 Doc 22356
BROWN Harriet (c) by Poplin 1844 Doc 21216
BROWN Hitty (c) by Pittsfield 1800 Doc 19247
BROWN Horace by Portsmouth 1828 Doc 9200
BROWN Hugh by Portsmouth 1827 Doc 8073
BROWN Hugh by Portsmouth 1826 Doc 7634
BROWN Jacob by Kensington 1794 Doc 14528
BROWN James by Portsmouth 1851 Doc 931
BROWN James by Portsmouth 1831 Doc 13081
BROWN James by Portsmouth 1851 Doc 932
BROWN James by Portsmouth 1851 Doc 311
BROWN James (c) by Pittsfield 1801 Doc 19665
BROWN Jane by Kingston 1786 Doc 9151
BROWN Jane (c) by Kingston 1786 Doc 9151

BROWN Jonathan (c) by Pittsfield 1800 Doc 19247
BROWN Joseph by Pittsfield 1800 Doc 19247
BROWN Joseph by Poplin 1796 Doc 15598
BROWN Joseph by Danville 1843 Doc 20928
BROWN Joseph by Poplin 1845 Doc 21835
BROWN Joseph (c) by Poplin 1846 Doc 22356
BROWN Joseph (c) by Poplin 1844 Doc 21216
BROWN Lois (alias) Shaw by Kensington 1792 Doc 13190
BROWN Lois (alias) Shaw by Kensington 1793 Doc 13190
BROWN Marsha by Poplin 1853 Doc 2371
BROWN Martha by Poplin 1845 Doc 21835
BROWN Mary by Kingston 1786 Doc 9151
BROWN Mary (c) by Poplin 1844 Doc 21216
BROWN Michael by Exeter 1773 Doc 2472
BROWN Michael by Hampton Falls 1786 Doc 9631
BROWN Molly by Kensington 1794 Doc 14528
BROWN Rebeccah by Brentwood 1773 Doc 2472
BROWN Robert by Kensington 1794 Doc 14528
BROWN Ruth by Poplin 1801 Doc 20206
BROWN Ruth by Windham 1788 Doc 10525
BROWN Ruth by Danville 1843 Doc 20928
BROWN Samuel by Portsmouth 1833 Doc 14119
BROWN Sarah by Kingston 1786 Doc 9151
BROWN Susan by Brentwood 1830 Doc 11710
BROWN Timothy (Rev) by Kingston 1781 Doc 4749
BROWN Ursula (c) by Pittsfield 1800 Doc 19247
BROWN William by Portsmouth 1808 Doc 29235
BRUBANK Hale by Kingston 1795 Doc 14648
BRUCE Charles by Nottingham 1843 Doc 20629
BRUCE Stephen by Nottingham 1843 Doc 20629
BRUER Stephen by Nottingham 1843 Doc 20928
BRYANT Jemima by Allenstown 1814 Doc 37727
BRYANT Jemima by Newmarket 1789 Doc 10229
BUCANNON Catherine by Portsmouth 1831 Doc 13081
BUCHANAN Alexander by Portsmouth 1840 Doc 19137
BUCHANAN Duncan by Rockingham County 1831 Doc 13399
BUCHANNAN Duncan by Portsmouth 1832 Doc 13755
BUCHANNAN Mary Ann by Portsmouth 1832 Doc 13755
BUCHANNAN Mary Ann by Portsmouth 1836 Doc 16214
BUCHANNAN Mary Ann by Portsmouth 1837 Doc 16931
BUCK Ann by Portsmouth 1842 Doc 20107
BUCKANNAN Alex'd by Portsmouth 1841 Doc 19510
BUCKINS Cocat by Portsmouth 1852 Doc 1554
BUCKLAND Create by Portsmouth 1852 Doc 1554
BUCKLEY Gideon by Londonderry 1812 Doc 35625
BUCKLEY Gideon by Pembroke 1812 Doc 35625
BUCKLEY James by Portsmouth 1840 Doc 19137
BUCKLEY James by Portsmouth 1840 Doc 18857
BUCKLEY James by Portsmouth 1841 Doc 19510
BUCKMAN Mary Ann by Portsmouth 1838 Doc 18267
BULLARD George by Portsmouth 1833 Doc 14415
BUNKER John by Portsmouth 1852 Doc 1554

BURAP Betsey by Deerfield 1851 Doc 931
BURAP Rufus by Deerfield 1851 Doc 931
BURBANK Ann (c) by Poplin 1779 Doc 4164
BURBANK Betsy (w) by Deerfield 1816 Doc 38438
BURBANK Betty (c) by Deerfield 1793 Doc 13587
BURBANK Caleb (c) by Deerfield 1793 Doc 13587
BURBANK David by Deerfield 1793 Doc 13587
BURBANK Eliz See Corliss by Plaistow 1839 Doc 17185
BURBANK Elizabeth by Brentwood 1828 Doc 9823
BURBANK Elizabeth by Deerfield 1793 Doc 13587
BURBANK Elizabeth (c) by Deerfield 1793 Doc 13587
BURBANK Enoch (c) by Poplin 1779 Doc 4164
BURBANK Eunis by Poplin 1779 Doc 4164
BURBANK Eunis (c) by Poplin 1779 Doc 4164
BURBANK Ezra by Poplin 1779 Doc 4164
BURBANK Holley by Deerfield 1793 Doc 13587
BURBANK Huldah (c) by Poplin 1779 Doc 4164
BURBANK Mary by Newmarket 1796 Doc 15359
BURBANK Nathl by Portsmouth 1852 Doc 1554
BURBANK Richard (c) by Deerfield 1793 Doc 13587
BURBANK Ruth by Deerfield 1793 Doc 13587
BURBANK Sarah (c) by Poplin 1779 Doc 4164
BURBANK Thomas by Deerfield 1845 Doc 21835
BURCH Jane by Chester 1828 Doc 9823
BURCH Robert by Concord 1812 Doc 34232
BURCHARD Elisha by Exeter 1844 Doc 21216
BURCHARD Elisha by Exeter 1843 Doc 20629 A
BURDEEN Lucy by Newmarket 1782 Doc 5630
BURILL Louisa by Hampstead 1866 Doc 9409
BURILL Lydia by Derry 1843 Doc 20629 S
BURK Pat by Windham 1849 Doc 311
BURK Philip (Negro) by Raymond 1791 Doc 12228
BURKA Phillis (Negro) by Exeter 1791 Doc 12531
BURLEY Josiah by Brentwood 1796 Doc 15359
BURLEY Judith by Poplin 1789 Doc 10229
BURLEY Judith by Brentwood 1796 Doc 15359
BURNAM Deborah by Nottingham 1790 Doc 11910
BURNES Ann by Portsmouth 1830 Doc 12197
BURNES Wm by Portsmouth 1852 Doc 1554
BURNHAM Elizabeth by Portsmouth 1834 Doc 14818
BURNHAM Joseph by Portsmouth 1834 Doc 14818
BURNHAM Thomas by Goffstown 1832 Doc 13399
BURNS Mary by Seabrook 1850 Doc 311
BURNS Philip by Pittsfield 1812 Doc 34232
BURNS Sarah by Hampton 1850 Doc 311
BURPEE Martha by Candia 1842 Doc 20107
BURPEE Martha by Candia 1842 Doc 20424
BURPEE Martha by Candia 1843 Doc 20629 S
BURPEY Elizabeth by Epping 1789 Doc 11611
BURPEY Elizabeth (c) by Epping 1789 Doc 11611
BURPEY Esther (c) by Epping 1789 Doc 11611
BURPEY Jeremiah by Epping 1789 Doc 16611

BURPEY Jeremiah (c) by Epping 1789 Doc 11610
BURPEY Nathaniel (c) by Epping 1789 Doc 11611
BURRELL John by Atkinson 1796 Doc 16050
BURRELL Lydia by Atkinson 1796 Doc 16050
BURRELL Lydia by Derry 1844 Doc 21216
BURRELL Lydia by Derry 1836 Doc 16214
BURRELL Lydia by Derry 1832 Doc 13399
BURRELL Lydia by Derry 1839 Doc 18267
BURRELL Lydia by Derry 1840 Doc 18856
BURRELL Lydia by Derry 1841 Doc 19510
BURRILL Lydia by Derry 1837 Doc 16931
BURRILL Cynthia A by Hampstead 1866 Doc 9128
BURRILL Cynthia A by Hampstead 1867 Doc 9409
BURRILL Louisa (c) by Hampstead 1867 Doc 9409
BURRILL Lydia by Derry 1850 Doc 311
BURRILL Lydia by Derry 1845 Doc 21835
BURRILL Lydia by Derry 1846 Doc 22356
BURRILL Lydia by Derry 1853 Doc 2085
BURRILL Lydia by Derry 1852 Doc 1554
BURROUGHS Richard by Rockingham County 1831 Doc 13399
BURRVILL Lydia by Derry 1851 Doc 931
BURT Moses L by Newmarket 1853 Doc 2371
BURT William by Poplin 1790 Doc 11611
BURTON (alias) Sarah by Poplin 1792 Doc 12531
BURTON Hannah by Hampton 1817 Doc 44178
BURUM Samuel by Northwood 1778 Doc 4199
BUSWELL Charles K by Bridgewater 1866 Doc 9409
BUSWELL Cynthia L by Deerfield 1807 Doc 27572
BUSWELL Elizabeth by Bridgewater 1866 Doc 9409
BUSWELL Lydia H by Deerfield 1807 Doc 27572
BUSWELL Samuel G by Deerfield 1807 Doc 27572
BUSWELL William by S Hampton 1827 Doc 8655
BUSWELL William J by Deerfield 1807 Doc 27572
BUSWELL Willie S (c) by Bridgewater 1866 Doc 9409
BUTLER Elizabeth by Seabrook 1789 Doc 11611
BUTLER James by Hampton 1799 Doc 18299
BUTLER Joseph by Atkinson 1795 Doc 15018
BUTLER Margaret by Portsmouth 1833 Doc 14122
BUTLER Patrick by Portsmouth 1833 Doc 14122
BUTLER Sarah by Atkinson 1795 Doc 15018
BUTMAN Susanne by Exeter 1846 Doc 22592
BUTNAM Susannah by Exeter 1846 Doc 22356
BUZWELL Aron Colby (c) by S Hampton 1800 Doc 19247
BUZWELL Daniel (c) by S Hampton 1800 Doc 19247
BUZWELL Molly by S Hampton 1800 Doc 19247
BUZWELL Molly (c) by S Hampton 1800 Doc 19247
BUZWELL William by S Hampton 1800 Doc 19247
BUZWELL William (c) by S Hampton 1800 Doc 19247
BUZELL William by S Hampton 1826 Doc 8073
BYAN Sarah by Portsmouth 1842 Doc 20107
BYANS John by Portsmouth 1841 Doc 20107
BYARS Nana by Portsmouth 1839 Doc 18267

BYARS Nancy by Portsmouth 1839 Doc 18856
BYERS Mehitable (c) by Portsmouth 1846 Doc 22356
BYERS Sarah by Portsmouth 1851 Doc 931
BYERS Sarah by Portsmouth 1842 Doc 20107
BYONS John by Exeter 1833 Doc 16214
BYONS John by Rockingham County 1831 Doc 13399
CABAN Samuel by Exeter 1831 Doc 13399
CABB Ann W by Portsmouth 1852 Doc 1554
CAFE Rachael by Deerfield 1844 Doc 21216
CAHILL Thomas by Portsmouth 1837 Doc 16931
CAHLING James by Portsmouth 1852 Doc 1555
CAILE Patrick by Portsmouth 1841 Doc 19511
CAILES Patrick by Portsmouth 1841 Doc 19510
CAILIS (Mrs) Patrick by Portsmouth 1841 Doc 19511
CALBFUS Elizabeth by Gilford 1852 Doc 1842
CALBFUS John by Gilford 1852 Doc 1842
CALBFUS John (c) by Gilford 1852 Doc 1842
CALDEN Betsey by Candia 1842 Doc 20107
CALDEN Betsy by Candia 1842 Doc 20424
CALDON Mary by Newmarket 1844 Doc 21209
CALFE John by Sanbornton 1772 Doc 731
CALLAUGH Roger W by Portsmouth 1852 Doc 1554
CALLEY Caroline by Stratham 1846 Doc 22356
CALLEY Caroline H by Stratham 1851 Doc 931
CALLEY Caroline M by Stratham 1850 Doc 311
CALLEY Caroline M by Stratham 1852 Doc 1554
CALLEY Parson by Kingston 1786 Doc 9151
CALLEY Richard by Windham 1846 Doc 22356
CALLEY Sarah by Stratham 1853 Doc 2085
CALLOUGH Roger by Portsmouth 1851 Doc 311
CALNAN Thomas by Epsom 1810 Doc 33660
CALORD Eliphalet C by Nottingham 1794 Doc 14339
CAMBELL David by Bradford 1827 Doc 8077
CAMBELL John by Bradford 1827 Doc 8077
CAMBELL John by Salem 1843 Doc 20629
CAMBELL Joseph by Portsmouth 1851 Doc 311
CAMBELL Joseph by Portsmouth 1835 Doc 15900
CAMBELL Joseph by Portsmouth 1842 Doc 20107
CAMBELL Joseph by Portsmouth 1852 Doc 1554
CAMBELL Joseph by Portsmouth 1836 Doc 16214
CAMBELL Martha by Salem 1843 Doc 20629
CAMBELL Martha by Salem 1854 Doc 2371
CAMBELL Martha by Salem 1843 Doc 20928
CAMBELL Martha by Salem 1846 Doc 22356
CAMBELL Martha (c) by Salem 1843 Doc 20928
CAMBELL Martha 3rd by Bradford 1827 Doc 8077
CAMBELL Martha Jr by Bradford 1827 Doc 8077
CAMBELL Mary Jane by Salem 1846 Doc 22356
CAMBELL Nancy by Salem 1843 Doc 20928
CAMPBELL Betty by Windham 1793 Doc 13587
CAMPBELL Isaac by Derry 1832 Doc 13399
CAMPBELL John by Bradford 1818 Doc 45992

CAMPBELL Joseph by Portsmouth 1837 Doc 16931
CAMPBELL Joseph by Portsmouth 1846 Doc 22356
CAMPBELL Joseph by Portsmouth 1851 Doc 931
CAMPBELL Martha by Salem 1850 Doc 311
CAMPBELL Martha by Stratham 1851 Doc 931
CAMPBELL Martha by Salem 1853 Doc 2085
CAMPBELL Martha by Portsmouth 1845 Doc 21835
CAMPBELL Samuel by Windham 1792 Doc 13587
CAMPFIELD John by Deerfield 1836 Doc 16931
CAMREN Benjamin by Portsmouth 1830 Doc 12197
CAMREN Catherine by Portsmouth 1830 Doc 12197
CAMREN Catherine by Portsmouth 1830 Doc 12197
CAMREN Joseph by Portsmouth 1830 Doc 12197
CAMREN Martha by Portsmouth 1830 Doc 12197
CAMREN Martha by Portsmouth 1830 Doc 12197
CANE Robert by Pembroke 1797 Doc 16546
CAPEN Samuel by Portsmouth 1830 Doc 12197
CAPEN Samuel by Portsmouth 1830 Doc 12197
CAR Ann (c) by Greenland 1777 Doc 4164
CAR Archelus (c) by Greenland 1777 Doc 4164
CAR Betty by Greenland 1777 Doc 4164
CAR Betty (c) by Greenland 1777 Doc 4164
CAR Charles (c) by Greenland 1777 Doc 4164
CAR Daniel (c) by Greenland 1777 Doc 4164
CAR Molley (c) by Greenland 1777 Doc 4164
CAR Richard (c) by Greenland 1777 Doc 4164
CAR Samuel by Greenland 1777 Doc 4164
CAR Sarah by Newington 1775 Doc 3695
CAR Sarah (c) by Greenland 1777 Doc 4164
CARD Sarah by Portsmouth 1830 Doc 12197
CARD Sarah by Portsmouth 1830 Doc 12197
CAREY Anna by Kingston 1799 Doc 17750
CARLIS Patrick by Portsmouth 1842 Doc 20107
CARLTON Benjamin by Portsmouth 1851 Doc 931
CARLTON Benjamin by Portsmouth 1852 Doc 1554
CARLTON Benjamin by Portsmouth 1846 Doc 22356
CARLTON Benjamin L by Portsmouth 1851 Doc 311
CARLTON Benjamin L by Portsmouth 1851 Doc 1554
CARLTON Ruth by Derry 1842 Doc 20107
CARLTON Thomas by Exeter 1846 Doc 22356
CARMAN Joseph by Portsmouth 1827 Doc 8073
CARMAN Joseph by Portsmouth 1827 Doc 8073
CARPENTER Samuel by Portsmouth 1830 Doc 12197
CARR Abern by Brentwood 1792 Doc 12882
CARR Ann by Epping 1842 Doc 20107
CARR Parker by Rockingham County 1831 Doc 13399
CARR Parker by Portsmouth 1833 Doc 14119
CARR Polly by Loudon 1792 Doc 12882
CARRMAN Joseph by Portsmouth 1828 Doc 9200
CARROLL Ann (c) by Portsmouth 1851 Doc 311
CARROLL Elizabeth (c) by Portsmouth 1851 Doc 311
CARROLL Ellen (c) by Portsmouth 1851 Doc 311

CARROLL Jane by Portsmouth 1851 Doc 311
CARROLL Jane by Portsmouth 1839 Doc 18857
CARROLL Jane by Portsmouth 1841 Doc 19510
CARROLL Jane by Portsmouth 1840 Doc 18857
CARROLL Jeremiah by Portsmouth 1851 Doc 311
CARROLL Julia (c) by Portsmouth 1851 Doc 311
CARROLL Margaret by Derry 1829 Doc 12682
CARROLL Margaret by Derry 1829 Doc 10409
CARROLL Margaret by Derry 1831 Doc 13081
CARROLL Margaret by Rockingham County 1831 Doc 13399
CARROLL Margaret by Londonderry 1845 Doc 21835
CARROLL Mary (c) by Portsmouth 1851 Doc 311
CARROLL Mary Ann by Portsmouth 1840 Doc 18857
CARROLL Michael by Portsmouth 1841 Doc 19510
CARROLL Michael by Portsmouth 1840 Doc 19137
CARROLL Michael by Portsmouth 1842 Doc 20107
CARROLL Peter by Londonderry 1845 Doc 21835
CARROLL Philip by Portsmouth 1840 Doc 18857
CARROLL Phillip by Portsmouth 1840 Doc 18857
CARROLL Phillip by Portsmouth 1841 Doc 19510
CARSON James by Portsmouth 1842 Doc 20107
CARSON Joanna by Portsmouth 1842 Doc 20107
CARTER Abigail by Kingston 1853 Doc 2085
CARTER Abigail by Epping 1853 Doc 2086
CARTER Benjamin by Newton 1810 Doc 33660
CARTER Betty (c) by Kingston 1806 Doc 26134
CARTER Dalby (Mrs) by Kingston 1853 Doc 2085
CARTER Dorothy (c) by E Kingston 1805 Doc 24720
CARTER Elizabeth by Nottingham 1779 Doc 4293
CARTER Enoch by Newton 1855 Doc 4985
CARTER Enoch (c) by E Kingston 1805 Doc 24720
CARTER Gideon by Kingston 1806 Doc 26134
CARTER Hannah by Kingston 1806 Doc 26134
CARTER Hannah (c) by E Kingston 1805 Doc 24720
CARTER James by Greenland 1796 Doc 15359
CARTER John by Brentwood 1842 Doc 20424
CARTER John by Brentwood 1835 Doc 15557
CARTER John by Brentwood 1842 Doc 20629 A
CARTER John by Brentwood 1843 Doc 20629 S
CARTER John by Kingston 1789 Doc 10754
CARTER John by Brentwood 1844 Doc 21216
CARTER John (c) by E Kingston 1805 Doc 24720
CARTER John Jr by E Kingston 1805 Doc 24720
CARTER Orlando by Exeter 1773 Doc 2268
CARTER Sarah by E Kingston 1805 Doc 24720
CARTER Sarah (c) by E Kingston 1805 Doc 24720
CARUTH James by Kensington 1777 Doc 3797
CARY Dinah by Portsmouth 1842 Doc 20424
CARY Liberty by Portsmouth 1842 Doc 20424
CARY Ths by Portsmouth 1852 Doc 1554
CASARA (Negro) by Exeter 1774 Doc 2656
CASE James by Portsmouth 1846 Doc 22356

CASE James by Portsmouth 1822 Doc 3416
CASEY Daniel by Portsmouth 1840 Doc 19137
CASEY Daniel by Portsmouth 1840 Doc 18857
CASEY Daniel by Portsmouth 1841 Doc 19510
CASS Luci (w) by Candia 1816 Doc 40757
CASS Rachael by Deerfield 1846 Doc 22356
CASS Rachel by Deerfield 1845 Doc 21835
CASS Rachel by Deerfield 1850 Doc 311
CASWELL Betty by Northwood 1807 Doc 27572
CASWELL Betty (c) by Northwood 1807 Doc 27572
CASWELL Dolly by Exeter 1826 Doc 6965
CASWELL John by Northwood 1807 Doc 27572
CASWELL Judy (c) by Northwood 1807 Doc 27572
CASWELL Margaret by Windham 1797 Doc 16897
CASWELL Nuel (c) by Northwood 1807 Doc 27572
CASWELL Samuel by Rye 1842 Doc 20424
CASWELL Samuel by Rye 1841 Doc 19510
CASWELL Samuel by Portsmouth 1840 Doc 18856
CASWELL Samuel by Rye 1838 Doc 17909
CASY Liberty by Portsmouth 1846 Doc 22356
CAT (Negro) by Pembroke 1780 Doc 4331
CATE Jonathan by Newmarket 1844 Doc 21209
CATE Mary by Greenland 1788 Doc 10397
CATE Sarah (w) by Stratham 1801 Doc 20206
CAULEY Hannah (c) by Newmarket 1800 Doc 19247
CAULEY Polly (c) by Newmarket 1800 Doc 19247
CAULEY Richard (c) by Newmarket 1800 Doc 19247
CAULEY Samuel by Newmarket 1800 Doc 19247
CENTER Betsey by Chester 1858 Doc 4985
CENTER Charles by Chester 1858 Doc 4985
CENTER James (c) by Chester 1858 Doc 4985
CESAR (Negro) by Kingston 1799 Doc 18299
CHALDING James by Portsmouth 1852 Doc 1554
CHALLIS Dolly by Hawke 1811 Doc 33660
CHALLIS Ephraim by Hawke 1798 Doc 17408
CHALLIS Hannah by Hawke 1798 Doc 17408
CHALLIS Joseph (c) by Hawke 1798 Doc 17408
CHANDLER Jabez by Greenland 1786 Doc 9151
CHANDLER Lydia by Bridgewater 1814 Doc 37727
CHANDLER Thomas by Bridgewater 1814 Doc 37727
CHAPMAN John by Portsmouth 1826 Doc 7634
CHAPMAN Jonathan by Greenland 1781 Doc 4574
CHAPMAN Phebe by Poplin 1790 Doc 11611
CHAPMAN William by Derry 1852 Doc 1554
CHARLTON Thomas (Negro) by Exeter 1845 Doc 20629 A
CHARLTON Thomas by Portsmouth 1840 Doc 18857
CHARLTON Thomas by Exeter 1840 Doc 19510
CHARLTON Thomas by Portsmouth 1839 Doc 18856
CHARLTON Thomas by Portsmouth 1841 Doc 19510
CHASE Abigail by Salem 1796 Doc 15598
CHASE Arvilla (c) by Deerfield 1859 Doc 5505
CHASE Beckey (c) by Deerfield 1780 Doc 4480

CHASE Betsey (c) by Salem 1796 Doc 15598
CHASE Betsy (c) by Deerfield 1780 Doc 4480
CHASE Betty (c) by Hampton Falls 1788 Doc 10640
CHASE Charles by Hampton Falls 1788 Doc 10640
CHASE Chirety by Plaistow 1794 Doc 14339
CHASE Dorothy by Newmarket 1850 Doc 931
CHASE Edmund by Salem 1796 Doc 15598
CHASE Edmund (c) by Salem 1796 Doc 15598
CHASE Elizabeth by Deerfield 1780 Doc 4480
CHASE Elizabeth by Salem 1773 Doc 2472
CHASE Hannah by S Hampton 1783 Doc 5630
CHASE Henry by Stratham 1846 Doc 22356
CHASE Henry by Stratham 1852 Doc 1554
CHASE Henry by Stratham 1843 Doc 20629 S
CHASE Henry by Rye 1841 Doc 19510
CHASE Henry by Stratham 1853 Doc 2085
CHASE Henry by Stratham 1842 Doc 20424
CHASE Henry by Stratham 1851 Doc 931
CHASE John by Atkinson 1796 Doc 16050
CHASE John Leach (c) by Hampton Falls 1788 Doc 10640
CHASE Jonathan by Hampton Falls 1784 Doc 7804
CHASE Joseph by Hampstead 1811 Doc 32876
CHASE Joseph by S Hampton 1783 Doc 5630
CHASE Joseph (c) by Deerfield 1859 Doc 5505
CHASE Joshua by Portsmouth 1830 Doc 12197
CHASE Joshua by Portsmouth 1830 Doc 12197
CHASE Josiah by Exeter 1842 Doc 20107
CHASE Leach (c) by Hampton Falls 1788 Doc 10640
CHASE Mary (c) by Plaistow 1794 Doc 14339
CHASE Mathew by Exeter 1827 Doc 8655
CHASE Moses by Plaistow 1793 Doc 13587
CHASE Nancy by Deerfield 1859 Doc 5505
CHASE Nathaniel by Salem 1773 Doc 2472
CHASE Parker by Deerfield 1780 Doc 4480
CHASE Parker by Atkinson 1805 Doc 24720
CHASE Paul by S Hampton 1783 Doc 5630
CHASE Polly by Poplin 1799 Doc 18299
CHASE Rhoda (c) by Hampton Falls 1788 Doc 10640
CHASE Richard by Portsmouth 1789 Doc 10754
CHASE Robert (c) by Deerfield 1780 Doc 4480
CHASE Ruth by Kingston 1779 Doc 4293
CHASE Ruth by Atkinson 1805 Doc 24720
CHASE Sarah (c) by Deerfield 1780 Doc 4480
CHASE Sary by Plaistow 1793 Doc 13587
CHASE Seth by Deerfield 1859 Doc 5505
CHASE Silas by S Hampton 1783 Doc 5630
CHEFLEY Alpheus (Col) by ? 1782 Doc 5272
CHERLE Phillip by Northwood 1796 Doc 15359
CHESKE Deboroah by Northwood 1796 Doc 15359
CHESLEY Benjamin (c) by Nottingham 1796 Doc 15948
CHESLEY Deborah by Nottingham 1795 Doc 15948
CHESLEY Elizabeth by Nottingham 1796 Doc 15948

CHESLEY Hannah (c) by Nottingham 1795 Doc 15948
CHESLEY Joseph (c) by Nottingham 1795 Doc 15948
CHESLEY Philip by Nottingham 1795 Doc 15948
CHESLEY Philip (c) by Nottingham 1795 Doc 15948
CHESLEY Samuel by Nottingham 1823 Doc 3965
CHESLEY Winthrop by Nottingham 1796 Doc 15948
CHILDS Elizabeth by Salem 1819 Doc 47427
CHILDS Benjamin by Temple 1852 Doc 1842
CHILDS Elizabeth by Newmarket 1774 Doc 2656
CHRITCHET Hannah by Nottingham 1791 Doc 12228
CHURCH Enoch by Chester 1851 Doc 931
CILLEY Amos by Deerfield 1819 Doc 47427
CILLEY Amos Jr by Deerfield 1819 Doc 47427
CILLEY Lucindia by Rockingham County 1825 Doc 6965
CILLEY Lucindia by Rockingham County 1825 Doc 6505
CLAENBODE Richard by Portsmouth 1841 Doc 19510
CLAGSTON William by Portsmouth 1832 Doc 13755
CLAGSTON William by Portsmouth 1830 Doc 12197
CLAIRBOLE Richard by Portsmouth 1851 Doc 311
CLAIRENBOLE Richard by Portsmouth 1852 Doc 1554
CLAIRNBOL Richard by Portsmouth 1851 Doc 1554
CLANSLEY Mary by Portsmouth 1852 Doc 1554
CLARENBODE Richard by Brentwood 1836 Doc 16931
CLARENBOLD George H by Portsmouth 1827 Doc 8073
CLARENBOLD James by Portsmouth 1827 Doc 8073
CLARENBOLD James by Portsmouth 1828 Doc 9200
CLARENBOLD Richard by Portsmouth 1828 Doc 9200
CLARENBOLD Sarah by Portsmouth 1828 Doc 9200
CLARENBOLD Sarah by Portsmouth 1827 Doc 8073
CLARENBOLE Richard by Portsmouth 1839 Doc 18856
CLARENBOLE Richard by Portsmouth 1834 Doc 14818
CLARENBOLE Richard by Portsmouth 1836 Doc 16214
CLARENBOTT Mary by Portsmouth 1832 Doc 13755
CLARENBOTT Richard by Portsmouth 1832 Doc 13755
CLARINBOLE Richard by Portsmouth 1852 Doc 1554
CLARINBOLE Richard by Portsmouth 1842 Doc 20107
CLARINBOLE Richard by Portsmouth 1851 Doc 931
CLARK Anna Maria by Portsmouth 1833 Doc 14415
CLARK Betty by Brentwood 1800 Doc 19247
CLARK Betty by Kingston 1786 Doc 9151
CLARK Bridget (c) by Portsmouth 1843 Doc 20629
CLARK Daniel by Rockingham County 1831 Doc 13399
CLARK George by Portsmouth 1851 Doc 311
CLARK Henry by Candia 1842 Doc 20107
CLARK Henry by Candia 1852 Doc 1554
CLARK Henry by Candia 1853 Doc 2085
CLARK Henry by Candia 1845 Doc 21835
CLARK Henry by Chester 1842 Doc 20424
CLARK Henry by Candia 1842 Doc 20424
CLARK Henry by Candia 1846 Doc 22356
CLARK Henry by Candia 1851 Doc 931
CLARK Henry by Brentwood 1844 Doc 21216

CLARK Henry by Candia 1843 Doc 20629 S
CLARK Henry & Wife by Candia 1850 Doc 311
CLARK James by Derry 1840 Doc 18856
CLARK James by Derry 1841 Doc 19510
CLARK James by Londonderry 1852 Doc 1554
CLARK James by Londonderry 1854 Doc 2371
CLARK James by Londonderry 1846 Doc 22356
CLARK James by Windham 1834 Doc 15123
CLARK Jane by Portsmouth 1845 Doc 21835
CLARK John by Portsmouth 1845 Doc 21835
CLARK John by Portsmouth 1843 Doc 20629
CLARK John by Portsmouth 1833 Doc 14415
CLARK John by Portsmouth 1839 Doc 18267
CLARK John (c) by Portsmouth 1843 Doc 20629
CLARK Joshua by Londonderry 1821 Doc 2382
CLARK Maria by Portsmouth 1835 Doc 15900
CLARK Maria by Portsmouth 1836 Doc 16214
CLARK Martha by Derry 1841 Doc 19510
CLARK Mary by Portsmouth 1843 Doc 20629
CLARK Molly by Hampstead 1831 Doc 12683
CLARK Nancy by Candia 1842 Doc 20424
CLARK Nancy by Candia 1852 Doc 1554
CLARK Nancy by Londonderry 1854 Doc 2371
CLARK Nancy by Londonderry 1853 Doc 2085
CLARK Nancy by Candia 1853 Doc 2085
CLARK Nancy by Candia 1846 Doc 22356
CLARK Phillis (Negro) by Deerfield 1793 Doc 14018
CLARK Richard by Portsmouth 1791 Doc 12228
CLARK Sally by Kingston 1799 Doc 18299
CLARK William by Nottingham 1789 Doc 10911
CLARK William by Northwood 1805 Doc 24720
CLARKE James by Derry 1840 Doc 18856
CLARKS James by Londonderry 1842 Doc 20424
CLARKSON Polley by Poplin 1802 Doc 21391
CLARKSON Polly by Brentwood 1801 Doc 19665
CLARNBOLD Richard by Portsmouth 1827 Doc 8073
CLARY Patrick by Portsmouth 1840 Doc 18857
CLARY Patrick by Portsmouth 1840 Doc 18857
CLARY Patrick by Portsmouth 1841 Doc 19510
CLEAN Alex W by Portsmouth 1831 Doc 13081
CLEMENT Dorothy by Pittsfield 1811 Doc 32876
CLEMENT Drew by Pittsfield 1811 Doc 32876
CLEMENT Mary by Newmarket 1783 Doc 5630
CLERKSON Sarah by Atkinson 1791 Doc 11910
CLEVELY Isaac (Negro) by Exeter 1792 Doc 12882
CLIFFORD Benjamin by S Hampton 1827 Doc 8073
CLIFFORD Molley by Poplin 1804 Doc 23419
CLIFFORD Nathaniel by Poplin 1804 Doc 23419
CLIFFORD Polly by Candia 1815 Doc 39186
CLIFFORD William by ? 1823 Doc 3965
CLIFFORD William (c) by Poplin 1804 Doc 23419
CLINTON John by Rockingham County 1851 Doc 931

CLINTON John by Portsmouth 1851 Doc 311
CLINTON John by Portsmouth 1851 Doc 931
CLINTON John by Portsmouth 1845 Doc 21835
CLINTON John by Portsmouth 1852 Doc 1554
CLINTON John (c) by Portsmouth 1846 Doc 22356
CLOUGH Daniel Sampson by Kingston 1778 Doc 4111
CLOUGH Elizabeth (w) by Deerfield 1799 Doc 17750
CLOUGH Jabez by Poplin 1807 Doc 27572
CLOUGH Jonathan by Sandown 1788 Doc 10397
CLOUGH Mary by Hampton Falls 1774 Doc 3061
CLOUGH Mary by Northfield 1796 Doc 15598
CLOUGH William by Portsmouth 1838 Doc 18267
CLUGSTON Ann by Portsmouth 1830 Doc 12197
CLUGSTON Ann by Portsmouth 1830 Doc 12197
CLUGSTON Ann by Portsmouth 1830 Doc 12197
CLUGSTON William by Portsmouth 1832 Doc 13754
CLUGSTON William by Portsmouth 1832 Doc 13755
CLYE Ebenezer by Pembroke 1792 Doc 13587
COBBEY James by S Hampton 1778 Doc 4164
COBBEY James by Kingston 1777 Doc 3797
COCHRAN Ann by Portsmouth 1851 Doc 931
COCHRAN Ann by Portsmouth 1851 Doc 311
COCHRAN Anna by Portsmouth 1852 Doc 1554
COEL John by Portsmouth 1841 Doc 19511
COENEY Morris by Windham 1849 Doc 311
COENS Henry by Gosport 1850 Doc 311
COFFIN Molly by Brentwood 1801 Doc 19665
COFFIN Peter by Brentwood 1801 Doc 19665
COGGSWELL Sophia by Exeter 1853 Doc 1842
COGSWELL Sophia Peters by Exeter 1842 Doc 20107
COGSWELL Arvilla (c) by Exeter 1845 Doc 21835
COGSWELL Arvilla (c) by Exeter 1843 Doc 20629 S
COGSWELL Arvilla by Exeter 1844 Doc 21216
COGSWELL Augusta (c) by Exeter 1845 Doc 21835
COGSWELL Augusta Ann by Exeter 1844 Doc 21216
COGSWELL Augusta Ann (c) by Exeter 1843 Doc 20629 S
COGSWELL Lucy by Exeter 1852 Doc 1554
COGSWELL Lucy by Exeter 1851 Doc 931
COGSWELL Lucy by Exeter 1853 Doc 2085
COGSWELL Lucy by Exeter 1850 Doc 311
COGSWELL Lucy (c) (Negro) by Exeter 1843 Doc 20629 A
COGSWELL Lucy C by Exeter 1844 Doc 21216
COGSWELL Lucy C (c) by Exeter 1845 Doc 21835
COGSWELL Lucy C (c) (Negro) by Exeter 1842 Doc 20107
COGSWELL Sophia (Negro) by Exeter 1842 Doc 20107
COGSWELL Sophia by Exeter 1845 Doc 20629 A
COGSWELL Sophia by Exeter 1843 Doc 20629 S
COGSWELL Sophia by Exeter 1845 Doc 21835
COGSWELL Sophia by Exeter 1844 Doc 21216
COGSWELL Sophia by Exeter 1853 Doc 2085
COLBATH Elizabeth by Newington 1854 Doc 2371
COLBATH Elizabeth by Newington 1850 Doc 311

COLBATH Elizabeth by Newington 1852 Doc 1554
COLBATH Elizabeth by Newington 1850 Doc 931
COLBE Abigail by Kingston 1780 Doc 4406
COLBE Anna (c) by Pembroke 1797 Doc 16546
COLBE Josiah (c) by Pembroke 1797 Doc 16546
COLBE Mary by Pembroke 1797 Doc 16546
COLBE Peter by Pembroke 1797 Doc 16546
COLBY Abigail by Effingham 1842 Doc 20425
COLBY Anna by Kensington 1786 Doc 9151
COLBY Anna by Newton 1821 Doc 2397
COLBY Anna by Haverhill 1830 Doc 11710
COLBY Anna by Kingston 1852 Doc 1554
COLBY Anna by Kingston 1853 Doc 2371
COLBY Antionette (c) by Canterbury 1841 Doc 19512
COLBY Catherine by Hampstead 1822 Doc 2912
COLBY David by Rockingham County 1831 Doc 13399
COLBY Ebenezer by Salisbury 1830 Doc 11710
COLBY Harriette (c) by Canterbury 1841 Doc 19512
COLBY Jane by Canterbury 1841 Doc 19512
COLBY Jestha by Canterbury 1841 Doc 19512
COLBY Jestha by Sandown 1819 Doc 47427
COLBY Love by Chester 1841 Doc 19510
COLBY Love by Chester 1839 Doc 18267
COLBY Love by Chester 1842 Doc 20107
COLBY Love by Chester 1836 Doc 16931
COLBY Love by Chester 1837 Doc 17575
COLBY Love by Chester 1840 Doc 18856
COLBY Lovey by Chester 1844 Doc 21216
COLBY Lovey by Chester 1845 Doc 21835
COLBY Richard by Strafford 1846 Doc 22592
COLBY Sarah by Strafford 1846 Doc 22592
COLBY Soanni (c) by Canterbury 1841 Doc 19512
COLE George Edward by Portsmouth 1851 Doc 932
COLE Gilman by Northwood 1822 Doc 3416
COLE John by Portsmouth 1842 Doc 20107
COLE Mary by Greenland 1788 Doc 10397
COLE Mary by Portsmouth 1851 Doc 932
COLE Mary by Portsmouth 1851 Doc 931
COLE Salley by Londonderry 1846 Doc 22356
COLE Sally by Londonderry 1851 Doc 931
COLE Sally by Londonderry 1842 Doc 20424
COLE Sally by Londonderry 1854 Doc 2371
COLE Sally by Londonderry 1853 Doc 2085
COLE Sally by Londonderry 1843 Doc 21216
COLE Sally by Greenland 1794 Doc 14648
COLE Sally by Londonderry 1842 Doc 20107
COLE Sally by Londonderry 1852 Doc 1554
COLE Sally by Londonderry 1850 Doc 311
COLEBATH Elizabeth by Newington 1853 Doc 2085
COLEMAN Elizabeth by Newington 1846 Doc 22592
COLEMAN Joseph by Portsmouth 1840 Doc 18857
COLEMAN Joseph by Portsmouth 1841 Doc 19510

COLEMAN Joseph by Portsmouth 1839 Doc 18856
COLEMAN Joseph by Portsmouth 1840 Doc 18857
COLEMAN Joseph by Portsmouth 1842 Doc 20107
COLEMAN Nathaniel by Rye 1846 Doc 22356
COLEORD Elizabeth by Nottingham 1794 Doc 14339
COLEORD Nancy by Nottingham 1794 Doc 14339
COLHAN Dennis by Deerfield 1851 Doc 931
COLLBERTH Dudley by Portsmouth 1846 Doc 22592
COLLBERTH Elizabeth by Portsmouth 1846 Doc 22592
COLLING Mary by Danville 1853 Doc 2085
COLLINS Benjamin by Danville 1842 Doc 20424
COLLINS Dorothy (w) by Danville 1842 Doc 20424
COLLINS Elizabeth by Windham 1843 Doc 20928
COLLINS Elizabeth by Windham 1842 Doc 20424
COLLINS Elizabeth by Portsmouth 1841 Doc 19511
COLLINS Elizabeth by Portsmouth 1841 Doc 19510
COLLINS Elizabeth by Portsmouth 1843 Doc 20629
COLLINS Elizabeth by Portsmouth 1842 Doc 20107
COLLINS Elizabeth by Windham 1843 Doc 21503
COLLINS Israel by Danville 1842 Doc 20424
COLLINS John by Windham 1842 Doc 20424
COLLINS Jonathan by Epping 1794 Doc 14339
COLLINS Joseph by Danville 1842 Doc 20424
COLLINS Lois by Derry 1843 Doc 20629 A
COLLINS Mary by Danville 1843 Doc 20629 S
COLLINS Mary by Danville 1851 Doc 931
COLLINS Mary by Danville 1844 Doc 21216
COLLINS Mary by Danville 1842 Doc 20424
COLLINS Mary L by Danville 1850 Doc 311
COLLINS Mary S by Danville 1842 Doc 20424
COLLINS Mary S by Danville 1846 Doc 22356
COLLINS Mary S by Danville 1845 Doc 21835
COLLINS Mary S by Danville 1852 Doc 1554
COLLINS Mary S by Danville 1853 Doc 2371
COLLINS Patrick by Brentwood 1850 Doc 311
COLLINS Ruth by Epping 1794 Doc 14339
COLLINS Samuel by Deerfield 1845 Doc 21835
COLLINS Samuel by Portsmouth 1841 Doc 19511
COLLINS Sarah by Danville 1842 Doc 20424
COLLINS William by Derry 1831 Doc 12682
COLLINS William by Derry 1830 Doc 12197
COLLINS William by Derry 1843 Doc 20629 A
COLMAN John by Rye 1798 Doc 16897
CONDY James F by Hawke 1794 Doc 14339
CONE Catherine by Portsmouth 1828 Doc 9200
CONE Catherine (c) by Portsmouth 1828 Doc 9200
CONE James (c) by Portsmouth 1828 Doc 9200
CONE Olive (c) by Portsmouth 1828 Doc 9200
CONNALLY Elizabeth by Portsmouth 1851 Doc 931
CONNALLY Elizabeth by Portsmouth 1851 Doc 311
CONNALLY Sarah by Portsmouth 1851 Doc 931
CONNALLY Sarah Jane by Portsmouth 1851 Doc 311

CONNER James S by Poplin 1809 Doc 30749
CONNER Ruth K by Poplin 1809 Doc 30749
CONNER Thomas by Deerfield 1852 Doc 2086
CONNOR Daniel by S Hampton 1772 Doc 1407
CONNOR Elizabeth by S Hampton 1772 Doc 1407
CONNOR Samuel by S Hampton 1772 Doc 1407
CONNOR Samuel (c) by S Hampton 1772 Doc 1407
CONNOR Sarah by Concord 1812 Doc 34232
CONNORS Gideon by Epping 1780 Doc 4574
CONOLY Michael by Portsmouth 1841 Doc 19510
CONOLY Michael by Portsmouth 1840 Doc 19137
CONOLY Michael by Portsmouth 1842 Doc 20107
CONWAY Clorinda by Exeter 1842 Doc 20107
COOK Cyrene by Londonderry 1815 Doc 39186
COOK Elizabeth by Greenland 1792 Doc 12882
COOK Irene by Chester 1844 Doc 21216
COOK Irene by Chester 1842 Doc 20424
COOK Irene by Chester 1843 Doc 20629 S
COOK John by Exeter 1784 Doc 7181
COOKE Hannah by Newmarket 1790 Doc 11611
COOKE Rebecker by Kingston 1796 Doc 15733
COOMBS Betty by Brentwood 1801 Doc 20206
COOMBS David by Brentwood 1801 Doc 20206
COOMBS Francis (c) by Brentwood 1800 Doc 18692
COOMBS John by Brentwood 1800 Doc 18692
COOMBS John by Poplin 1786 Doc 9631
COOMBS Polley (c) by Brentwood 1800 Doc 18692
COOMES John by Stratham 1807 Doc 27572
COOMEX Betty by Poplin 1794 Doc 14339
COOMEX John by Poplin 1794 Doc 14339
COOPER Hannah by Newtown 1805 Doc 24720
COOPER Hannah by Plaistow 1789 Doc 11025
COPS Sarah by Plaistow 1771 Doc 731
CORLISS Anne by Windham 1794 Doc 14018
CORLISS Elizabeth by Brentwood 1837 Doc 17185
CORLISS Solomon by Windham 1794 Doc 14018
CORNEL Frances by Sandown 1797 Doc 16897
CORNELL Margery by Deerfield 1820 Doc 2385
CORNING Nathan by Londonderry 1839 Doc 18267
COTTON Ezekiel by Brentwood 1786 Doc 9151
COTTON Loas by Brentwood 1786 Doc 9151
COTTON Nathaniel by Epsom 1803 Doc 22771
COUIS Saml F by Portsmouth 1851 Doc 311
COWDERY Sarah by Derry 1852 Doc 1554
COWDEY Sarah by Derry 1851 Doc 931
COWDRY Sarah by Derry 1850 Doc 311
COWEN George E by Portsmouth 1851 Doc 311
COX James by Barrington 1822 Doc 2912
COX Samuel by Derry 1841 Doc 19510
COYNE Laurence by Derry 1852 Doc 1842
COZINE Sarah by Brentwood 1836 Doc 16931
CRAGG James by Windham 1787 Doc 10229

CRAGG Jannet by Windham 1787 Doc 10229
CRAIGIE John by Sandown 1816 Doc 40757
CRAVEN Deborah by Nottingham 1794 Doc 14339
CRAWLEY John by Portsmouth 1840 Doc 18856
CREEL Ann by Portsmouth 1827 Doc 8073
CREEL Richard by Portsmouth 1830 Doc 12197
CREW John by Portsmouth 1846 Doc 22356
CRICKET Benjamin by Atkinson 1771 Doc 2656
CRITCHETT Elizabeth by Greenland 1773 Doc 2472
CRITCHETT Susannah by Newmarket 1784 Doc 7181
CROCKER Mehitable by Derry 1831 Doc 12682
CROCKET Mary by Keningston 1785 Doc 9466
CROCKET Sachuriah by Portsmouth 1791 Doc 12228
CROFTS Ann by Atkinson 1774 Doc 2656
CROFTS Ann (c) by Atkinson 1774 Doc 2656
CROFTS Ephraim by Atkinson 1774 Doc 2656
CROFTS Ephraim (c) by Atkinson 1774 Doc 2656
CROFTS William (c) by Atkinson 1774 Doc 2656
CROOKER John by Portsmouth 1836 Doc 16216
CROSS Aaron by Windham 1793 Doc 14018
CROSS Aaron (c) by Windham 1793 Doc 14018
CROSS Bettey by Windham 1793 Doc 14018
CROSS Bettey (c) by Windham 1793 Doc 14018
CROSS Nancy (c) by Windham 1793 Doc 14018
CROSS Rachel by Deerfield 1843 Doc 20629 S
CROWLEY James by Exeter 1795 Doc 14648
CROWLEY John by Portsmouth 1838 Doc 18267
CROWLEY John by Portsmouth 1843 Doc 20629
CROWLEY John by Portsmouth 1839 Doc 18856
CROWLEY Margaret by Portsmouth 1843 Doc 20629
CROWLEY Susan by Portsmouth 1851 Doc 311
CROWN Deborah by Northwood 1817 Doc 44178
CROXFORD Mary by Portsmouth 1780 Doc 4331
CRUEL Richard by Portsmouth 1832 Doc 13755
CUKEN Betsey by Londonderry 1821 Doc 1592
CUMIER Joshua by Sandown 1796 Doc 15598
CUMMEY Lavina A by Exeter 1846 Doc 22356
CUMMINGHAM Catherine by Portsmouth 1842 Doc 20629
CUMMINGHAM Patrick by Portsmouth 1842 Doc 20629
CUMREY Laura by Exeter 1843 Doc 20629 S
CUNNINGHAM Alanson by Chester 1825 Doc 6965
CURRIER Abigail by Portsmouth 1808 Doc 29235
CURRIER Catharine by Epping 1844 Doc 21216
CURRIER David by Newtown 1843 Doc 20928
CURRIER Isaac by E Kingston 1845 Doc 21835
CURRIER John L by Epping 1843 Doc 20629 S
CURRIER Joseph by E Kingston 1845 Doc 21835
CURRIER Lucinda by Seabrook 1792 Doc 13051
CURRIER Mary by Newtown 1845 Doc 21835
CURRIER Mary by Newton 1852 Doc 1554
CURRIER Mary by Newton 1850 Doc 931
CURRIER Mary by Newtown 1843 Doc 20928

CURRIER Mary by Newtown 1844 Doc 21503
CURRIER Mary by Newton 1850 Doc 311
CURRIER Mary by Newton 1853 Doc 2085
CURRIER Nancy by Epping 1843 Doc 20629 S
CURRIER Philis (Negro) by Poplin 1796 Doc 15598
CURRIER Phillip (Negro) by Poplin 1796 Doc 15598
CURRIER Polly by E Kingston 1852 Doc 1554
CURRIER Polly by E Kingston 1845 Doc 21835
CURRIER Polly by Deerfield 1795 Doc 15018
CURRIER Polly by E Rochester 1853 Doc 2371
CURRIER Polly by E Kingston 1851 Doc 931
CURRIER Polly by E Kingston 1846 Doc 22356
CURRIER Polly by E Kingston 1843 Doc 20928
CURRIER Polly (Negro) by E Kingston 1850 Doc 311
CURRIER Rachael by Epping 1843 Doc 20629 S
CURRIER Rachael by Epping 1844 Doc 21216
CURRIER Rachael by Epping 1842 Doc 20424
CURRIER Roxan by Epping 1844 Doc 21216
CURRIER Seco (Negro) by Poplin 1796 Doc 15598
CURRIER Thomas by Epping 1842 Doc 20107
CURRY Lucinda by Exeter 1791 Doc 11910
CURTES Dolley by Kingston 1852 Doc 1554
CURTIS Charles by Portsmouth 1826 Doc 7634
CURTIS Charles by Portsmouth 1827 Doc 8073
CURTIS Charles by Plaistow 1861 Doc 7174
CURTIS Eizar Ann by Plaistow 1861 Doc 7174
CURTIS George (c) by Plaistow 1861 Doc 7174
CURTIS Ida (c) by Plaistow 1861 Doc 7174
CURTIS Mary by Portsmouth 1828 Doc 9200
CURTIS Rachal by Raymond 1798 Doc 17408
CURTIS Rachel by Poplin 1801 Doc 19665
CURTIS Thomas by Portsmouth 1828 Doc 9200
CUSHEN Sarah by Brentwood 1796 Doc 15359
CUSHEN William by Brentwood 1796 Doc 15359
CUSHING James by Derry 1853 Doc 2085
CUSHING James by Derry 1844 Doc 21216
CUSHING James by Derry 1840 Doc 18856
CUSHING James by Derry 1850 Doc 311
CUSHING James by Derry 1853 Doc 2371
CUSHING James by Derry 1845 Doc 21835
CUSHING James by Derry 1843 Doc 20629 S
CUSHING James by Derry 1841 Doc 19510
CUSHING James by Derry 1852 Doc 1554
CUSHING James by Brentwood 1836 Doc 16931
CUSHING James by Derry 1839 Doc 18267
CUSHING James by Derry 1846 Doc 22356
CUSHING James by Derry 1851 Doc 931
CUSHING Mary by Brentwood 1781 Doc 4749
CUTLER Caroline by Exeter 1836 Doc 16931
CUTLER Jerusha by Loudon 1786 Doc 9151
CUTLER Nancy by Exeter 1836 Doc 16931
CUTLER Nancy by Exeter 1846 Doc 22356

CUTLER Nancy by Exeter 1840 Doc 18856
CUTLER Nancy by Exeter 1841 Doc 19510
CUTLER Nancy by Exeter 1839 Doc 18267
CUTLER Nancy by Exeter 1842 Doc 20107
CUTLER Rufus by Exeter 1842 Doc 20107
CUTLER Rufus by Exeter 1841 Doc 19510
CUTLER Rufus by Exeter 1840 Doc 18856
CUTLER Rufus (c) by Exeter 1839 Doc 18267
CUTTER Sarah by Portsmouth 1852 Doc 1555
CUTTS Margary by Portsmouth 1851 Doc 311
CUTTS Margary by Portsmouth 1852 Doc 1554
CUTTS Margery by Portsmouth 1852 Doc 1555
CUTTS Margery by Portsmouth 1846 Doc 22356
CUTTS Margery by Portsmouth 1851 Doc 931
CUTTS Margery by Portsmouth 1853 Doc 2086
CUTTS Margery by Portsmouth 1843 Doc 20629
DACY Jeremiah by ? 1821 Doc 1592
DACY Jeremiah by Portsmouth 1827 Doc 8073
DAILEY James by Portsmouth 1841 Doc 19510
DAILEY James by Portsmouth 1839 Doc 18856
DAILEY London by Exeter 1784 Doc 7181
DALE Timothy by Stratham 1792 Doc 13190
DALE Timothy by Exeter 1794 Doc 14018
DALEY James by Portsmouth 1835 Doc 15900
DALEY James by Portsmouth 1836 Doc 16214
DALEY John by Portsmouth 1845 Doc 21835
DALLING (w) by Stratham 1793 Doc 14018
DALLING Dyoniica by Portsmouth 1846 Doc 22356
DALLING Sarah by Nottingham 1789 Doc 11025
DALVIN Thos by Portsmouth 1852 Doc 1554
DAME Asa by Durham 1843 Doc 20629
DAME Joseph by Durham 1843 Doc 20629
DAME Joseph by Portsmouth 1842 Doc 20424
DAME Nancy by Portsmouth 1842 Doc 20424
DAME Nancy by Portsmouth 1845 Doc 21835
DAME Timothy by Portsmouth 1842 Doc 20424
DAME Timothy by Durham 1843 Doc 20629
DAMIREL Sarah by Kensington 1777 Doc 3797
DANA William by Exeter 1832 Doc 13754
DANA William by Exeter 1831 Doc 13399
DANE Polly by Exeter 1791 Doc 12531
DANE Walter C by Deerfield 1827 Doc 9822
DANFORTH Lydea by Loudon 1706 Doc 15359
DANFORTH Zedidiah by Loudon 1706 Doc 15359
DANIEL James by Plaistow 1793 Doc 13587
DANIEL Moses (c) by Plaistow 1793 Doc 13587
DANIEL Reuben by Durham 1818 Doc 45992
DANIELS Anny by Pittsfield 1801 Doc 19665
DANIELS Eliphalet by Deerfield 1798 Doc 16897
DANIELS Ephraim Jr (c) by Pittsfield 1801 Doc 19665
DANIELS Ephriam by Pittsfield 1801 Doc 19665
DANIELS James W by Portsmouth 1832 Doc 13755

DANIELS Jonathan by Kingston 1786 Doc 9151
DANIELS Jonathan (c) by Pittsfield 1801 Doc 19665
DANIELS Love by Newmarket 1789 Doc 10754
DANIELS Lucey by Deerfield 1798 Doc 16897
DANIELS Mary by Newmarket 1789 Doc 10754
DANIELS Mary by Kingston 1786 Doc 9151
DANIELS Nancy by Portsmouth 1832 Doc 13755
DANIELS Sarah by Newmarket 1789 Doc 10754
DANIELS Sarah by Newmarket 1801 Doc 20206
DANIELS William (minor) by Kingston 1797 Doc 16546
DANIELS William Glidden by Poplin 1798 Doc 17408
DANNELS Stephen by Plaistow 1791 Doc 12228
DARBY Thomas by Portsmouth 1832 Doc 13755
DARBY Thomas P by Portsmouth 1832 Doc 13754
DARBY Thomas Parson by Portsmouth 1832 Doc 13399
DARETY Caroline by Brentwood 1853 Doc 2085
DARETY George by Brentwood 1853 Doc 2085
DARETY John by Brentwood 1853 Doc 2085
DARETY Mary by Brentwood 1853 Doc 2085
DARETY Mary by Brentwood 1853 Doc 2085
DARETY Michael by Brentwood 1853 Doc 2085
DARGIN Levi by Kingston 1793 Doc 14018
DARLING Eunice (c) by Hawke 1777 Doc 3797
DARLING John by Brentwood 1782 Doc 4997
DARLING John by Hawke 1777 Doc 3797
DARLING John (c) by Hawke 1777 Doc 3797
DARLING Lois (c) by Hawke 1777 Doc 3797
DARLING Lydia (c) by Hawke 1777 Doc 3797
DARLING Mary by Hawke 1777 Doc 3797
DARLING Mary (c) by Hawke 1777 Doc 3797
DARLING Thankfull by Hawke 1777 Doc 3797
DAVERSON Salley by Pembroke 1797 Doc 16546
DAVIDSON Anna by Windham 1842 Doc 20424
DAVIDSON Sarah by Derry 1836 Doc 16214
DAVIDSON Sarah by Derry 1832 Doc 13754
DAVIDSON Sarah by Derry 1831 Doc 12682
DAVIDSON Sarah by Derry 1829 Doc 10409
DAVIDSON Sarah by Derry 1831 Doc 13081
DAVIDSON Sarah by Rockingham County 1831 Doc 13399
DAVIDSON Sarah by Chester 1825 Doc 6965
DAVIDSON Sarah by Derry 1829 Doc 11709
DAVIDSON Sarah by Derry 1830 Doc 12197
DAVIDSON William (Negro) by Exeter 1850 Doc 311
DAVIS Abagail by Gosport 1852 Doc 1554
DAVIS Benjamin by Gosport 1852 Doc 1554
DAVIS Betsey by Candia 1852 Doc 1554
DAVIS Betsey by Epping 1834 Doc 15899
DAVIS Betsy by Candia 1850 Doc 311
DAVIS Deborah by Hampton 1799 Doc 18299
DAVIS Ephraim by Chester 1849 Doc 24261
DAVIS Ezekiel by ? 1805 Doc 23965
DAVIS George W by Newton 1842 Doc 20424

DAVIS Hazen by Newton 1842 Doc 20424
DAVIS Henry by Gosport 1852 Doc 1554
DAVIS Jeremiah by Poplin 1774 Doc 3514
DAVIS Jonathan by Nottingham 1789 Doc 11183
DAVIS Jonathan by Newmarket 1789 Doc 10911
DAVIS Jonathan by Kingston 1806 Doc 26134
DAVIS Joseph by Plaistow 1799 Doc 18299
DAVIS Lidia by Plaistow 1799 Doc 18299
DAVIS Lidia (c) by Plaistow 1799 Doc 18299
DAVIS Loisannah by Stratham 1799 Doc 18299
DAVIS Lydia by Kensington 1795 Doc 14648
DAVIS Lydia by Newmarket 1845 Doc 21835
DAVIS Mary by Plaistow 1783 Doc 7181
DAVIS Mary by Poplin 1777 Doc 3797
DAVIS Mary by Kingston 1789 Doc 10754
DAVIS Molley/Mary by Stratham 1786 Doc 9151
DAVIS Nancy by Kingston 1806 Doc 26134
DAVIS Nathaniel by Kingston 1806 Doc 26134
DAVIS Nathaniel by Poplin 1777 Doc 3797
DAVIS Polly by Kingston 1806 Doc 26134
DAVIS Samuel by Newmarket 1845 Doc 21835
DAVIS Sarah (c) by Plaistow 1799 Doc 18299
DAVIS Simeon by Meredith 1836 Doc 16215
DAVIS Simeon by Newmarket 1829 Doc 10410
DAVIS Simeon (c) by Merrideth 1836 Doc 16215
DAVIS Simeon (c) by Meredith 1831 Doc 12683
DAVIS Thomas by Portsmouth 1839 Doc 18267
DAVIS Thomas by Poplin 1797 Doc 16546
DAVIS William by Portsmouth 1827 Doc 8073
DAVIS William by Kensington 1795 Doc 14648
DAVISON Abigail by Pembroke 1797 Doc 16546
DAVISON Robert by Pembroke 1797 Doc 16546
DAVISON Wm by Portsmouth 1851 Doc 311
DAY Jane by Portsmouth 1830 Doc 12197
DAY Mary Jane by Portsmouth 1830 Doc 12197
DAY Mary Jane by Portsmouth 1836 Doc 16214
DAY Mary Jane by Portsmouth 1836 Doc 16216
DAY Mary Jane by Portsmouth 1837 Doc 16931
DAY Mary Jane by Portsmouth 1830 Doc 12197
DAY Mary June by Portsmouth 1836 Doc 16216
DE Wit Leonard C by Portsmouth 1852 Doc 1555
DEACON Joseph by Portsmouth 1851 Doc 931
DEAEOFF Joseph by Portsmouth 1851 Doc 311
DEARBORN Abraham by Gilford 1819 Doc 47427
DEARBORN Benjamin by Brentwood 1794 Doc 14339
DEARBORN John by Northfield 1819 Doc 47427
DEARBORN Jonathan by Hampton Falls 1841 Doc 19510
DEARBORN Joseph by Poplin 1808 Doc 29235
DEARBORN Mary by Nottingham 1786 Doc 9151
DEARBORN Mary by Nottingham 1790 Doc 11310
DEARBORN Matilda by Candia 1861 Doc 6710
DEARBORN Moses W by Candia 1861 Doc 6710

DEARBORN Sally (c) by Gilford 1819 Doc 47427
DEARBORN Samuel by Nottingham 1790 Doc 11310
DEARBORN Sarah by Derry 1829 Doc 11709
DEARBORN Sarah by Derry 1829 Doc 11709
DEARBY Thomas by Rockingham County 1831 Doc 13399
DEARING Eleanor by Portsmouth 1780 Doc 4331
DEARING Mary Ann by Portsmouth 1851 Doc 931
DEARING Mary Ann by Portsmouth 1839 Doc 18856
DEARING Mary Ann by Portsmouth 1852 Doc 1554
DEARING Mary Ann by Portsmouth 1851 Doc 311
DEARING Mary Ann by Portsmouth 1839 Doc 18267
DECATER Cornelius by Portsmouth 1839 Doc 18856
DECATER Cornelius by Portsmouth 1839 Doc 18267
DEIREE Jane (Negro) by Stratham 1795 Doc 15359
DELANA Ann by Portsmouth 1830 Doc 12197
DELANA Augusta (c) by Newmarket 1846 Doc 22356
DELANA Charles W by Newmarket 1850 Doc 311
DELANA Charles W (c) by Newmarket 1846 Doc 22356
DELANA Chas W by Newmarket 1850 Doc 931
DELANA Michael by Londonderry 1852 Doc 1554
DELANA Polly by Newmarket 1844 Doc 21216
DELANA Polly by Newmarket 1843 Doc 20629
DELANA Thomas by Newmarket 1843 Doc 20629
DELANA Thomas by Portsmouth 1832 Doc 13399
DELANA Thomas by Portsmouth 1832 Doc 13754
DELANCE Augusta by Newmarket 1850 Doc 311
DELAND John by Londonderry 1840 Doc 18856
DELAND Polly by Newmarket 1843 Doc 20928
DELANEY John by Londonderry 1840 Doc 19136
DELANEY John (c) by Londonderry 1840 Doc 19510
DELANEY Joseph (c) by Londonderry 1840 Doc 19510
DELANEY Michael by Londonderry 1840 Doc 19510
DELANEY Michael by Exeter 1852 Doc 1554
DELANEY Michael (c) by Londonderry 1840 Doc 19136
DELANEY Sally by Londonderry 1840 Doc 19136
DELANEY Sarah by Londonderry 1840 Doc 19510
DELANG John by Londonderry 1840 Doc 18856
DELANG Joseph (c) by Londonderry 1840 Doc 18856
DELANG Michael (c) by Londonderry 1840 Doc 18856
DELANG Sarah by Londonderry 1840 Doc 18856
DELAP James by Epping 1788 Doc 10754
DELICATE Ellen by Newmarket 1853 Doc 2371
DELLINGS Eliza by Portsmouth 1852 Doc 1555
DENNETT George by Portsmouth 1843 Doc 20629
DESMAR Patrick by Portsmouth 1842 Doc 20107
DETTING Elizabeth by Portsmouth 1852 Doc 1554
DEVELING Felise by Portsmouth 1830 Doc 12197
DEVELING Felix by Portsmouth 1830 Doc 12197
DEVELING Felix by Portsmouth 1830 Doc 12197
DEVENPORT Johanah by Portsmouth 1795 Doc 14648
DEVIVAN Joanna by Portsmouth 1851 Doc 311
DEWIT Sarah by Portsmouth 1852 Doc 1555

DEXTER Aaron (c) by Atkinson 1796 Doc 16050
DEXTER David by Atkinson 1796 Doc 16050
DEXTER Molly by Atkinson 1796 Doc 16050
DEXTER Nathaniel (c) by Atkinson 1796 Doc 16050
DEXTER Rebeccah (c) by Atkinson 1796 Doc 16050
DEXTER Samuel (c) by Atkinson 1796 Doc 16050
DIAMOND Elizabeth by Epping 1789 Doc 11611
DIAMOND Enos (c) by Epping 1789 Doc 11611
DIAMOND Hannah (c) by Epping 1789 Doc 11611
DIAMOND Isaac (c) by Epping 1789 Doc 11611
DIAMOND Mary (c) by Epping 1789 Doc 11611
DIAMOND Samuel (c) by Epping 1789 Doc 11611
DICKEY Rachal by Windham 1790 Doc 11611
DILL (Negro woman) by Greenland 1797 Doc 16546
DIMON Thomas by Exeter 1772 Doc 1880
DINAH (Negro) by Portsmouth 1789 Doc 11310
DINNES Lucy by Windham 1790 Doc 11910
DIONS Love by Rye 1836 Doc 16214
DIRE John by Epping 1778 Doc 4043
DIX Abigail by Newtown 1840 Doc 18856
DIX Marica Rachel by Newtown 1840 Doc 18856
DOCKAM Hannah by Poplin 1788 Doc 10640
DOCKHAM John by Exeter 1773 Doc 2268
DOCKHAM Nathaniel by Exeter 1773 Doc 2268
DOCKHAM Phebe by Stratham 1807 Doc 27572
DOCKMAN Phebe by Greenland 1792 Doc 12882
DODGE Thomas by Hopkinton 1829 Doc 11710
DOE Jonathan by Epping 1788 Doc 10397
DOE Sarah by Newington 1804 Doc 22771
DOHERTY Patrick by Portsmouth 1842 Doc 20424
DOHERTY William by Portsmouth 1842 Doc 20424
DOIONS Joseph W by Portsmouth 1840 Doc 18856
DOLBEE Isaac by Warner 1818 Doc 45992
DOLE Scipo by Exeter 1779 Doc 4199
DOLLESS Love by Epping 1790 Doc 11310
DOLLIEE Israel by Warner 1818 Doc 45992
DOLLOFF Rebecca by Meredith 1819 Doc 47427
DONNELL John O by Portsmouth 1852 Doc 1554
DONNOVAN Timothy by Portsmouth 1852 Doc 1554
DONOVAN Daniel by Portsmouth 1851 Doc 932
DONOVAN Daniel by Portsmouth 1828 Doc 9200
DONOVAN Timothy by Portsmouth 1851 Doc 931
DOOLEY Andrew (c) by Londonderry 1852 Doc 1554
DOOLEY Elizabeth by Londonderry 1852 Doc 1554
DORETY Mary by Brentwood 1852 Doc 1554
DOREY Jeremiah by Portsmouth 1830 Doc 12197
DORIN Richard by Londonderry 1840 Doc 18856
DORING Samuel by Newmarket 1843 Doc 20928
DORNEY John by Portsmouth 1830 Doc 12197
DORNEY John by Portsmouth 1827 Doc 8073
DORNEY John by Portsmouth 1830 Doc 12197
DOROTY Caroline by Brentwood 1854 Doc 2371

DOROTY George by Brentwood 1854 Doc 2371
DOROTY John by Brentwood 1854 Doc 2371
DOROTY John & Family by Epping 1852 Doc 1554
DOROTY Mary A by Brentwood 1854 Doc 2371
DOROTY Mary N by Brentwood 1854 Doc 2371
DOROTY Michael by Brentwood 1854 Doc 2371
DORREN Catherine by Londonderry 1840 Doc 19136
DORREY John by Portsmouth 1827 Doc 8073
DORRON Richard by Londonderry 1840 Doc 19136
DORSEY Jeremiah by Portsmouth 1830 Doc 12197
DORSEY Jeremiah by Portsmouth 1830 Doc 12197
DOUCY Gus by Exeter 1827 Doc 8655
DOURY George by Exeter 1825 Doc 6965
DOURY George by Exeter 1821 Doc 2381
DOURY Jon by Exeter 1827 Doc 8073
DOURY Jon by Exeter 1825 Doc 6505
DOURY Sally Hunt by Exeter 1821 Doc 2912
DOVER Katharine by Londonderry 1840 Doc 19510
DOVER Richard by Londonderry 1840 Doc 19510
DOW Aaron (c) by Seabrook 1788 Doc 10754
DOW Abiah by Hampton 1774 Doc 3061
DOW Abigail by Kensington 1793 Doc 13587
DOW Betty by Pittsfield 1812 Doc 34232
DOW Betty (c) by Pittsfield 1812 Doc 34232
DOW Charlotte by Portsmouth 1846 Doc 22356
DOW Charlotte by Portsmouth 1845 Doc 21835
DOW Claron (c) by Kensington 1792 Doc 13190
DOW David (c) by Kensington 1792 Doc 13190
DOW Deborah (c) by Pittsfield 1812 Doc 34232
DOW Elizabeth (c) by Portsmouth 1846 Doc 22356
DOW Hannah by Hampton Falls 1795 Doc 15359
DOW Harriet by Kensington 1794 Doc 14528
DOW Harriet by Hampton Falls 1795 Doc 15359
DOW Isaiah by Pittsfield 1812 Doc 34232
DOW Israel (c) by Kensington 1792 Doc 13190
DOW Israel (c) by Seabrook 1788 Doc 10754
DOW James by Greenland 1831 Doc 12682
DOW Jaquith by Hampton Falls 1795 Doc 15359
DOW Jaquith (c) by Hampton Falls 1795 Doc 15359
DOW Jeremiah by Hampton 1774 Doc 3061
DOW Jeremiah (c) by Pittsfield 1812 Doc 34232
DOW John by Portsmouth 1830 Doc 12197
DOW Lucinda by Kensington 1794 Doc 14528
DOW Lucinda by Hampton Falls 1795 Doc 15359
DOW Mary Elizabeth by Portsmouth 1845 Doc 21835
DOW Mary Elizabeth by Portsmouth 1846 Doc 22356
DOW Nancy (c) by Pittsfield 1812 Doc 34232
DOW Nathan by Plaistow 1795 Doc 15018
DOW Richard by Kensington 1794 Doc 14528
DOW Richard by Hampton Falls 1795 Doc 15359
DOW Robert by Kensington 1792 Doc 13190
DOW Robert by Seabrook 1788 Doc 10754

DOW Robert Jr (c) by Seabrook 1788 Doc 10754
DOW Robert Jr (c) by Kensington 1792 Doc 13190
DOW Sally by Kensington 1853 Doc 2371
DOW Sally (c) by Pittsfield 1812 Doc 34232
DOW Sarah (c) by Kensington 1792 Doc 13190
DOW Susanna by Kensington 1792 Doc 13190
DOW Susanna by Seabrook 1788 Doc 10754
DOW Susanna (c) by Seabrook 1788 Doc 10754
DOW Vienney (c) by Hampton Falls 1795 Doc 15359
DOW William by Hampstead 1795 Doc 14648
DOWN Aaron by Portsmouth 1839 Doc 18267
DOWN Mary by Plaistow 1771 Doc 731
DOWNEY John by Portsmouth 1831 Doc 13081
DOWNEY John by Portsmouth 1828 Doc 9200
DOWNING Elizabeth by Newmarket 1843 Doc 20629
DOWNING Esther by Nottingham 1804 Doc 23419
DOWNING Samuel by Newmarket 1843 Doc 20629
DOWNING Samuel by Newmarket 1844 Doc 21216
DOWNING Susan by Exeter 1817 Doc 44178
DOWNS Aaron by Portsmouth 1839 Doc 18856
DOWNS Abagail by Gosport 1854 Doc 2371
DOWNS Abigail by Gosport 1846 Doc 22356
DOWNS Abigail by Gosport 1846 Doc 22356
DOWNS Abigail by Gosport 1850 Doc 311
DOWNS Abigail by Isle Of Shoals 1845 Doc 21835
DOWNS Abigail by Hampton Falls 1792 Doc 12882
DOWNS Benjamin by Isle Of Shoals 1845 Doc 21835
DOWNS Benjamin by Gosport 1854 Doc 2371
DOWNS Benjamin by Gosport 1850 Doc 311
DOWNS Benjamin by Gosport 1846 Doc 22356
DOWNS Benjamin by Rye 1853 Doc 2085
DOWNS Berry by Gosport 1846 Doc 22356
DOWNS Betty (c) by Hampton Falls 1790 Doc 11611
DOWNS Eunice by Kensington 1795 Doc 14648
DOWNS Henry by Isle Of Shoals 1845 Doc 21835
DOWNS Henry by Gosport 1846 Doc 22356
DOWNS Henry by Eastport 1853 Doc 2085
DOWNS Henry by Gosport 1851 Doc 931
DOWNS John by Hampton Falls 1783 Doc 6644
DOWNS Jonathan by Hampton Falls 1790 Doc 11611
DOWNS Joseph by Rye 1836 Doc 16214
DOWNS Joseph W by Rye 1836 Doc 16214
DOWNS Joseph W by Rye 1837 Doc 16931
DOWNS Lida by Hampton Falls 1790 Doc 11611
DOWNS Love by Rye 1830 Doc 12682
DOWNS Lydia by Hampton Falls 1783 Doc 6644
DOWNS Mary by Rye 1831 Doc 12682
DOWNS Sally by Hampton Falls 1790 Doc 11611
DOWNS William by Rye 1831 Doc 12682
DOWNS William by Rye 1829 Doc 11709
DOWNS William by Rye 1829 Doc 10409
DOYEN Sarah by Concord 1822 Doc 3416

DOYLE Eneas by Portsmouth 1840 Doc 18857
DOYLE Eneas by Portsmouth 1841 Doc 19510
DOYLE Eneas by Portsmouth 1840 Doc 18857
DOYLE Eneas by Portsmouth 1840 Doc 19137
DOYLE John by Portsmouth 1837 Doc 16931
DOYLE William by Exeter 1828 Doc 9200
DRAKE Betty (c) by Hawke 1794 Doc 14339
DRAKE Jesse (c) by Hawke 1794 Doc 14339
DRAKE Simon by Hawke 1794 Doc 14339
DRAKE Tamson by Hawke 1794 Doc 14339
DREW Clement (c) by Loudon 1790 Doc 11611
DREW Deborah by Greenland 1797 Doc 16546
DREW Deborah (c) by Northwood 1793 Doc 13190
DREW Esther by Loudon 1789 Doc 10911
DREW Hannah by Northwood 1793 Doc 13190
DREW Hannah (c) by Northwood 1793 Doc 13190
DREW Joseph (c) by Loudon 1789 Doc 10911
DREW Joshia by Northwood 1793 Doc 13190
DREW Lydia (c) by Northwood 1793 Doc 13190
DREW Mary by Loudon 1789 Doc 10911
DREW Mary (c) by Northwood 1793 Doc 13190
DREW Obadiah by Loudon 1789 Doc 10911
DREW Samuel (c) by Northwood 1793 Doc 13190
DROIN Sarah Ann by Newmarket 1833 Doc 14122
DUDA Samuel (alias) Tucke by Newmarket 1794 Doc 14339
DUDLEY Anna by Brentwood 1801 Doc 20206
DUDLEY Anna by Kingston 1799 Doc 17750
DUDLEY Anna (c) by Kingston 1799 Doc 17750
DUDLEY Anna (w) by Brentwood 1801 Doc 19665
DUDLEY Daniel by Poplin 1809 Doc 30749
DUDLEY Darah by Epping 1792 Doc 12531
DUDLEY Daverson by Brentwood 1801 Doc 20206
DUDLEY David (c) by Kingston 1799 Doc 17750
DUDLEY Davison by Poplin 1808 Doc 29235
DUDLEY Hannah by Newington 1775 Doc 3695
DUDLEY John S by Brentwood 1815 Doc 39186
DUDLEY Jonathan by Brentwood 1798 Doc 17408
DUDLEY Mary by Kingston 1799 Doc 17750
DUDLEY Peter Coffin by Kingston 1799 Doc 17750
DUDLEY Polley by Brentwood 1801 Doc 20206
DUDLEY Polly (c) by Kingston 1799 Doc 17750
DUDLEY Rusha by Poplin 1808 Doc 29235
DUDLEY Rushea (c) by Kingston 1799 Doc 17750
DUDLEY Susanna by Brentwood 1801 Doc 20206
DUDLEY Susanna (c) by Kingston 1799 Doc 17750
DUDLEY Terrisha by Brentwood 1801 Doc 20206
DUFFEY George by Portsmouth 1832 Doc 13754
DUFFEY Owen by Portsmouth 1835 Doc 15900
DUFFY George by Portsmouth 1832 Doc 13755
DUFFY Owen by Portsmouth 1836 Doc 16214
DUFFY Owen by Portsmouth 1836 Doc 16214
DUNCAN John by Londonderry 1845 Doc 21835

DUNCAN Julia Ann by Portsmouth 1836 Doc 16214
DUNCAN Sarah by Newcastle 1829 Doc 10409
DUNCAN Sarah by New Castle 1827 Doc 9200
DUNCAN Sarah by Newcastle 1827 Doc 9822
DUNHAM Charlotte (Indian) by Deerfield 1826 Doc 6965
DUNKIN Julianna by Portsmouth 1835 Doc 15900
DUNLAP David by Atkinson 1831 Doc 12682
DUNLAP David (c) by Atkinson 1831 Doc 12682
DUNLAP Elizabeth (c) by Atkinson 1831 Doc 12682
DUNLAP George W (c) by Atkinson 1831 Doc 12682
DUNLAP Jacob by Salem 1831 Doc 13399
DUNLAP James (c) by Atkinson 1831 Doc 12682
DUNLAP Mary (c) by Atkinson 1831 Doc 12682
DUNLAP Samuel (c) by Atkinson 1831 Doc 12682
DUNLAP Sarah (c) by Atkinson 1831 Doc 12682
DUNLAP Sophia by Atkinson 1831 Doc 12682
DUNLAP Sophia by Salem 1850 Doc 311
DUNLAP Sophia by Stratham 1851 Doc 931
DUNLAP Sophia by Salem 1854 Doc 2371
DUNLAP Sophia by Salem 1853 Doc 2085
DUNN Mary by Newmarket 1853 Doc 2085
DUNTAN James by Hampton Falls 1795 Doc 15359
DUNTAN John B by Hampton Falls 1795 Doc 15359
DUNTLEY Hannah by Bow 1796 Doc 15598
DUNTLEY Jonathan (c) by Bow 1796 Doc 15598
DUNTLEY Joseph by Bow 1796 Doc 15598
DUNTLEY Olive (c) by Bow 1796 Doc 15598
DUNTLEY Robert (c) by Bow 1796 Doc 15598
DUNWELL Daniel by Windham 1853 Doc 2371
DURGIN Abigail by Deerfield 1851 Doc 932
DURGIN Abigail by Newmarket 1850 Doc 931
DURGIN Jonathan by ? 1816 Doc 40757
DURGIN Levi by Poplin 1792 Doc 12882
DURGIN Levi by Durham 1822 Doc 2912
DURGIN Sarah by Loudon 1789 Doc 11611
DURY John by Portsmouth 1832 Doc 13754
DURY John by Portsmouth 1836 Doc 16214
DURY John by Portsmouth 1839 Doc 18856
DURY John by Portsmouth 1840 Doc 18857
DURY John by Portsmouth 1841 Doc 19510
DURY John by Portsmouth 1837 Doc 16931
DURY John by Portsmouth 1840 Doc 19137
DURY John by Portsmouth 1830 Doc 12197
DURY John by Portsmouth 1842 Doc 20107
DURY John by Portsmouth 1846 Doc 22356
DURY John by Portsmouth 1830 Doc 12197
DURY John by Portsmouth 1838 Doc 18267
DURY John by Portsmouth 1832 Doc 13755
DURY John by Portsmouth 1836 Doc 16214
DUSTEN Sarah by Atkinson 1785 Doc 8644
DUSTIN Benjamin by Derry 1843 Doc 20629 A
DUSTIN Sally by Derry 1843 Doc 20629 A

DUSTIN William by Derry 1843 Doc 20629 A
DUTCH Samuel by S Hampton 1822 Doc 2912
DUTCH Samuel by Lee 1821 Doc 1592
DUTY Mark by Bow 1792 Doc 13587
DUTY Sally (c) by Bow 1792 Doc 13587
DWIER John by Portsmouth 1851 Doc 311
DWIN George by Portsmouth 1851 Doc 932
DWINELL Christopher (c) by Litchfield 1830 Doc 11710
DWINELL Sally by Londonderry 1846 Doc 22356
DWINELL Sally by Londonderry 1844 Doc 21503
DWINELL Sally by Londonderry 1843 Doc 21216
DWINELL Stephen by Londonderry 1844 Doc 21503
DYAS James by Portsmouth 1825 Doc 6965
DYAS William by Portsmouth 1827 Doc 8073
DYER George by Portsmouth 1851 Doc 311
DYER Goerge by Portsmouth 1851 Doc 931
DYER Henry by Portsmouth 1852 Doc 1555
DYER Henry by Portsmouth 1852 Doc 1554
DYER Jonathan by Portsmouth 1808 Doc 29235
DYER Kerziak by Epping 1782 Doc 4882
DYER Samuel by Epping 1782 Doc 4882
EASTMAN Anna by Stratham 1792 Doc 13190
EASTMAN Anna by Windham 1819 Doc 47427
EASTMAN Anne by Greenland 1780 Doc 4574
EASTMAN Betsey by Windham 1789 Doc 11183
EASTMAN Ebenezer (c) by Windham 1819 Doc 47427
EASTMAN Elizabeth (c) by Windahm 1819 Doc 47427
EASTMAN Jacob by Hampstead 1820 Doc 2397
EASTMAN Jacob by Hampstead 1822 Doc 2912
EASTMAN Richard by Windham 1789 Doc 11183
EASTMAN Samuel G by Windham 1819 Doc 47427
EASTMAN Sarah by Hampstead 1823 Doc 3965
EASTMAN Sarah by Hawke 1790 Doc 11310
EASTMAN Timothy (c) by Windham 1819 Doc 47427
EATON Jane by Kensington 1791 Doc 12228
EATON Phebe by Asylum 1846 Doc 22592
EATON Stephen by S Hampton 1841 Doc 19510
EAVANS Holton by Epping 1845 Doc 21835
EAVANS Holton by Deerfield 1845 Doc 21835
EAVANS Molly by Deerfield 1845 Doc 21835
EAVANS Waldon by Deerfield 1845 Doc 21835
EDER George by Rockingham County 1825 Doc 6965
EDGARLY Betty by Epping 1800 Doc 19247
EDGELY Samuel by Exeter 1775 Doc 3703
EDGERLY John by Newmarket 1802 Doc 21391
EDGERLY Temperence by Newmarket 1802 Doc 21391
EDWARDS John by Kensington 1812 Doc 34232
EDWARDS John by Newmarket 1810 Doc 32331
EDWARDS John by Stratham 1810 Doc 33660
EDWARDS Mary by Greenland 1780 Doc 4574
EIDON Peter by Portsmouth 1841 Doc 19510
EILLIOT J A by Exeter 1853 Doc 2371

ELIOT Abigail (c) by Poplin 1804 Doc 23419
ELIOT Anna (c) by Pittsfield 1805 Doc 23965
ELIOT Billey (c) by Pittsfield 1805 Doc 23965
ELIOT Hannah (c) by Pittsfield 1805 Doc 23965
ELIOT Harris (c) by Pittsfield 1805 Doc 23965
ELIOT Jacob (c) by Pittsfield 1805 Doc 23965
ELIOT Joseph (c) by Pittsfield 1805 Doc 23965
ELIOT Joseph (c) by Poplin 1804 Doc 23419
ELIOT Nathaniel by Pittsfield 1805 Doc 23965
ELIOT Polley (c) by Pittsfield 1805 Doc 23965
ELIOT Rosamond by Poplin 1804 Doc 23419
ELIOT Ross by Brentwood 1785 Doc 8644
ELIOT Sarah by Nottington 1789 Doc 11310
ELKINS Richard by Newmarket 1842 Doc 20107
ELLERD Ruth by Greenland 1777 Doc 4164
ELLIOT Elenor by Allenstown 1822 Doc 3416
ELLIOT Hannah by Londonderry 1821 Doc 1592
ELLIOT John A by Exeter 1850 Doc 311
ELLIOTT John A by Exeter 1853 Doc 2371
ELLIOTT John A by Exeter 1853 Doc 2085
ELLIOTT Nancy by Exeter 1850 Doc 311
ELLIOTT Nancy by Exeter 1852 Doc 1554
ELLIOTT Nancy by Exeter 1851 Doc 931
ELLISON Mary by Northfield 1821 Doc 1592
EMERSON Amos by Windham 1845 Doc 21835
EMERSON Abigail (c) by Pittsfield 1801 Doc 20206
EMERSON Benjamin (c) by Bow 1791 Doc 12228
EMERSON Betty by Bow 1791 Doc 12228
EMERSON Betty (c) by Bow 1791 Doc 12228
EMERSON Daniel (c) by Pittsfield 1801 Doc 20206
EMERSON Elizabeth by Loudon 1790 Doc 11611
EMERSON George by Loudon 1790 Doc 11611
EMERSON George by Bow 1791 Doc 12228
EMERSON James (c) by Bow 1791 Doc 12228
EMERSON John by Rockingham County 1825 Doc 6505
EMERSON Jonathan by Pelham 1835 Doc 15557
EMERSON Lawrence by Epping 1838 Doc 17575
EMERSON Lois by Epping 1838 Doc 17575
EMERSON Polly (c) by Bow 1791 Doc 12228
EMERSON Sally (c) by Bow 1791 Doc 12228
EMERSON Samuel by Pittsfield 1801 Doc 20206
EMERSON Samuel (c) by Bow 1791 Doc 12228
EMERSON Sarah by Pittsfield 1801 Doc 20206
EMERY Daniel by Brentwood 1836 Doc 16931
EMERY Daniel by Portsmouth 1832 Doc 13754
EMERY Daniel by Portsmouth 1836 Doc 16214
EMERY Daniel by Portsmouth 1839 Doc 18856
EMERY Daniel by Portsmouth 1828 Doc 9200
EMERY Daniel by Portsmouth 1842 Doc 20107
EMERY Daniel by Portsmouth 1841 Doc 19510
EMERY Daniel by Portsmouth 1830 Doc 12197
EMERY Dolley by Portsmouth 1852 Doc 1554

EMERY Dolly by Portsmouth 1851 Doc 311
EMERY Dolly by Portsmouth 1851 Doc 931
EMERY Eliphelet by Atkinson 1774 Doc 2656
EMERY Elizabeth by Portsmouth 1840 Doc 18857
EMERY Elizabeth by Portsmouth 1840 Doc 18857
EMERY Elizabeth by Portsmouth 1841 Doc 19510
EMERY Laura Ann by Exeter 1843 Doc 20928
EMERY Nehemiah by Epping 1800 Doc 19247
EMERY Polly by Epping 1800 Doc 19247
EMERY Salley by Epping 1800 Doc 19247
EMERY Samuel by Newmarket 1844 Doc 21216
ENNISS Patrick by Nottingham 1810 Doc 33660
ENNISS Patrick by Nottingham 1813 Doc 36435
ENNISS Patrick by Nottingham 1812 Doc 34232
ENWOOD Joseph by Portsmouth 1851 Doc 311
ERDON Peter by Portsmouth 1841 Doc 19136
ERVING John by Sandown 1815 Doc 39186
ESMAN Ann by N Hampton 1789 Doc 10911
EVANS Holley by Epping 1846 Doc 22356
EVANS David by Portsmouth 1839 Doc 18267
EVANS Holton by Epping 1846 Doc 22356
EVANS Ruth by Portsmouth 1849 Doc 311
EVANS Ruth by Poplin 1851 Doc 931
EVANS Walden by Epping 1846 Doc 22356
EVANS Waldron by Deerfield 1795 Doc 14879
EVANS William by Deerfield 1795 Doc 14879
EVERTON James by Londonderry 1841 Doc 19510
EVERTON William by Londonderry 1841 Doc 19510
EVERTON William by Londonderry 1843 Doc 21216
EVERTON William by Londonderry 1846 Doc 22356
EVERTON William by Londonderry 1842 Doc 20424
EVERTON Willian by Londonderry 1842 Doc 20107
FALLS Sarah (w) by Newington 1795 Doc 14879
FANNING David by Portsmouth 1851 Doc 931
FANNING David by Portsmouth 1851 Doc 311
FANNING David by Portsmouth 1845 Doc 21835
FANNING David by Portsmouth 1852 Doc 1554
FANNING David by Portsmouth 1852 Doc 1554
FANNING David by Portsmouth 1851 Doc 1554
FARLEY Peter by Portsmouth 1851 Doc 311
FARMER Andrew by Pembroke 1780 Doc 4331
FARMER Betey by Bow 1796 Doc 15598
FARMER Jonathan by Bow 1796 Doc 15598
FARMER Joseph (c) by Bow 1796 Doc 15598
FARMER Susannah (c) by Bow 1796 Doc 15598
FARMER Thomas (c) by Bow 1796 Doc 15598
FARNHAM Sarah by Newmarket 1851 Doc 932
FARWELL Henry by Derry 1850 Doc 311
FARWELL Henry by Chester 1851 Doc 931
FARWELL Henry by Chester 1850 Doc 311
FAVOR Betsey by Portsmouth 1846 Doc 22356
FAVOR Daniel by Kingston 1790 Doc 10911

FAVOR Daniel by Kingston 1790 Doc 11611
FAVOUR Daniel by Kingston 1773 Doc 2095
FAVOUR Elizabeth by Newmarket 1773 Doc 2095
FAWLEY C by Portsmouth 1852 Doc 1554
FEBENEL Luis by Portsmouth 1846 Doc 22356
FELKER Mary by Nottingham 1842 Doc 20424
FELKER Mary by Nothingham 1844 Doc 21216
FELKER Mary by Nottingham 1845 Doc 21835
FELLOWS Hannah by Hawke 1801 Doc 19665
FERDINAND Dorothy by Portsmouth 1832 Doc 13754
FERDINAND Dorothy by Portsmouth 1832 Doc 13755
FERDINAND Elizabeth by Portsmouth 1832 Doc 13755
FERDINAND Elizabeth by Portsmouth 1832 Doc 13754
FERDINAND Peter by Portsmouth 1832 Doc 13755
FERGERSON Daniel by Portsmouth 1827 Doc 9200
FERGUSON Betsy by Rockingham County 1831 Doc 13399
FERINGTON John by Epping 1799 Doc 18299
FERINGTON Mary by Epping 1799 Doc 18299
FERINGTON Mary by Epsom 1810 Doc 33660
FERN Colby (Mrs) by Kingston 1853 Doc 2085
FERNALD Patrick by Nottingham 1794 Doc 14339
FERNST John (c) by Portsmouth 1846 Doc 22356
FIFI Mary (c) by Chichester 1867 Doc 8216
FIFI Moses by Chichester 1867 Doc 8216
FIFIELD Abigail by Poplin 1792 Doc 12882
FIFIELD Abigail by Hampton Falls 1780 Doc 4331
FIFIELD Jonathan by Seabrook 1793 Doc 13190
FIFIELD Margaret by Hampton Falls 1780 Doc 4331
FIFIELD Margaret by Atkinson 1780 Doc 4331
FINN Michael by Portsmouth 1841 Doc 19136
FISH Eleas by Portsmouth 1841 Doc 19510
FISH Eleazer by Portsmouth 1840 Doc 19137
FISH Eleazer by Portsmouth 1842 Doc 20107
FISHER Rueben by Pembroke 1793 Doc 13587
FISHLEY John by Rye 1802 Doc 22285
FISHLEY Sarah by Rye 1802 Doc 22285
FISK Cata by Exeter 1787 Doc 9740
FISK Cato by Poplin 1799 Doc 17750
FISK Cato by Raymond 1796 Doc 16050
FISK Cato (Negro) by Deerfield 1801 Doc 20206
FISK Ebenezer (Negro) by Deerfield 1801 Doc 20206
FISK Ebenezer (c) by Poplin 1799 Doc 17750
FISK Elizabeth (Negro) by Deerfield 1801 Doc 20206
FISK Else by Poplin 1799 Doc 17750
FISK James by Exeter 1853 Doc 2085
FISK James by Exeter 1853 Doc 2371
FISK James (c) by Poplin 1799 Doc 17750
FISK James (Negro) by Deerfield 1801 Doc 20206
FISK John (c) by Poplin 1799 Doc 17750
FISK John (Negro) by Deerfield 1801 Doc 20206
FISK Nancy (c) by Poplin 1799 Doc 17750
FISK Nancy (Negro) by Deerfield 1801 Doc 20206

FISK Polly by Windham 1791 Doc 12531
FISK Sarah by Deerfield 1802 Doc 21796
FITZGERALD Dennis by Portsmouth 1843 Doc 20629
FITZGERALD Edward by Portsmouth 1850 Doc 932
FITZGERALD Garrett by Portsmouth 1852 Doc 1554
FITZGERALD Garrett by Portsmouth 1853 Doc 2086
FITZGERALD James by Portsmouth 1827 Doc 8073
FITZGERALD Jeremiah by Portsmouth 1850 Doc 932
FITZGERALD Jeremiah by Portsmouth 1851 Doc 931
FITZGERALD John by Portsmouth 1852 Doc 1555
FITZPATRICK Elizabeth by Nottingham 1789 Doc 10229
FLANDERS Abigail by Candia 1827 Doc 9822
FLANDERS Adeline by Plaistow 1839 Doc 17185
FLANDERS Anna by Plaistow 1773 Doc 2268
FLANDERS Christopher (c) by Sandown 1788 Doc 10229
FLANDERS Daniel P by Plaistow 1839 Doc 17185
FLANDERS David by Londonderry 1840 Doc 18856
FLANDERS Elizabeth by Sandown 1788 Doc 10229
FLANDERS Ezekiel by Plaistow 1773 Doc 2268
FLANDERS Ezekiel Jr (c) by Plaistow 1773 Doc 2268
FLANDERS Frances by Plaistow 1839 Doc 17185
FLANDERS Frances (c) by Plaistow 1773 Doc 2268
FLANDERS Gorham by Plaistow 1839 Doc 17185
FLANDERS Hannah by Chester 1861 Doc 6144
FLANDERS James by Chester 1846 Doc 22356
FLANDERS Jarvis by Chester 1844 Doc 21216
FLANDERS Jarvis by Rockingham County 1831 Doc 13399
FLANDERS Jarvis by Derry 1832 Doc 13754
FLANDERS Jarvis by Kingston 1842 Doc 20424
FLANDERS Jarvis by Derry 1833 Doc 14122
FLANDERS Jarvis by Chester 1845 Doc 21835
FLANDERS Jarvis by Chester 1843 Doc 20629 S
FLANDERS John (c) by Chester 1861 Doc 6144
FLANDERS Jonathan (c) by Plaistow 1773 Doc 2268
FLANDERS Joseph (c) by Plaistow 1773 Doc 2268
FLANDERS Mary C by Plaistow 1839 Doc 17185
FLANDERS Nathaniel (c) by Plaistow 1773 Doc 2268
FLANDERS Philip by Chester 1861 Doc 6144
FLANDERS Philip by Chester 1853 Doc 2371
FLANDERS Philip by Chester 1852 Doc 1554
FLANDERS Prince by Plaistow 1839 Doc 17185
FLANDERS Sarah (s) by Plaistow 1773 Doc 2268
FLANDERS Stephen (c) by Plaistow 1773 Doc 2268
FLANDERS Thomas by Plaistow 1839 Doc 17185
FLANDERS William J by Plaistow 1839 Doc 17185
FLANNAGAN Michael by Portsmouth 1852 Doc 1842
FLEMING Thomas (minor) by ? 1816 Doc 40757
FLINN John by Portsmouth 1852 Doc 1842
FLINN Lucy by Portsmouth 1832 Doc 13754
FLINN Lucy by Portsmouth 1830 Doc 12197
FLINN Timothy by Portsmouth 1851 Doc 311
FLINT Edward by Exeter 1831 Doc 12682

FLINT Edward by Exeter 1836 Doc 16931
FLINT Edward by Exeter 1825 Doc 6965
FLINT Edward by Exeter 1830 Doc 12197
FLINT Edward by Exeter 1829 Doc 11709
FLINT Edward by Exeter 1827 Doc 8073
FLINT Edward by Exeter 1831 Doc 13081
FLINT Edward by Exeter 1831 Doc 13399
FLINT Edward by Exeter 1828 Doc 9822
FLINT Edward by Exeter 1827 Doc 8655
FLINT Edward by Exeter 1832 Doc 13754
FLINT Edward by Exeter 1835 Doc 16214
FLINT Edward by Exeter 1838 Doc 18267
FLOOD Allen (c) by Loudon 1789 Doc 10911
FLOOD Elizabeth by Brentwood 1790 Doc 11910
FLOOD Hannah (c) by Plaistow 1773 Doc 2268
FLOOD James by Plaistow 1773 Doc 2268
FLOOD John by Kensington 1772 Doc 731
FLOOD Joseph by Brentwood 1790 Doc 11910
FLOOD Lydia by E Kingston 1805 Doc 24720
FLOOD Mary by Kingston 1801 Doc 19665
FLOOD Mary by Kensington 1772 Doc 731
FLOOD Mary (c) by Kingston 1801 Doc 19665
FLOOD Mary by Loudon 1789 Doc 10911
FLOOD Polly (c) by Kingston 1801 Doc 19665
FLOOD Rachael (c) by Kingston 1801 Doc 19665
FLOOD Rachael (c) by Loudon 1789 Doc 10911
FLOOD Rhoda (c) by Loudon 1789 Doc 10911
FLOOD Richard by Loudon 1789 Doc 10911
FLOOD Richard by Kingston 1801 Doc 19665
FLOOD Richard by Hampstead 1769 Doc 1612
FLOOD Samuel by Brentwood 1790 Doc 11910
FLOOD Sarah by Plaistow 1773 Doc 2268
FLOOD Sarah (c) by Plaistow 1773 Doc 2268
FLOOD William by E Kingston 1805 Doc 24720
FLOW Molly by Epping 1846 Doc 22356
FLOWRANCE Hannah by Exeter 1779 Doc 4199
FLOYD John by Portsmouth 1835 Doc 15900
FLOYD John by Portsmouth 1836 Doc 16214
FOGG Gerrett (c) by Portsmouth 1835 Doc 15557
FOGG John by Portsmouth 1835 Doc 15557
FOGG Sarah by Portsmouth 1835 Doc 15557
FOLCEY Peter (Negro) by Exeter 1845 Doc 20629 A
FOLENSBEE John (c) by Sandown 1813 Doc 36435
FOLENSBEE Sally by Sandown 1813 Doc 36435
FOLENSBEE Sally (c) by Sandown 1813 Doc 36435
FOLENSBEE William by Sandown 1813 Doc 36435
FOLENSBEE William (c) by Sandown 1813 Doc 36435
FOLLANSBEE Abigail by Candia 1826 Doc 7524
FOLLANSBEE Abigail by Candia 1827 Doc 8073
FOLLANSBEE Abigail by Candia 1826 Doc 6965
FOLLANSBEE Abigail by Candia 1827 Doc 8655
FOLLANSBEE Abigail by Candia 1825 Doc 6505

FOLLET John by Northwood 1827 Doc 8077
FOLSOM Abigail by Dorchester 1831 Doc 12683
FOLSOM Eunice by Durham 1808 Doc 29235
FOLSOM Samuel by Northfield 1785 Doc 8391
FOLSOM Unice by Newmarket 1783 Doc 5630
FORD John by Portsmouth 1840 Doc 19137
FORD John by Portsmouth 1841 Doc 19510
FORD John by Portsmouth 1842 Doc 20107
FOREDEN Michael by Portsmouth 1842 Doc 20107
FOREDEN Michael by Portsmouth 1841 Doc 20107
FOREMAN Charlotte (c) by Exeter 1836 Doc 16214
FOREMAN Charlotte (c) by Portsmouth 1836 Doc 16214
FOREMAN Edward (c) by Portsmouth 1836 Doc 16214
FOREMAN Edward (c) by Exeter 1836 Doc 16214
FOREMAN Edward (c) by Portsmouth 1833 Doc 14415
FOREMAN George (c) by Portsmouth 1833 Doc 14415
FOREMAN Harriet (c) by Portsmouth 1833 Doc 14415
FOREMAN Jesse by Portsmouth 1833 Doc 14415
FOREMAN Jesse by Exeter 1836 Doc 16214
FOREMAN Ninz (c) by Portsmouth 1833 Doc 14415
FOREMAN Sarah by Portsmouth 1833 Doc 14415
FOREMAN Sarah by Portsmouth 1836 Doc 16214
FOREMAN Sarah by Exeter 1836 Doc 16214
FOREST David by Portsmouth 1851 Doc 311
FOREST Sara by Portsmouth 1851 Doc 931
FORMAN Charlott by Exeter 1836 Doc 16931
FORMAN Charlotte by Exeter 1840 Doc 18856
FORMAN Edward (c) by Exeter 1839 Doc 18267
FORMAN Sarah by Exeter 1840 Doc 18856
FORMAN Sarah by Exeter 1836 Doc 16931
FORMAN Sarah (c) by Exeter 1839 Doc 18267
FORREST Catherine by Portsmouth 1846 Doc 22356
FORREST Catherine by Portsmouth 1852 Doc 1555
FORREST Catherine by Portsmouth 1851 Doc 932
FORREST Catherine by Portsmouth 1851 Doc 931
FORREST Catherine by Portsmouth 1853 Doc 2086
FORREST Catherine by Portsmouth 1851 Doc 311
FORREST Catherine by Portsmouth 1852 Doc 1554
FORREST Catherine by Portsmouth 1845 Doc 21835
FORREST John (c) by Portsmouth 1845 Doc 21835
FORREST John (c) by Portsmouth 1846 Doc 22356
FORREST Larry by Portsmouth 1842 Doc 20107
FORREST Larry by Portsmouth 1842 Doc 20107
FORREST Sara by Portsmouth 1852 Doc 1554
FORREST Sarah by Portsmouth 1851 Doc 311
FORREST Lawry by Portsmouth 1845 Doc 21835
FORRESTER Lawry by Portsmouth 1846 Doc 22356
FORRESTER W Garein by Portsmouth 1851 Doc 311
FORTIER Joseph by Salem 1808 Doc 29949
FOSS Benjamin (c) by Newmarket 1776 Doc 3712
FOSS Deborah by Tamworth 1822 Doc 3416
FOSS Elizabeth by Newmarket 1776 Doc 3712

FOSS Hannah by Tamworth 1822 Doc 3416
FOSS Jedidiah by Portsmouth 1842 Doc 20107
FOSS John by Newmarket 1776 Doc 3712
FOSS John by Exeter 1840 Doc 19510
FOSS John Jr (c) by Newmarket 1776 Doc 3712
FOSS Lydia (c) by Newmarket 1776 Doc 3712
FOSS Robert by Derry 1836 Doc 16215
FOSS Robert by Poplin 1836 Doc 16215
FOSS Sarah (c) by Newmarket 1776 Doc 3712
FOSS William by Greenland 1790 Doc 11611
FOSTER William by Portsmouth 1851 Doc 931
FOSTER Edward by Portsmouth 1833 Doc 14122
FOSTER James by Windham 1827 Doc 8073
FOSTER Mary by Windham 1789 Doc 11183
FOSTER William by Portsmouth 1846 Doc 22356
FOSTER William by Portsmouth 1842 Doc 20424
FOSTER William by Portsmouth 1852 Doc 1554
FOSTER William by Portsmouth 1851 Doc 311
FOWLER Abigail by Hampton 1798 Doc 18299
FOWLER Abigail (c) by S Hampton 1792 Doc 12882
FOWLER Elizabeth (c) by Poplin 1806 Doc 26821
FOWLER Ezekiel by Poplin 1806 Doc 26821
FOWLER Ezekiel (c) by Poplin 1806 Doc 26821
FOWLER Isaac (c) by Poplin 1806 Doc 26821
FOWLER Jacob (c) by S Hampton 1792 Doc 12882
FOWLER Martha by S Hampton 1792 Doc 12882
FOWLER Mary by Poplin 1806 Doc 26821
FOWLER Mehitabel (c) by S Hampton 1792 Doc 12882
FOWLER Philip by ? 1803 Doc 2352
FOWLER Robert (c) by Poplin 1806 Doc 26821
FOWLER Samuel by S Hampton 1792 Doc 12882
FOWLER Sarah by Hampton 1801 Doc 19665
FOWLS Robert by Brentwood 1796 Doc 15359
FOWLS Robert L by Brentwood 1796 Doc 15359
FOWLS Sarah by Brentwood 1796 Doc 15359
FRACKE Cattern (c) by Northwood 1791 Doc 11910
FRACKE Hannah (c) by Northwood 1791 Doc 11910
FRACKE Robert (c) by Northwood 1791 Doc 11910
FRACKE Samuel by Northwood 1791 Doc 11910
FRACKE Samuel Jr (c) by Northwood 1791 Doc 11910
FRACKE Sanday M (c) by Northwood 1791 Doc 11910
FRACKE Sarah by Northwood 1791 Doc 11910
FRANCIS Betsey (minor) by Kingston 1791 Doc 12531
FRANCIS Betty by Poplin 1797 Doc 16546
FRASHER Samuel by Nothingham 1785 Doc 8391
FRASHER Susana by Nothingham 1785 Doc 8391
FRAZIER Alexander by Portsmouth 1842 Doc 20107
FRAZIER Nancy by Concord 1813 Doc 36435
FREEMAN Diah by Derry 1831 Doc 13399
FREEMAN Edward (c) by Exeter 1835 Doc 16214
FREEMAN Sarah by Exeter 1835 Doc 16214
FRENCH Abigail by Exeter 1795 Doc 14648

FRENCH Anna (c) by Bow 1791 Doc 12228
FRENCH Beckey by Deerfield 1798 Doc 16897
FRENCH Clarrisa by Landraff 1834 Doc 14817
FRENCH Edward by Deerfield 1798 Doc 16897
FRENCH Edward by Epsom 1810 Doc 33660
FRENCH Elisha by Northfield 1785 Doc 8391
FRENCH Elvira (c) by Landraff 1834 Doc 14817
FRENCH Hannah (c) by Bow 1791 Doc 12228
FRENCH Lucy by Bow 1791 Doc 12228
FRENCH Mary A by Stratham 1851 Doc 931
FRENCH Mary A by Stratham 1852 Doc 1554
FRENCH Mary A by Stratham 1853 Doc 2085
FRENCH Mehitabel (c) by Bow 1791 Doc 12228
FRENCH Moses by Landraff 1834 Doc 14817
FRENCH Moses by Rockingham County 1831 Doc 13399
FRENCH Rebekah (c) by Bow 1791 Doc 12228
FRENCH Samuel by Nottingham 1850 Doc 311
FRENCH Sarah by Newmarket 1789 Doc 10911
FRENCH Stephen (c) by Landraff 1834 Doc 14817
FRENCH Susanna by Bow 1791 Doc 12228
FRENCH William (c) by Bow 1791 Doc 12228
FRENCH William by Bow 1791 Doc 12228
FRENCY Mary by Stratham 1853 Doc 2371
FRIDELL (Negro) by Exeter 1795 Doc 14648
FRITZGERALD James by Windham 1793 Doc 13587
FRITZGERALD Sarah by Deerfield 1780 Doc 4406
FROST Elizabeth (c) by Portsmouth 1846 Doc 22356
FROST Jane by Portsmouth 1846 Doc 22356
FROST Jane by Portsmouth 1851 Doc 931
FROST John by Portsmouth 1846 Doc 22356
FROST John (c) by Portsmouth 1846 Doc 22356
FROST John Jr (c) by Portsmouth 1846 Doc 22356
FROST Nathaniel (c) by Portsmouth 1846 Doc 22356
FRYE Martha Ann by Portsmouth 1834 Doc 14818
FULLER Abigail by Seabrook 1841 Doc 19512
FULLER Abigail (c) by Seabrook 1841 Doc 19512
FULLER Clairissa (c) by Seabrook 1841 Doc 19512
FULLER Elizabeth (c) by Seabrook 1841 Doc 19512
FULLER James by Exeter 1773 Doc 2472
FULLER John by Seabrook 1841 Doc 19512
FULLER John Jr (c) by Seabrook 1841 Doc 19512
FULLER Jonathan (c) by Seabrook 1841 Doc 19512
FULLER Phebe J (c) by Seabrook 1841 Doc 19512
FULLINGTON Ebenezer by Poplin 1801 Doc 20206
FULLINGTON Ebenezer (c) by Poplin 1801 Doc 20206
FULLINGTON Lydia by Poplin 1801 Doc 20206
FULLINGTON Lydia (c) by Poplin 1801 Doc 20206
FUNNEL Hannah by Pittsfield 1802 Doc 20738
FUNNISTON Polly by Londonderry 1814 Doc 37172
FURBER Nancy by Portsmouth 1843 Doc 20629
FURBER Nancy by Portsmouth 1846 Doc 22356
FURNHAM Sarah H by Newmarket 1852 Doc 1554

GALE Eli by Exeter 1827 Doc 8655
GALE Hannah by Exeter 1827 Doc 8655
GALLAWAY Abigail by Newtown 1772 Doc 731
GALLAWAY Elizabeth by Newtown 1772 Doc 731
GALLAWAY Faith Elizabeth by Newtown 1772 Doc 731
GALLAWAY Job by Newtown 1772 Doc 731
GALLAWAY Lydea by Newtown 1772 Doc 731
GALLAWAY Martha by Newtown 1772 Doc 731
GALLAWAY Mary by Newtown 1772 Doc 731
GALLAWAY Trueworth by Newtown 1772 Doc 731
GALNAGH Charles (c) by Farmington 1861 Doc 6144
GALNAGH Elizabeth by Farmington 1861 Doc 6144
GALNAGH Elizabeth by Farmington 1861 Doc 6144
GALNAGH Elizabeth by Brentwood 1852 Doc 1842
GALNAGH Emma (c) by Farmington 1861 Doc 6144
GALNAGH George H (c) by Farmington 1861 Doc 6144
GALNAGH James by Farmington 1861 Doc 6144
GALNAGH James by Brentwood 1852 Doc 1842
GALNAGH James F (c) by Farmington 1861 Doc 6144
GALNAGH Laura E (c) by Farmington 1861 Doc 6144
GALNAGH Mary A (c) by Farmington 1861 Doc 6144
GALNAGH Mary E (c) by Brentwood 1852 Doc 1842
GALNAUGH Elizabeth by Brentwood 1854 Doc 2371
GALNAUGH James by Brentwood 1854 Doc 2371
GALT Benjamin (c) by Windham 1790 Doc 11611
GALT Margaret by Windham 1790 Doc 11611
GALT Martha (c) by Windham 1790 Doc 11611
GAMMON Abigail by Portsmouth 1842 Doc 20424
GAMMON Charles by Portsmouth 1840 Doc 19137
GAMMON Dorcas by Greenland 1804 Doc 23419
GAMMON Dorcas by Portsmouth 1842 Doc 20424
GAMMON Dorcas by Portsmouth 1852 Doc 1554
GAMMON Doreas by Portsmouth 1851 Doc 311
GAMMON Doreas by Portsmouth 1851 Doc 931
GANNON Bridget by Portsmouth 1852 Doc 1555
GANNON Bridgett by Portsmouth 1852 Doc 1554
GANNON Charles by Portsmouth 1841 Doc 19510
GARDE John by Portsmouth 1832 Doc 13754
GARDE John by Portsmouth 1832 Doc 13755
GARDENER Lydia by Hampton 1817 Doc 44178
GARDIMS George by Portsmouth 1830 Doc 12197
GARDING George by Portsmouth 1830 Doc 12197
GARDNER Delevarance by Brentwood 1786 Doc 9151
GARDNER John by Rockingham County 1825 Doc 6505
GARDY Hannah by Sandown 1788 Doc 10397
GARNER Erastus by Portsmouth 1833 Doc 14122
GARY Mary by Portsmouth 1839 Doc 18856
GAULT Isaac by Auburn 1853 Doc 1842
GAUTT Elizabeth (c) by Pembroke 1795 Doc 15359
GAUTT Hazen (c) by Pembroke 1795 Doc 15359
GAUTT Marthaw (c) by Pembroke 1795 Doc 15359
GAUTT Nancy by Pembroke 1795 Doc 15359

GAUTT William by Pembroke 1795 Doc 15359
GAUTT William (c) by Pembroke 1795 Doc 15359
GEORGE Charles A by Brentwood 1852 Doc 1842
GEORGE David by Hampstead 1770 Doc 1612
GEORGE Jonathan by Hampstead 1770 Doc 1612
GERRISH Moses by Kensington 1789 Doc 11310
GERRY Joseph by Exeter 1830 Doc 12197
GERRY Nancy by Exeter 1830 Doc 12197
GIBBS Molly by Hampton Falls 1783 Doc 5630
GIBBS Rachael by Hampton Falls 1783 Doc 5630
GIBSON George by Poplin 1843 Doc 20629 A
GIBSON John by Exeter 1774 Doc 2656
GIFFIN Rachael by Deerfield 1846 Doc 22356
GIFFIN John by Auburn 1843 Doc 311
GILE Eli by Exeter 1828 Doc 9822
GILE Ezekiel by ? 1823 Doc 3965
GILE Ezekiel by Plaistow 1844 Doc 21216
GILE Ezekiel by Plaistow 1846 Doc 22356
GILE Ezekiel by Plaistow 1842 Doc 20424
GILE Ezekiel by Plymouth 1821 Doc 1592
GILE Ezekiel by Plaistow 1845 Doc 21835
GILE Ezekiel Jr (c) by ? 1823 Doc 3965
GILE Jonathan (c) by ? 1823 Doc 3965
GILE Polly by ? 1823 Doc 3965
GILE Ruth by ? 1823 Doc 3965
GILE Timothy W (c) by ? 1823 Doc 3965
GILES Mary/Polly by Deerfield 1795 Doc 14879
GILES Polly/Mary by Stratham 1799 Doc 18299
GILL Fay by Exeter 1790 Doc 11910
GILL Joel (c) by Exeter 1790 Doc 11910
GILL Larry by Exeter 1790 Doc 11910
GILLESPY James by Windham 1772 Doc 1880
GILLISPEE George by Portsmouth 1851 Doc 311
GILMAN Abigail by Poplin 1807 Doc 27572
GILMAN Abigail (c) by Poplin 1807 Doc 27572
GILMAN Faireny (c) by Poplin 1807 Doc 27572
GILMAN Richard by Poplin 1807 Doc 27572
GILMAN Benjamin by Exeter 1826 Doc 7524
GILMAN Benjamin by Exeter 1773 Doc 2472
GILMAN Cezar by Portsmouth 1835 Doc 15900
GILMAN Cozar by Portsmouth 1836 Doc 16214
GILMAN John by Kingston 1790 Doc 11310
GILMAN Mariah by Nottingham 1781 Doc 4574
GILMAN Olive by Greenland 1797 Doc 16546
GILMAN Robert by Exeter 1830 Doc 11710
GILMAN Robert by Newmarket 1832 Doc 13399
GILMAN Robert by Hawke 1798 Doc 17408
GILMAN Robert by Brentwood 1803 Doc 22285
GILMAN Sarah by Newmarket 1828 Doc 9201
GIRDEY Hannad by Sandown 1788 Doc 10229
GITCHEL Ezekiel by Deerfield 1801 Doc 19665
GITCHEL Ezekiel (c) by Deerfield 1801 Doc 19665

GITCHEL Ezra (c) by Deerfield 1801 Doc 19665
GITCHEL Huledy by Deerfield 1801 Doc 19665
GITCHEL Lydia (c) by Deerfield 1801 Doc 19665
GITCHEL Nathan (c) by Deerfield 1801 Doc 19665
GITTINS John by Stratham 1851 Doc 931
GLEASON Michael by Portsmouth 1833 Doc 14122
GLIDDEN Betty by Poplin 1783 Doc 5630
GLIDDEN Jonathan by Poplin 1798 Doc 17408
GLIDEN Joanan by Brentwood 1772 Doc 1407
GLINES Jonathan by Sandown 1844 Doc 21503
GLINES Lydia by Sandown 1844 Doc 21503
GLINN John W by Portsmouth 1851 Doc 311
GLOU Moylly by Epping 1844 Doc 21216
GLOVER John by Boscawen 1818 Doc 45992
GLOVER John by Northfield 1818 Doc 45992
GODDARDS D William by Portsmouth 1841 Doc 19510
GOFF James by Portsmouth 1836 Doc 16214
GOFF James by Portsmouth 1835 Doc 15900
GOLDEN Jane by Kingston 1778 Doc 4111
GOLDEN Mary by Portsmouth 1852 Doc 1554
GOOCH James by Northwood 1790 Doc 11611
GOOCH James Jr by Northwood 1790 Doc 11611
GOOCH Polle by Northwood 1790 Doc 11611
GOOCH Salle by Northwood 1790 Doc 11611
GOODFREY Abigail by Stratham 1794 Doc 14648
GOODHUE Mary by Pelham 1810 Doc 32331
GOODHUE Widow by Pelham 1810 Doc 31571
GOODIN Abigail by Hampton 1807 Doc 26821
GOODWIN Elizabeth (c) by S Hampton 1849 Doc 24261
GOODWIN Ivory by Portsmouth 1852 Doc 1554
GOODWIN Amos (c) by S Hampton 1849 Doc 24261
GOODWIN Benjamin by Portsmouth 1835 Doc 15900
GOODWIN Benjamin by Portsmouth 1836 Doc 16214
GOODWIN Ezekiel by S Hampton 1849 Doc 24261
GOODWIN Francis (c) by S Hampton 1849 Doc 24261
GOODWIN Larry by Portsmouth 1852 Doc 1555
GOODWIN Sarah by Candia 1843 Doc 20928
GOODWIN Sarah (c) by S Hampton 1849 Doc 24261
GORDEN John by Portsmouth 1852 Doc 1554
GORDEN Joseph by Kensington 1792 Doc 13190
GORDEN Nicholas by Brentwood 1795 Doc 15018
GORDEN Polly (c) by Kensington 1792 Doc 13190
GORDEN Robert by Portsmouth 1839 Doc 18542
GORDEN Sarah by Kensington 1792 Doc 13190
GORDEN Thomas by Raymond 1795 Doc 14648
GORDEN Thomas by Poplin 1792 Doc 12531
GORDING Hannah by Deerfield 1788 Doc 10229
GORDON Jesse by Hampstead 1833 Doc 14414
GORDON Robert by Portsmouth 1840 Doc 18856
GOSS Polly by Pittsfield 1822 Doc 2912
GOTT Abigail by Portsmouth 1830 Doc 12197
GOTT Abigail by Portsmouth 1832 Doc 13754

GOTT Adaline by Portsmouth 1834 Doc 14818
GOUCH Dolle (c) by Northwood 1788 Doc 10640
GOUCH James Jr (c) by Northwood 1788 Doc 10640
GOUCH Salle by Northwood 1788 Doc 10640
GOULD Jane T by Portsmouth 1836 Doc 16216
GOULD Jane T by Portsmouth 1836 Doc 16214
GOVE Enoch by Seabrook 1852 Doc 1554
GOVE Enoch by Seabrook 1850 Doc 311
GOVE Enoch by Seabrook 1846 Doc 22356
GOVE Enoch by Seabrook 1853 Doc 2371
GOVE Enoch by Seabrook 1853 Doc 2085
GOVE Enoch by Seabrook 1850 Doc 931
GOVE Hannah by Hampton Falls 1842 Doc 20107
GOVE Jerimiah by Hampton Falls 1842 Doc 20107
GOVE Nathan by Sandown 1814 Doc 37727
GOVE Polly by Sandown 1814 Doc 37727
GOWIN John by Portsmouth 1852 Doc 1554
GRACE John by Portsmouth 1852 Doc 1554
GRADE John by Portsmouth 1832 Doc 13755
GRAFTON Abigail by Exeter 1850 Doc 311
GRAFTON Mary E by Exeter 1850 Doc 311
GRAFTON Thomas W by Exeter 1850 Doc 311
GRANGE Barnard W by Portsmouth 1842 Doc 20107
GRANGE Abigail by Deerfield 1785 Doc 9466
GRANGE Eben by Deerfield 1785 Doc 9466
GRANT Abigail by Portsmouth 1830 Doc 12197
GRANT Alex by Greenland 1780 Doc 4331
GRANT Benjamin by Loudon 1789 Doc 10911
GRANT Doras by Portsmouth 1830 Doc 12197
GRANT Dorcas by Portsmouth 1830 Doc 12197
GRANT George by Plaistow 1793 Doc 14018
GRANT John Jr by Portsmouth 1827 Doc 8073
GRANT Mary by Northwood 1773 Doc 2268
GRANT Peter by Portsmouth 1851 Doc 311
GRANT Polly by Sandown 1796 Doc 15598
GRANT Rebeccah by Epping 1794 Doc 14339
GRANT Susy by Derry 1842 Doc 20424
GRAVES Abagial by Hawke 1811 Doc 32876
GRAVES Abigail by Poplin 1816 Doc 40757
GRAVES Isarel by Brentwood 1842 Doc 20629 A
GRAVES Isarel by Exeter 1785 Doc 8391
GRAVES Israel by Brentwood 1842 Doc 20424
GRAVES Israel by Brentwood 1845 Doc 21835
GRAVES Israel by Poplin 1816 Doc 40757
GRAVES Israel by Brentwood 1852 Doc 1554
GRAVES Israel by Hawke 1811 Doc 32876
GRAVES Israel by Brentwood 1846 Doc 22356
GRAVES Israel by Brentwood 1843 Doc 20629 S
GRAVES Israel by Brentwood 1854 Doc 2371
GRAVES Israel by Brentwood 1844 Doc 21216
GRAVES Isreas by Brentwood 1853 Doc 2085
GRAW William W by Portsmouth 1852 Doc 1555

GRAY John by Exeter 1774 Doc 3514
GRAY Mary by Portsmouth 1841 Doc 19510
GRAY Mary by Portsmouth 1851 Doc 311
GRAY Mary by Portsmouth 1842 Doc 20107
GRAY Mary by Portsmouth 1840 Doc 18267
GRAY Mary by Portsmouth 1851 Doc 931
GRAY Mary by Portsmouth 1852 Doc 1554
GRAY William F by Portsmouth 1840 Doc 18267
GREAN Barnard by Portsmouth 1841 Doc 20107
GREELEY Betty by Kensington 1792 Doc 13190
GREELEY Jonathan by Deerfield 1801 Doc 19665
GREELEY Jonathan by E Kingston 1810 Doc 32331
GREELEY Nathan by E Kingston 1843 Doc 20629 A
GREELEY Nathan by E Kingston 1846 Doc 22356
GREELEY Nathan by E Kingston 1843 Doc 20928
GREEN Elizabeth by Exeter 1852 Doc 1554
GREEN Polly by Portsmouth 1843 Doc 20629
GREEN Sarah by Loudon 1789 Doc 11025
GREEN Thomas by Portsmouth 1851 Doc 311
GREENAWAY Abraham by E Kingston 1810 Doc 33660
GREENAWAY Abraham by E Kingston 1809 Doc 32331
GREENAWAY Abraham by E Kingston 1813 Doc 36435
GREENAWAY Abraham by Kingston 1783 Doc 5630
GREENLEAF Mary by Derry 1850 Doc 311
GREENLEAF William by Salem 1853 Doc 2085
GREENLEAF William by Salem 1854 Doc 2371
GREENOUGH Charles (c) by Atkinson 1858 Doc 4985
GREENOUGH Deborah by Atkinson 1858 Doc 4985
GREENOUGH Fanny (c) by Atkinson 1858 Doc 4985
GREENOUGH George B (c) by Atkinson 1858 Doc 4985
GREENOUGH Robert by Atkinson 1858 Doc 4985
GREENOUGH Sarah E (c) by Atkinson 1858 Doc 4985
GREETY Nathan by Meridith 1819 Doc 47427
GREGORY Thomas by Hampton 1840 Doc 18856
GRENSUGH Samuel by Stratham 1800 Doc 18692
GREORGE Dorothy by Poplin 1796 Doc 15598
GRIFFES Robert by Portsmouth 1835 Doc 15900
GRIFFIN Ebenezer by Atkinson 1771 Doc 2656
GRIFFIN Elizabeth by Londonderry 1846 Doc 22358
GRIFFIN Elizabeth by Londonderry 1854 Doc 2371
GRIFFIN Jeremiah by Raymond 1790 Doc 11611
GRIFFIN John by Portsmouth 1842 Doc 20107
GRIFFIN John by Londonderry 1842 Doc 20107
GRIFFIN John by Londonderry 1850 Doc 311
GRIFFIN John by Portsmouth 1841 Doc 19511
GRIFFIN John by Portsmouth 1841 Doc 19510
GRIFFIN John by Portsmouth 1840 Doc 19137
GRIFFIN John by Londonderry 1845 Doc 21835
GRIFFIN John by Londonderry 1851 Doc 931
GRIFFIN John by Londonderry 1846 Doc 22356
GRIFFIN Jonathan by Londonderry 1854 Doc 2371
GRIFFIN Jonathan by Pelham 1817 Doc 44178

GRIFFIN Nathan by Derrfield 1846 Doc 22356
GRIFFIN Rachael by Deerfield 1838 Doc 17575
GRIFFIN Rachael by Deerfield 1836 Doc 16215
GRIFFIN Rachael by Deerfield 1836 Doc 16215
GRIFFIN Rachel by Deerfield 1850 Doc 311
GRIFFIN Rachel by Derrfield 1846 Doc 22356
GRIFFIS Robert by Portsmouth 1836 Doc 16214
GRIMALL John by Greenland 1791 Doc 11910
GRIMES Bettey by Windham 1795 Doc 15359
GRIMES Rebecka by Windham 1794 Doc 14648
GROO Sarah by Brentwood 1790 Doc 11310
GROVER Abigail by Portsmouth 1834 Doc 14818
GROVER Mary Cotes by Portsmouth 1791 Doc 12228
GROW Sarah by Poplin 1792 Doc 12531
GUMMON Doras by Portsmouth 1846 Doc 22356
GWINE John W by Portsmouth 1852 Doc 1554
HACKET Allen (c) by Epping 1799 Doc 18299
HACKET Charles by Epping 1799 Doc 18299
HACKET Hannah by Epping 1799 Doc 18299
HACKET Hannah by Epping 1778 Doc 4043
HACKET Hannah (c) by Epping 1799 Doc 18299
HACKET Warren (c) by Epping 1799 Doc 18299
HACKETT James by Portsmouth 1827 Doc 8073
HADDEN W by Portsmouth 1852 Doc 1554
HADENS Robert by Portsmouth 1852 Doc 1842
HADLOCK Benjamin (c) by Kingston 1798 Doc 17408
HADLOCK Mary by Kingston 1798 Doc 17408
HADLOCK Mary (c) by Kingston 1798 Doc 17408
HADLOCK Susanna by Allenstown 1789 Doc 11025
HAGGERTY Dennis by Portsmouth 1833 Doc 14122
HAILS James by Newmarket 1789 Doc 10754
HAINES Elizabeth by Newmarket 1789 Doc 10911
HAINES Gideon by Newmarket 1789 Doc 10911
HAINES James by Epping 1792 Doc 12531
HAINES James by Greenland 1795 Doc 15018
HALE Abigail by Atkinson 1780 Doc 4331
HALE Clarrisa by Exeter 1817 Doc 45992
HALE Juderisa by Exeter 1817 Doc 45992
HALEY Martha by Nottingham 1780 Doc 4331
HALEY Nathan by E Kingston 1844 Doc 21216
HALFPENNEY Ann by Portsmouth 1851 Doc 931
HALFPENNEY James (c) by Portsmouth 1846 Doc 22356
HALFPENNEY Martha by Portsmouth 1851 Doc 931
HALFPENNEY Martha by Portsmouth 1852 Doc 1554
HALFPENNEY Mary by Portsmouth 1851 Doc 311
HALFPENNEY Sarah by Portsmouth 1846 Doc 22356
HALFPENNY Martha (c) by Portsmouth 1851 Doc 311
HALISAND James by Nottingham 1794 Doc 14339
HALL Elizabeth Chase by Exeter 1842 Doc 20107
HALL Edwin by Exeter 1851 Doc 931
HALL Sarah Roberts by Brentwood 1850 Doc 311
HALL Abigail (c) by Exeter 1846 Doc 22356

HALL Aron (Negro) by Exeter 1795 Doc 14648
HALL Augustus (c) by Exeter 1852 Doc 1554
HALL Betsey (Negro) by Exeter 1796 Doc 15359
HALL Clairissa (Negro) by Exeter 1795 Doc 14648
HALL Clarissa by Kensington 1817 Doc 44178
HALL Dolley (Negro) by Exeter 1795 Doc 14648
HALL Edwin by Exeter 1853 Doc 2085
HALL Edwin by Exeter 1853 Doc 2371
HALL Edwin (c) by Exeter 1846 Doc 22356
HALL Edwin (c) by Exeter 1850 Doc 311
HALL Edwin (c) by Exeter 1852 Doc 1554
HALL Elizabeth by Portsmouth 1843 Doc 20629 A
HALL Granville (c) by Exeter 1852 Doc 1554
HALL George by Exeter 1843 Doc 20629 S
HALL George by Exeter 1846 Doc 22356
HALL George (Negro) by Exeter 1842 Doc 20107
HALL George by Exeter 1844 Doc 21216
HALL Joseph by Rye 1846 Doc 22356
HALL Jude by Portsmouth 1843 Doc 20629 A
HALL Jude by Exeter 1787 Doc 9740
HALL Jude by Exeter 1842 Doc 20107
HALL Jude (Negro) by Stratham 1792 Doc 13190
HALL Judi (Negro) by Exeter 1795 Doc 14648
HALL Lovey by Nottingham 1846 Doc 22356
HALL Mark (c) by Exeter 1846 Doc 22356
HALL Mary & Child by Nottingham 1852 Doc 1554
HALL Mary & Child by Nottingham 1854 Doc 2371
HALL Mary (c) by Exeter 1846 Doc 22356
HALL Nathan by Nottingham 1850 Doc 311
HALL Nathan by Nottingham 1854 Doc 2371
HALL Nathan & Wife by Nottingham 1852 Doc 1554
HALL Nathaniel (Negro) by Exeter 1795 Doc 14648
HALL Rebecca (Negro) by Exeter 1792 Doc 12882
HALL Rhoda (Negro) by Exeter 1795 Doc 14648
HALL Rohada (Negro) by Stratham 1792 Doc 13190
HALL Sarah by Auburn 1843 Doc 311
HALL Susanna (Negro) by Exeter 1796 Doc 15359
HALL Susannah by Nothingham 1777 Doc 3981
HALL Thomas by Portsmouth 1838 Doc 18267
HALL Thomas by Deerfield 1781 Doc 4749
HALL William by Portsmouth 1830 Doc 12197
HALL William by Portsmouth 1831 Doc 13081
HALL William by Portsmouth 1828 Doc 9200
HALL William (Negro) by Exeter 1795 Doc 14648
HALL William by Portsmouth 1825 Doc 6965
HALL William by Portsmouth 1827 Doc 8073
HALL William by Portsmouth 1830 Doc 12197
HALLEY Martha by Greenland 1780 Doc 4331
HALPENNEY Ann (c) by Portsmouth 1846 Doc 22356
HALPENNEY Mary by Portsmouth 1852 Doc 1554
HALPENNEY Mary by Portsmouth 1851 Doc 931
HALPENNEY Sarah by Portsmouth 1851 Doc 931

HALPENNEY Sarah by Portsmouth 1852 Doc 1554
HALPENNEY Sarah by Portsmouth 1851 Doc 311
HALPENNY Ann by Portsmouth 1842 Doc 20107
HALPENNY Ann (c) by Portsmouth 1841 Doc 19510
HALPENNY James by Portsmouth 1841 Doc 19510
HALPENNY James by Portsmouth 1842 Doc 20107
HALPENNY Sarah by Portsmouth 1842 Doc 20107
HALPENNY Sarah by Portsmouth 1841 Doc 19137
HALPENNY Sarah by Portsmouth 1841 Doc 19510
HALSGROVE James by Portsmouth 1841 Doc 19510
HAM Charles by Stratham 1850 Doc 6393
HAM Jacob by Newmarket 1801 Doc 20738
HAM William (Mrs) (w) by Portsmouth 1817 Doc 44178
HAMILTON John by Exeter 1795 Doc 14648
HAMILTON Oliver by Portsmouth 1852 Doc 1554
HAMILTON Oliver by Portsmouth 1852 Doc 1555
HAMILTON Phebe by Newmarket 1792 Doc 12882
HAMMET Doley by Windham 1793 Doc 13587
HAMMET John by Windham 1793 Doc 13587
HAMMETT George by Portsmouth 1846 Doc 22356
HAMMOND Hannah by Portsmouth 1851 Doc 931
HAMMOND Inu by Portsmouth 1831 Doc 13082
HAMMOND Ira by Derry 1831 Doc 13081
HAMMOND Ira by Portsmouth 1832 Doc 13082
HAMMOND Ira by Portsmouth 1832 Doc 13754
HAMMOND Susan D by Portsmouth 1836 Doc 16214
HAMMOND Susan Deborah by Portsmouth 1835 Doc 15900
HANES Rachael by Rye 1803 Doc 22285
HANES Reuben by Rye 1803 Doc 22285
HANES Samuel by Loudon 1796 Doc 15359
HANES Susannah by Loudon 1796 Doc 15359
HANNAFORD Amos F by Exeter 1844 Doc 20629
HANNET Daniel by Portsmouth 1851 Doc 932
HANNETT David by Portsmouth 1850 Doc 932
HANOVER Thomas by Portsmouth 1841 Doc 19510
HANOVER Thomas by Portsmouth 1840 Doc 19137
HANSON Plummer by Raymond 1852 Doc 2086
HANSON Isaac by Kingston 1842 Doc 20424
HANSON John by Portsmouth 1851 Doc 311
HANSON Plummer by Raymond 1853 Doc 2371
HANSON Samuel by Raymond 1853 Doc 2371
HANSON Samuel by ? 1850 Doc 311
HANSON Samuel by Raymond 1850 Doc 1554
HANSON Samuel by Raymond 1850 Doc 931
HANSON Sarah by Kingston 1844 Doc 21503
HANSON Sarah by Kingston 1846 Doc 22356
HANSON Sarah by Newton 1850 Doc 311
HANSON Sarah by Kingston 1842 Doc 20424
HARAVEY John S by Nottingham 1854 Doc 2371
HARDEN Samuel by Hampton 1850 Doc 311
HARDEY Afa by Salem 1792 Doc 13051
HARDEY Bial by Kingston 1790 Doc 11611

HARDEY Caleb (c) by Salem 1792 Doc 13051
HARDEY Fabethy (c) by Salem 1792 Doc 13051
HARDEY Fibey (c) by Salem 1792 Doc 13051
HARDEY Meditable by Salem 1792 Doc 13051
HARDEY Rebeckah (c) by Salem 1792 Doc 13051
HARDEY Sarah (c) by Salem 1792 Doc 13051
HARDEY Tabethy (c) by Salem 1792 Doc 13051
HARDIE Anna by Poplin 1786 Doc 9631
HARDIE Biley by Poplin 1786 Doc 9631
HARDIE Biley Jr by Poplin 1786 Doc 9631
HARDIE Joseph by Poplin 1786 Doc 9631
HARDIE Marcy by Poplin 1786 Doc 9631
HARDIE Rebeckah by Poplin 1786 Doc 9631
HARDING Jesse by Portsmouth 1839 Doc 18267
HARDING Mary by Portsmouth 1839 Doc 18267
HARDING Mary by Portsmouth 1842 Doc 20107
HARDING Mary by Portsmouth 1839 Doc 18856
HARDING Mary by Portsmouth 1841 Doc 19510
HARDING Mary by Portsmouth 1841 Doc 19511
HARDY Bradbuy by Hampton Falls 1854 Doc 2371
HARDY David by Poplin 1808 Doc 29235
HARDY Hannah by Poplin 1808 Doc 29235
HARDY Jacob by ? 1782 Doc 5272
HARDY John by Haverhill 1828 Doc 9201
HARDY Jonathan (alias) by Hampton Falls 1779 Doc 4237
HARDY Lucy by Haverhill 1828 Doc 9201
HARDY Lydia by Windham 1793 Doc 14018
HARDY Silas by Windham 1793 Doc 14018
HARDY Thomas (Major) by Windham 1793 Doc 14018
HARFORD Dolly by Newmarket 1794 Doc 14339
HARFORD Dolly (c) by Newmarket 1794 Doc 14339
HARFORD Hannah (c) by Newmarket 1794 Doc 14339
HARFORD James (c) by Deerfield 1851 Doc 932
HARFORD John by Newmarket 1794 Doc 14339
HARFORD John (c) by Newmarket 1794 Doc 14339
HARFORD Polly (c) by Newmarket 1794 Doc 14339
HARGRAVES Jabez by N Hampton 1838 Doc 17575
HARGRAVES Jabez by N Hampton 1827 Doc 8655
HARGRAVES Jabez by N Hampton 1827 Doc 8073
HARGRAVES Jabez by N Hampton 1829 Doc 11709
HARGRAVES Jabez by N Hampton 1832 Doc 13754
HARGRAVES Jabez by N Hampton 1830 Doc 12197
HARGRAVES Jabez by N Hampton 1833 Doc 14122
HARGRAVES Jabez by N Hampton 1831 Doc 12682
HARGRAVES Jabez by N Hampton 1831 Doc 13081
HARGRAVES Jabez by N Hampton 1831 Doc 13399
HARGRAVES Jabez by Exeter 1825 Doc 6505
HARGRAVES James by Rye 1802 Doc 22285
HARMETON Peter by Portsmouth 1841 Doc 19510
HARMETON Peter by Portsmouth 1838 Doc 18267
HARMON Hannah by Portsmouth 1851 Doc 311
HARMOND Hannah by Portsmouth 1852 Doc 1554

HARRCHEU Edward by Portsmouth 1852 Doc 1554
HARRETT Johanna by Exeter 1852 Doc 1554
HARRIGAIN Patrick by Portsmouth 1841 Doc 19510
HARRIGAIN Patrick by Portsmouth 1841 Doc 19136
HARRIGAN Daniel by Portsmouth 1833 Doc 14122
HARRIMAN Abigail by Plaistow 1784 Doc 7181
HARRIMAN Anna by Londonderry 1841 Doc 19510
HARRIMAN David by Salem 1777 Doc 3981
HARRIMAN Eunes by Plaistow 1784 Doc 7181
HARRIMAN Jonathan by Plaistow 1784 Doc 7181
HARRINGTON Catherine by Newmarket 1853 Doc 2371
HARRIS Joseph by Salem 1774 Doc 3514
HARRIS Joseph by Portsmouth 1830 Doc 12197
HARRIS Mariah by Brentwood 1836 Doc 16931
HARRIS Martha by Salem 1843 Doc 20629 A
HARRIS Martha by Salem 1843 Doc 20928
HARRIS Merrthia by Salem 1774 Doc 3514
HARRIS William by Portsmouth 1837 Doc 16931
HARRISON Jemima by Kingston 1782 Doc 5384
HARRISON Polly by Kensington 1792 Doc 13190
HARRISON Polly by Kingston 1793 Doc 13190
HARRISON William by Kingston 1782 Doc 5384
HART Ceazar (Negro) by Portsmouth 1843 Doc 20629
HART Charlotte by County-roch 1853 Doc 2371
HART Charlotte by Exeter 1844 Doc 21503
HART Sarah by Newmarket 1791 Doc 12228
HARTFORD Hannah by Deerfield 1851 Doc 932
HARTFORD John Jr by Allenstown 1796 Doc 15598
HARTFORD Joseph by Deerfield 1853 Doc 2086
HARTFORD Sarah by Deerfield 1853 Doc 2086
HARTGRAVES Zabez by Exeter 1836 Doc 16214
HARTHORN Hannah by Hampton Falls 1785 Doc 8391
HARTHORN Nathaniel by Hampton Falls 1785 Doc 8391
HARTSHONE Hannah by Hampton Falls 1779 Doc 4237
HARTSHONE Jonathan by Hampton Falls 1779 Doc 4237
HARTSHORN Hannah by Hampton Falls 1783 Doc 5630
HARVE James by Piermont 1773 Doc 1972
HARVE Joshua by Piermont 1773 Doc 1972
HARVE Mary by Piermont 1773 Doc 1972
HARVE Peter by Piermont 1773 Doc 1972
HARVE William by Piermont 1773 Doc 1972
HARVERY Anna by Hampstead 1814 Doc 37172
HARVERY Thomas by Hampstead 1814 Doc 37172
HARVEY Ann by Sandown 1786 Doc 9151
HARVEY Anne by Sandown 1817 Doc 44178
HARVEY Betty by Sandown 1786 Doc 9151
HARVEY Jabez by Sandown 1786 Doc 9151
HARVEY John by Nottingham 1852 Doc 1554
HARVEY John by Nottingham 1850 Doc 931
HARVEY John by ? 1846 Doc 22356
HARVEY John by Exeter 1791 Doc 11910
HARVEY Sally by Hampton Falls 1812 Doc 34232

HARVEY Thomas by Sandown 1817 Doc 44178
HARVEY Thomas by Plaistow 1818 Doc 45992
HARVEY Thomas by Plaistow 1817 Doc 44178
HARVEY Thomas by Sandown 1786 Doc 9151
HARVEY Unice by Wilmot 1835 Doc 15557
HASKEL Betse (c) by Kingston 1774 Doc 3061
HASKEL Eunice by Kingston 1774 Doc 3061
HASKEL Joseph by Kingston 1774 Doc 3061
HASSA Abiah by Atkinson 1784 Doc 7804
HASSA Sarah by Atkinson 1784 Doc 7804
HATCH John V by Greenland 1851 Doc 931
HATITINGS Julia A by Portsmouth 1851 Doc 311
HAUPSMAN William by Portsmouth 1835 Doc 15900
HAVEY John (c) by Nottingham 1851 Doc 932
HAWLEY Cornelius by Portsmouth 1852 Doc 1555
HAWLEY Cornelius by Portsmouth 1851 Doc 1554
HAWLEY Cornelius by Portsmouth 1852 Doc 1554
HAYNES Francis by Exeter 1773 Doc 2472
HAYNES William by Exeter 1773 Doc 2472
HAYWOOD Abigail by Portsmouth 1842 Doc 20629
HAYWOOD Thomas by Portsmouth 1842 Doc 20629
HEALEY Sarah by Raymond 1843 Doc 20928
HEALEY Sarah by Raymond 1843 Doc 20629 A
HEALEY William by Raymond 1843 Doc 20928
HEALY Lucretia by Raymond 1850 Doc 311
HEALY Levi by Raymond 1850 Doc 311
HEALY Samuel (c) by Raymond 1850 Doc 311
HEALY Sarah (c) by Raymond 1850 Doc 311
HEARD John by Hampstead 1810 Doc 31571
HEATH Abiel by Windham 1787 Doc 10229
HEATH Betsey (c) by Windham 1792 Doc 12531
HEATH Betty by Windham 1787 Doc 10229
HEATH Bradbury (c) by Windham 1791 Doc 12531
HEATH Ezekiel by Northfield 1785 Doc 9466
HEATH James by Windham 1792 Doc 12531
HEATH Joshua by Hampstead 1772 Doc 1612
HEATH Mary by Plaistow 1772 Doc 1407
HEATH Mary (c) by Plaistow 1772 Doc 1407
HEATH Mehitable by Hampstead 1772 Doc 1612
HEATH Moses (c) by Windham 1791 Doc 12531
HEATH Nancy (c) by Windham 1787 Doc 10229
HEATH Nathan (c) by Windham 1791 Doc 12531
HEATH Polley (c) by Windham 1791 Doc 12531
HEATH Rhoda by Windham 1791 Doc 12531
HEATH Richard by Hampstead 1772 Doc 1612
HEATH William by Hampstead 1772 Doc 1612
HEBERD Benjamin (c) by Salem 1792 Doc 13051
HEBERD Dorcas (c) by Salem 1792 Doc 13051
HEBERD Dorothy (c) by Salem 1792 Doc 13051
HEBERD Hannah (c) by Salem 1792 Doc 13051
HEBERD John by Salem 1792 Doc 13051
HEBERD Rhoda (c) by Salem 1792 Doc 13051

HEBERD Sarah by Salem 1792 Doc 13051
HEIGH Eleanor by Greenland 1780 Doc 4331
HENAGE Sophia by Portsmouth 1851 Doc 311
HENDERSON John by Pembroke 1821 Doc 1592
HENDERSON Joseph by Exeter 1781 Doc 4574
HENNESSEY Catherine by Portsmouth 1852 Doc 1555
HENNESSEY Catherine (c) by Portsmouth 1852 Doc 1554
HENNESSEY Ellen (c) by Portsmouth 1852 Doc 1554
HENNESSEY Joanna by Portsmouth 1852 Doc 1554
HENNESSEY Mary by Portsmouth 1852 Doc 1554
HENNESSEY Michael by Portsmouth 1852 Doc 1554
HENNESSEY Timothy by Portsmouth 1852 Doc 1554
HENNESSEY Timothy (Mrs) by Portsmouth 1852 Doc 1554
HENNESSY Catherine by Portsmouth 1851 Doc 931
HENNESSY Catherine (c) by Portsmouth 1851 Doc 311
HENNESSY Ellen (c) by Portsmouth 1851 Doc 311
HENNESSY Ellen (c) by Portsmouth 1851 Doc 931
HENNESSY Joanna by Portsmouth 1851 Doc 931
HENNESSY Joanna by Portsmouth 1851 Doc 311
HENNESSY Mary by Portsmouth 1851 Doc 311
HENNESSY Mary by Portsmouth 1851 Doc 931
HENNESSY Michael by Portsmouth 1851 Doc 931
HENNESY Mary by Portsmouth 1851 Doc 1554
HENRY Abner by Windham 1793 Doc 13587
HENRY Isabel by Windham 1793 Doc 13587
HENRY Thomas by Plaistow 1817 Doc 45992
HERBERT Ellen by Portsmouth 1851 Doc 931
HERBERT Ellen by Portsmouth 1852 Doc 1554
HERBERT Ellen by Portsmouth 1851 Doc 932
HERCY Mary by Newmarket 1796 Doc 15359
HERD John by Hampton 1810 Doc 32331
HERD John by Exeter 1810 Doc 31571
HESLTINE John by Salem 1780 Doc 4331
HESLTINE John (c) by Salem 1779 Doc 4331
HESLTINE Joseph (c) by Salem 1779 Doc 4331
HESLTINE Sarah by Salem 1779 Doc 4331
HIGGINS George by Newington 1772 Doc 731
HIGGINS John by Newington 1772 Doc 731
HIGGINS Kezia by Newington 1772 Doc 731
HIGGINS Martha by Raymond 1798 Doc 17408
HIGGINS Olive by Newington 1772 Doc 731
HIGHT Betsey by Exeter 1794 Doc 14018
HIGHT William by Exeter 1794 Doc 14018
HILDRETH Josiah by Deerfield 1853 Doc 2086
HILDRETH Polly by Deerfield 1853 Doc 2086
HILDRETH Polly by Candia 1853 Doc 2085
HILDRETH Polly by Candia 1854 Doc 2371
HILDRETH Polly by Candia 1851 Doc 931
HILDRETH Polly by Candia 1852 Doc 1554
HILL Abigail by Exeter 1792 Doc 12882
HILL Abner by Poplin 1804 Doc 23419
HILL Edmund by Exeter 1792 Doc 12882

HILL Elizabeth by Exeter 1783 Doc 5923
HILL Gregory (c) by Exeter 1792 Doc 12882
HILL Henry by Portsmouth 1851 Doc 311
HILL James (c) by Exeter 1792 Doc 12882
HILL John by Exeter 1783 Doc 5923
HILL John B by Nottingham 1792 Doc 12882
HILL John C by Nashua 1843 Doc 20629 S
HILL John Jr (c) by Nottingham 1792 Doc 12882
HILL Jonathan by Brentwood 1801 Doc 20206
HILL Joseph (c) by Nottingham 1792 Doc 12882
HILL Lucretia by Brentwood 1801 Doc 20206
HILL Margaret by Rye 1801 Doc 20206
HILL Margery (c) by Nottingham 1792 Doc 12882
HILL Mark by Brentwood 1801 Doc 20206
HILL Mary by Nashua 1843 Doc 20629 S
HILL Mary Jane (c) by Nashua 1843 Doc 20629 S
HILL Phebe by Nottingham 1792 Doc 12882
HILL Purmet by Brentwood 1801 Doc 20206
HILL Richard by Exeter 1784 Doc 7181
HILL Robert (c) by Nottingham 1792 Doc 12882
HILL Salley by Brentwood 1801 Doc 20206
HILL Samuel (c) by Nottingham 1792 Doc 12882
HILL Sarah by Brentwood 1801 Doc 20206
HILL Susan by Portsmouth 1808 Doc 29235
HILL William by Deerfield 1853 Doc 2086
HILLSGROVE James by Portsmouth 1840 Doc 18857
HILLSGROVE James by Portsmouth 1839 Doc 18856
HILLSGROVE James W by Portsmouth 1842 Doc 20107
HILLSGROVE James W by Portsmouth 1838 Doc 18267
HILTON Andrew by Exeter 1790 Doc 11310
HILTON Anna by Hampstead 1770 Doc 1612
HILTON Anna Lane (c) by Hampstead 1770 Doc 1612
HILTON Benjamin by Exeter 1790 Doc 11310
HILTON Henry by Hampstead 1770 Doc 1612
HILTON Henry (c) by Hampstead 1770 Doc 1612
HILTON Mary (c) by Hampstead 1770 Doc 1612
HINES Lydia by Deerfield 1850 Doc 311
HINES Lydia by Deerfield 1851 Doc 931
HINES Lydia P by Deerfield 1852 Doc 1554
HOAG Ebenezer by Stratham 1826 Doc 6965
HOAG Ebenezer by Stratham 1798 Doc 16897
HOAG Joseph by Stratham 1798 Doc 16897
HOBBS Mary (w) by Brentwood 1800 Doc 18692
HODGDON Abigail by Portsmouth 1842 Doc 20107
HODGDSON Abigail by Portsmouth 1841 Doc 19510
HODGDSON Abigail by Portsmouth 1841 Doc 19137
HODGKINS Elizabeth by Derry 1842 Doc 20107
HODSKINS Elizabeth by Derry 1842 Doc 20424
HOGAN Catharine by Loudon 1794 Doc 14339
HOGAN Erwine (c) by Loudon 1794 Doc 14339
HOGAN John by Loudon 1794 Doc 14339
HOGAN Lettey (c) by Loudon 1794 Doc 14339

HOGG Samuel by Portsmouth 1812 Doc 34232
HOIT Abigail by Brentwood 1800 Doc 18692
HOIT Cuff (Negro) by Exeter 1791 Doc 11910
HOIT Gerry (Negro) by Exeter 1791 Doc 11910
HOIT Grace by Exeter 1784 Doc 7181
HOIT Joanna (w) by Brentwood 1802 Doc 21796
HOIT Joseph by Brentwood 1801 Doc 20206
HOIT William by Portsmouth 1831 Doc 13081
HOLDON Abraham by Loudon 1790 Doc 11611
HOLDON Betty (c) by Loudon 1790 Doc 11611
HOLDON Polly (c) by Loudon 1790 Doc 11611
HOLDON Sarah by Loudon 1790 Doc 11611
HOLDRICK Sarah by Exeter 1829 Doc 11709
HOLLAND Fenny by Walpole 1826 Doc 7524
HOLLAND James by Portsmouth 1837 Doc 16931
HOLMAN Benjamin by Deerfield 1852 Doc 1554
HOLT (Mrs) Lovey by Nothingham 1844 Doc 21216
HOLT Enoch by Nottingham 1842 Doc 20424
HOLT Enoch by Salem 1843 Doc 20629 S
HOLT Love by Nottingham 1850 Doc 311
HOLT Lovey by Nottingham 1842 Doc 20424
HOLT Lovey by Nottingham 1850 Doc 931
HOLT Lovey by Nottingham 1851 Doc 932
HOLT Lovey by Nottingham 1852 Doc 1554
HOLT Lovey by Nottingham 1845 Doc 21835
HOLT Lovic by Newmarket 1838 Doc 17910
HOME Jeremiah by Greenland 1773 Doc 2472
HONES Sarah D by Portsmouth 1836 Doc 16216
HOOAG Abigail by Seabrook 1774 Doc 3061
HOOAG Eunice (c) by Seabrook 1774 Doc 3061
HOOAG Henry by Seabrook 1774 Doc 3061
HOOAG Louis (c) by Seabrook 1774 Doc 3061
HOOK Bettey (c) by Poplin 1801 Doc 19665
HOOK Ezekiel by Poplin 1801 Doc 19665
HOOK Ezekiel by Raymond 1799 Doc 17750
HOOK Ezekiel (c) by Poplin 1801 Doc 19665
HOOK Hannah by Poplin 1801 Doc 20738
HOOK Jeremiah (c) by Poplin 1801 Doc 19665
HOOK Molly (c) by Poplin 1801 Doc 19665
HOOK Sarah by Poplin 1801 Doc 19665
HOOPER Amos by Portsmouth 1852 Doc 1554
HOOPER Joseph by Derry 1850 Doc 311
HOOPER Pheby by Epsom 1801 Doc 19665
HOOPER Phillis by Exeter 1842 Doc 20107
HOOPER Stephen by Kingston 1790 Doc 11611
HORN Ebenezer by Kingston 1825 Doc 6505
HOULTON (Mrs) John by Portsmouth 1841 Doc 19511
HOULTON John by Portsmouth 1841 Doc 19510
HOULTON John by Portsmouth 1841 Doc 19511
HOULTON John by Portsmouth 1842 Doc 20107
HOVEY Isaac by Hampstead 1852 Doc 1554
HOW Abigail by Kensington 1791 Doc 12228

HOW Dart by Deerfield 1804 Doc 22771
HOW Dorothy by Deerfield 1804 Doc 22771
HOW Mary by Deerfield 1804 Doc 22771
HOWARD Abraham by Portsmouth 1852 Doc 1554
HOWARD Joseph by Portsmouth 1839 Doc 18856
HOWARD Joseph by Portsmouth 1838 Doc 18267
HOWARD Joseph by Portsmouth 1840 Doc 18857
HOWE Mark by Epping 1842 Doc 20107
HOWE Mary by Epping 1852 Doc 1554
HOWE Molly by Epping 1842 Doc 20107
HOWE Molly by Epping 1843 Doc 20629 S
HOWE Molly by Epping 1851 Doc 931
HOWE Molly by Epping 1842 Doc 20424
HOYT Harriot (infant) by Kingston 1807 Doc 27572
HOYT Mary by Plaistow 1783 Doc 7181
HOYT Sally by Plaistow 1794 Doc 14339
HUBBARD Nancy by Portsmouth 1852 Doc 1554
HUBBARD Nancy by Portsmouth 1851 Doc 311
HUBBARD Nancy by Portsmouth 1851 Doc 931
HUBBARD Richard by New Hampton 1818 Doc 45992
HUBBARD Richard by Kingston 1817 Doc 44178
HUCKINS Robert by Epsom 1778 Doc 4043
HUGES John by Portsmouth 1831 Doc 13081
HULL Nathan by Raymond 1855 Doc 3620
HUMMISON Ira by Portsmouth 1832 Doc 13755
HUNSCOMB Lucy by Newmarket 1780 Doc 4406
HUNT Marcy by Hampton Falls 1850 Doc 311
HUNT Bettey by Stratham 1793 Doc 14018
HUNT Hepzibah (c) by Hawke 1800 Doc 18692
HUNT Ichabod (c) by Hawke 1800 Doc 18692
HUNT Polley (c) by Hawke 1800 Doc 18692
HUNT Reuben by Hawke 1800 Doc 18692
HUNT Sarah by Hawke 1800 Doc 18692
HUNTER Hugh by Portsmouth 1852 Doc 1554
HUNTER Hugh by Portsmouth 1846 Doc 22356
HUNTER Hugh by Portsmouth 1851 Doc 931
HUNTER Hugh by Portsmouth 1851 Doc 311
HUNTOON David (minor) by Kingston 1790 Doc 11611
HUNTRESS Gideon (c) by Goffstown 1828 Doc 9201
HUNTRESS Hannah by Rockingham County 1831 Doc 13399
HUNTRESS Hanson by Rockingham County 1831 Doc 13399
HUNTRESS James by Stratham 1853 Doc 2371
HUNTRESS James L by Stratham 1851 Doc 931
HUNTRESS James L by Stratham 1853 Doc 2085
HUNTRESS Ruth by Goffstown 1828 Doc 9201
HUNTRESS Samuel by Newington 1842 Doc 20107
HUNTRESS Temperance by Newington 1842 Doc 20107
HUNTRESS Temperance by Londonderry 1842 Doc 20424
HUNTRESS Temperance by Newington 1843 Doc 20629
HUNTRESS Temperance by Newington 1844 Doc 21216
HUNTRESS William by Newington 1842 Doc 20107
HUPMAN William by ? 1836 Doc 16214

HURD Paul by Sandown 1815 Doc 39186
HURD Jeremiah (c) by Sandown 1815 Doc 39186
HURD Maria (c) by Sandown 1815 Doc 39186
HURD Mary by Sandown 1815 Doc 39186
HURHERSON John by Kingston 1773 Doc 2268
HUSO Cate by Raymond 1790 Doc 11910
HUSO Philip by Raymond 1790 Doc 11910
HUTCHINGS Charles by Portsmouth 1846 Doc 22356
HUTCHINGS David by Hampton 1771 Doc 1612
HUTCHINGS David (c) by Hampton 1771 Doc 1612
HUTCHINGS Hannah by Hampton 1771 Doc 1612
HUTCHINGS Joseph (c) by Hampton 1771 Doc 1612
HUTCHINGS Julia Ann by Portsmouth 1852 Doc 1554
HUTCHINGS Sarah by Portsmouth 1842 Doc 20107
HUTCHINGS Sarah by Portsmouth 1839 Doc 18856
HUTCHINGS Sarah by Portsmouth 1841 Doc 19136
HUTCHINGS Sarah by Portsmouth 1841 Doc 19511
HUTCHINGS Sarah by Portsmouth 1841 Doc 19510
HUTCHINS Julia Ann by Portsmouth 1851 Doc 931
INGALLS Francis by Portsmouth 1842 Doc 20107
INGALLS Francis by Portsmouth 1840 Doc 18857
INGALLS Francis by Portsmouth 1841 Doc 19510
INGALLS William by Portsmouth 1833 Doc 14415
INGALLS William by Exeter 1826 Doc 6965
INGALS Hannah by Kingston 1792 Doc 13190
INGALS Israel (c) by Kingston 1792 Doc 13190
INTINE Anges W by Portsmouth 1851 Doc 311
IRVING John by Hampstead 1814 Doc 37727
IWIRE John W by Portsmouth 1851 Doc 311
JACK Fortune (Negro) by Exeter 1791 Doc 12531
JACK Nancy by Greenland 1846 Doc 22356
JACK Nancy by Greenland 1845 Doc 21835
JACK Phyllis by Greenland 1846 Doc 22356
JACK Phyllis by Greenland 1843 Doc 21216
JACKMAN Sarah by Portsmouth 1845 Doc 21835
JACKMAN Sarah H by Portsmouth 1852 Doc 1554
JACKMAN Sarah H by Portsmouth 1851 Doc 311
JACKMAN Sarah N of Portsmouth 1846 Doc 22356
JACKMAN Sewall of Derry 1842 Doc 20107
JACKS Nancy of Greenland 1843 Doc 21216
JACKSON Ezekiel of Rye 1794 Doc 14339
JACKSON Pomp of North Hampton 1793 Doc 14018
JACKSON Pomprey (Negro) of Exeter 1794 Doc 14018
JACKWISH Harrit (c) of Seabrook 1792 Doc 13051
JACKWISH Vianna (c) of Seabrook 1792 Doc 13051
JACOBS Catharine of Portsmouth 1851 Doc 931
JACOBS Catherine (c) of Portsmouth 1852 Doc 1554
JACOBS Eleanor of Portsmouth 1852 Doc 1554
JACOBS Eleanor of Portsmouth 1850 Doc 932
JACOBS Eleanor of Portsmouth 1851 Doc 931
JACOBS Mary of Portsmouth 1851 Doc 931
JACOBS Mary of Kingston 1777 Doc 3797

JACOBS Mary (c) of Portsmouth 1852 Doc 1554
JAMES Abigail of Epsom 1801 Doc 20738
JAMES Abigil of Pittsfield 1801 Doc 20738
JAMES Ann Elizabeth of Portsmouth 1851 Doc 311
JAMES Ebenezer of Loudon 1796 Doc 15359
JAMES Hannah (c) of Pittsfield 1801 Doc 20738
JAMES Harriet of Portsmouth 1851 Doc 311
JAMES Harriet of Portsmouth 1851 Doc 931
JAMES Ira of Hampton 1858 Doc 4985
JAMES Joshua of Hampton 1858 Doc 4985
JAMES Levi of Loudon 1796 Doc 15359
JAMES Meribah of Loudon 1796 Doc 15359
JAMES Phebe of Loudon 1796 Doc 15359
JAMES Samuel of Hampton 1858 Doc 4985
JAMES Sarah of Hampton 1858 Doc 4985
JAMES Thomas of Candia 1851 Doc 931
JANE Dorcas of Portsmouth 1852 Doc 1554
JANE Margaret (c) of Portsmouth 1852 Doc 1554
JAQUES Henry C of Portsmouth 1827 Doc 8073
JAQUITH Henry of Exeter 1791 Doc 11910
JEFFERS Robert of Derry 1833 Doc 14122
JEMS Abigail of Northwood 1773 Doc 2268
JEMS Fransies of Northwood 1773 Doc 2268
JENKINS Caroline of Portsmouth 1851 Doc 311
JENNE Samuel of Auburn 1851 Doc 931
JENNES Mary of Hampton 1829 Doc 10410
JENNES Richard of Northwood 1787 Doc 9898
JENNESS Hannah of Candia 1817 Doc 44178
JENNIS Hannah of Greenland 1797 Doc 16897
JEWELL Elizabeth of Atkinson 1844 Doc 21503
JEWELL Elizabeth of Atkinson 1844 Doc 21503
JEWELL Elizabeth of Atkinson 1842 Doc 20424
JEWELL Elizabeth of Atkinson 1844 Doc 21216
JEWELL Elizabeth of Atkinson 1850 Doc 311
JEWELL Elizabeth of Atkinson 1852 Doc 1554
JEWELL Elizabeth of Atkinson 1843 Doc 20928
JEWELL Elizabeth of Atkinson 1843 Doc 20629 S
JEWELL Elizabeth of Atkinson 1851 Doc 931
JEWELL Elizabeth of Atkinson 1846 Doc 22356
JEWELL Elizabeth of Atkinson 1845 Doc 21835
JEWETT David of Brentwood 1800 Doc 18692
JINNE Samuel of Auburn 1851 Doc 932
JOHNSON Abigail of Nottingham 1795 Doc 14879
JOHNSON Abigail (c) of Nottingham 1795 Doc 14879
JOHNSON Abigal of Stratham 1808 Doc 29235
JOHNSON Amy (Negro) of Portsmouth 1852 Doc 1554
JOHNSON Amy (c) of Exeter 1843 Doc 20629 A
JOHNSON Ann (Negro) of Portsmouth 1851 Doc 311
JOHNSON Ann of Portsmouth 1851 Doc 931
JOHNSON Benjamin (c) of Nottingham 1795 Doc 14879
JOHNSON Betsy of Allenstown 1818 Doc 45992
JOHNSON Caroline of Exeter 1846 Doc 22356

JOHNSON Charles of Portsmouth 1840 Doc 18857
JOHNSON Charles of Portsmouth 1841 Doc 19510
JOHNSON Daniel (c) of Exeter 1843 Doc 20629 A
JOHNSON David of Portsmouth 1835 Doc 15900
JOHNSON David of Portsmouth 1837 Doc 16931
JOHNSON David of Portsmouth 1836 Doc 16214
JOHNSON Elisha of Pittsfield 1804 Doc 22771
JOHNSON George of Exeter 1842 Doc 20107
JOHNSON George of Exeter 1843 Doc 20629 S
JOHNSON Hannah of Loudon 1823 Doc 3965
JOHNSON Hiram of Pittsfield 1804 Doc 22771
JOHNSON Isaac of Stratham 1808 Doc 29235
JOHNSON Isaac (c) of Allenstown 1818 Doc 45992
JOHNSON Isaac (c) of Nottingham 1795 Doc 14879
JOHNSON Jeremiah of Pittsfield 1804 Doc 22771
JOHNSON John of Epping 1790 Doc 11310
JOHNSON John (Negro) of Portsmouth 1846 Doc 22356
JOHNSON John (c) of Pembroke 1795 Doc 15359
JOHNSON Joshua of Nottingham 1795 Doc 14879
JOHNSON Joshua (c) of Nottingham 1795 Doc 14879
JOHNSON Joshua M of Stratham 1808 Doc 29235
JOHNSON Louis (c) of Allenstown 1818 Doc 45992
JOHNSON Mahala of Pittsfield 1804 Doc 22771
JOHNSON Margaret of Loudon 1802 Doc 21796
JOHNSON Mary of Exeter 1843 Doc 20629 A
JOHNSON Mary of Stratham 1808 Doc 29235
JOHNSON Mary of Portsmouth 1843 Doc 20629
JOHNSON Moses of Pittsfield 1804 Doc 22771
JOHNSON Nathan (c) of Nottingham 1795 Doc 14879
JOHNSON Nathaniel (c) of Nottingham 1795 Doc 14879
JOHNSON Peter of Portsmouth 1839 Doc 18267
JOHNSON Philip of Greenland 1801 Doc 20206
JOHNSON Porter (c) of Allenstown 1818 Doc 45992
JOHNSON Richard of Portsmouth 1843 Doc 20629
JOHNSON Richard of Exeter 1843 Doc 20629 A
JOHNSON Richard (c) of Exeter 1843 Doc 20629 A
JOHNSON Ruth of Pittsfield 1804 Doc 22771
JOHNSON Samuel of Pembroke 1795 Doc 15359
JOHNSON Samuel of Epping 1790 Doc 11310
JOHNSON Sarah of Pembroke 1795 Doc 15359
JOHNSON Sarah of Stratham 1808 Doc 29235
JOHNSON Sarah (c) of Pembroke 1795 Doc 15359
JOHNSON Sylvia of Portsmouth 1846 Doc 22356
JOHNSON Sylvia of Portsmouth 1851 Doc 311
JOHNSON Sylvia of Portsmouth 1852 Doc 1554
JOHNSON Sylvia of Portsmouth 1851 Doc 931
JOHNSON Thomas (c) of Nottingham 1795 Doc 14879
JOHNSON Warren of Pittsfield 1804 Doc 22771
JOHNSON William of Portsmouth 1852 Doc 1555
JOHNSON Wm of Portsmouth 1852 Doc 1554
JONAS Robert of Portsmouth 1841 Doc 20107
JONES Thomas of Candia 1842 Doc 20424

JONES Anne of Hampton Falls 1783 Doc 5630
JONES Elizabeth of Newmarket 1781 Doc 4574
JONES Evans of Salem 1843 Doc 20629 A
JONES Fanny of Greenland 1792 Doc 12882
JONES James of Portsmouth 1839 Doc 18267
JONES John of Greenland 1794 Doc 14648
JONES Lydia of Kensington 1781 Doc 4574
JONES Mary of Salem 1846 Doc 22356
JONES Mary of Portsmouth 1845 Doc 21835
JONES Mary of Salem 1843 Doc 20928
JONES Mary of Salem 1843 Doc 20629 A
JONES Mary Ann of Portsmouth 1838 Doc 18267
JONES Mary Jane of Portsmouth 1839 Doc 18267
JONES Molly of Stratham 1794 Doc 14648
JONES Nabby of Deerfield 1800 Doc 18692
JONES Robert of Newmarket 1781 Doc 4574
JONES Robert of Greenland 1780 Doc 4574
JONES Robert of Portsmouth 1842 Doc 20107
JONES Sally of Portsmouth 1851 Doc 931
JONES Sally of Portsmouth 1852 Doc 1554
JONES Sally of Portsmouth 1851 Doc 311
JONES Sally of Portsmouth 1845 Doc 21835
JONES Samuel of Hampton Falls 1783 Doc 5630
JONES Sarah of Greenland 1780 Doc 4574
JONES Thomas of Candia 1842 Doc 20107
JONES Thomas of Candia 1844 Doc 21216
JONES Thomas of Candia 1843 Doc 20629 S
JORDAN John of Candia 1829 Doc 10409
JORDIN Abraham of Brentwood 1790 Doc 11310
JORDIN Charlotte of Brentwood 1790 Doc 11310
JOSEPH (An Indian) of Portsmouth 1852 Doc 1554
JOY John of Portsmouth 1851 Doc 311
JUDKINS Beatrice of Greenland 1789 Doc 10754
JUDKINS Mary of Poplin 1791 Doc 12228
JUDKINS Mary of Exeter 1793 Doc 13190
JUDKINS Molly of Brentwood 1790 Doc 11310
JUDKINS Peter (c) of Exeter 1793 Doc 13190
JUDKINS Robert of Exeter 1788 Doc 10640
JUDKINS Samuel of Exeter 1793 Doc 13190
JUDKINS Samuel of Epping 1785 Doc 9466
JUDKINS Sophia (c) of Exeter 1793 Doc 13190
KAISK Richard of Exeter 1810 Doc 31571
KANE Dennis of Portsmouth 1851 Doc 931
KANE Dennis of Portsmouth 1851 Doc 1554
KANE Francis of Portsmouth 1851 Doc 311
KANNA Patrick W of Portsmouth 1851 Doc 311
KARR William of Pembroke 1787 Doc 9898
KATE Martha of Rye 1843 Doc 20629 A
KATHRINE (Negro) of Exeter 1783 Doc 5923
KEASER James of Hawke 1810 Doc 32331
KEASER Lois of Hawke 1810 Doc 32331
KEASER Nanna of Plaistow 1792 Doc 13587

KEASER Susanah of Hawke 1810 Doc 32331
KEATING Geraldine A of Portsmouth 1852 Doc 1842
KEATING Marty of Portsmouth 1852 Doc 1842
KEATING Mary Ann (c) of Portsmouth 1852 Doc 1842
KEATING Thomas of Portsmouth 1841 Doc 19510
KEATING Thomas of Portsmouth 1840 Doc 19137
KEAZER Anna of Hampstead 1852 Doc 1554
KEAZER Nancy of Hampstead 1851 Doc 931
KEEF William of Londonderry 1812 Doc 35625
KEEGAN Nancy of Hampstead 1854 Doc 2371
KEEPEC Robert Neal of Portsmouth 1834 Doc 14818
KEGAN John of Kingston 1851 Doc 932
KEHOE James of Portsmouth 1845 Doc 21835
KEHOE James of Portsmouth 1851 Doc 311
KELANY Michel of Exeter 1853 Doc 2085
KELLEY Anna (w) of Newtown 1846 Doc 22356
KELLEY Annah of Loudon 1795 Doc 15018
KELLEY Anthony of Newtown 1843 Doc 20928
KELLEY Catharine of Stratham 1843 Doc 20629 S
KELLEY Catharine of Stratham 1845 Doc 21835
KELLEY Catherine of Stratham 1843 Doc 20629 A
KELLEY David of Portsmouth 1851 Doc 931
KELLEY David of Portsmouth 1851 Doc 311
KELLEY Gerd of Portsmouth 1832 Doc 13755
KELLEY Glad of Portsmouth 1832 Doc 13754
KELLEY Glad of Portsmouth 1830 Doc 12197 A
KELLEY John of Portsmouth 1839 Doc 18856
KELLEY John of Portsmouth 1842 Doc 20107
KELLEY John of Portsmouth 1840 Doc 18857
KELLEY John of Portsmouth 1841 Doc 19510
KELLEY Jonathan of Loudon 1795 Doc 15018
KELLEY Luanna of Brentwood 1800 Doc 18692
KELLEY Mahittable of Stratham 1852 Doc 1554
KELLEY Mehitable of Stratham 1850 Doc 311
KELLEY Mehitable (w) of Stratham 1851 Doc 931
KELLEY Nancy of Newton 1852 Doc 1554
KELLEY Nancy of Newtown 1844 Doc 21503
KELLEY Nancy of Newton 1853 Doc 2085
KELLEY Nancy of Newtown 1843 Doc 20928
KELLEY Nancy of Newtown 1845 Doc 21835
KELLEY Runney of Portsmouth 1846 Doc 22356
KELLEY Said? of Portsmouth 1831 Doc 13081
KELLEY Susannah of Stratham 1799 Doc 18299
KELLEY Susannah of Greenland 1795 Doc 15018
KELLY Edward of Sandown 1846 Doc 22356
KELLY Mary of Plaistow 1855 Doc 3620
KELLY Nancy of Newton 1850 Doc 931
KELLY Nancy of Newton 1850 Doc 311
KELLY Nathan of Plaistow 1791 Doc 12228
KELQUE John of Chester 1840 Doc 18856
KELSEY Betsey of Langdon 1832 Doc 13399
KELSEY Curtis (c) of Langdon 1832 Doc 13399

KELSEY Hannah (c) of Langdon 1832 Doc 13399
KELSEY John of Langdon 1832 Doc 13399
KELSEY John (c) of Langdon 1832 Doc 13399
KELSEY Willard (c) of Langdon 1832 Doc 13399
KEMP Asa of Sandown 1813 Doc 36435
KEMP Sarah of Sandown 1813 Doc 36435
KEMP Sarah (c) of Sandown 1813 Doc 36435
KENEDY John of Exeter 1843 Doc 20629 A
KENEDY Joseph (c) of Exeter 1843 Doc 20629 A
KENERDY Mary of Newmarket 1852 Doc 1554
KENESTON Eunice of Northfield 1831 Doc 12683
KENESYTON Abigail (c) of Stratham 1795 Doc 15018
KENESYTON Abigail of Stratham 1795 Doc 15018
KENESYTON Solomon (c) of Stratham 1795 Doc 15018
KENISSON Abraham (c) of Newmarket 1774 Doc 3695
KENISSON Hannah of Newmarket 1774 Doc 3695
KENISSON Samuel of Newmarket 1774 Doc 3695
KENISTON Sally of Epping 1853 Doc 2085
KENISTON Abigail of Greenland 1786 Doc 9466
KENISTON Abigail of Deerfield 1786 Doc 9466
KENISTON Eunice of Northwood 1850 Doc 311
KENISTON Eunice of Londonderry 1851 Doc 931
KENISTONE Mary (c) of Nottingham 1818 Doc 45992
KENISTONE Salley of Nottingham 1818 Doc 45992
KENISTONE Sarah of Deerfield 1779 Doc 4293
KENISTONE Thomas (c) of Nottingham 1818 Doc 45992
KENISTWON Abigail of Poplin 1786 Doc 9631
KENNEDAY John of Exeter 1850 Doc 311
KENNEDAY John of Exeter 1851 Doc 931
KENNEDAY John of Exeter 1852 Doc 1554
KENNEDY John of Exeter 1853 Doc 2371
KENNEDY John of Exeter 1844 Doc 21216
KENNEDY John of Exeter 1853 Doc 2085
KENNERSTON Elizabeth of Newcastle 1812 Doc 34232
KENNERSTON Lydia of Newcastle 1812 Doc 34232
KENNEY John of Portsmouth 1831 Doc 13081
KENNEY Maria of Greenland 1843 Doc 21216
KENNEYS Edward of Portsmouth 1842 Doc 20107
KENNEYS James of Portsmouth 1826 Doc 6965
KENNISON Betsey (c) of Newmarket 1795 Doc 14879
KENNISON Ebenezer of Newmarket 1795 Doc 14879
KENNISON Ebenezer (c) of Newmarket 1795 Doc 14879
KENNISON Elizabeth of Newmarket 1795 Doc 14879
KENNISON Eunice of Northwood 1842 Doc 20424
KENNISON Polly (c) of Newmarket 1795 Doc 14879
KENNISON Valentine of Northwood 1842 Doc 20424
KENNISTON Abigail of Epping 1800 Doc 19247
KENNISTON Eunice of Northwood 1844 Doc 21216
KENNISTONE Betsey of Epping 1791 Doc 12228
KENNISTONE Betsey (c) of Epping 1791 Doc 12228
KENNISTONE Ebenezer of Epping 1791 Doc 12228
KENNISTONE Martha of Brentwood 1794 Doc 14339

KENNISTONE Olla of Epping 1790 Doc 11310
KENNISTONE Polly (c) of Epping 1791 Doc 12228
KENNISTONE Robert (c) of Epping 1791 Doc 12228
KENNSINTON Eunice of Newmarket 1843 Doc 20629
KENSINTON Eunice of County 1853 Doc 2371
KENSTON Love of Northwood 1780 Doc 4331
KENT Albany of Exeter 1844 Doc 21216
KENT Mary of Exeter 1844 Doc 20629 A
KENT Peter (Negro) of N Hampton 1810 Doc 32876
KENTFIELD Betty (c) of Bow 1791 Doc 12228
KENTFIELD George of Bow 1791 Doc 12228
KENTFIELD George (c) of Bow 1791 Doc 12228
KENTFIELD Josiah (c) of Bow 1791 Doc 12228
KENTFIELD Nancy (c) of Bow 1791 Doc 12228
KENTFIELD Rebecca of Bow 1791 Doc 12228
KENTFIELD Rebecca (c) of Bow 1791 Doc 12228
KENTFIELD William (c) of Bow 1791 Doc 12228
KESYER Nancy of Hampstead 1850 Doc 311
KEYES William of Danville 1840 Doc 19136
KEZAR Harriet (c) of ? 1862 Doc 7016
KEZAR Isabelle (c) of ? 1862 Doc 7016
KEZER Albert (c) of Kingston 1861 Doc 7306
KEZER Harriet of Kingston 1861 Doc 7306
KEZER Harriet (c) of Kingston 1861 Doc 7306
KILEY Patrick of Portsmouth 1841 Doc 19510
KILEY Patrick of Portsmouth 1840 Doc 19137
KILGAUE John (c) of Chester 1839 Doc 18267
KILGAUE Rebecca of Chester 1839 Doc 18267
KILGREW John of Chester 1841 Doc 19510
KILGRUE John of Chester 1842 Doc 20107
KILGRUE John of Chester 1840 Doc 18856
KILLEYGRUE John of Chester 1844 Doc 21216
KILLEYGRUE John of Chester 1846 Doc 22356
KILVASEY Sally of Exeter 1846 Doc 22592
KIMBALL Benjamin of Concord 1809 Doc 31571
KIMBALL Betsy of Poplin 1843 Doc 20629 A
KIMBALL Charles W (c) of Atkinson 1846 Doc 22356
KIMBALL David of Atkinson 1846 Doc 22356
KIMBALL David of Poplin 1772 Doc 1407
KIMBALL David (c) of Poplin 1772 Doc 1407
KIMBALL David (c) of Atkinson 1846 Doc 22356
KIMBALL Elizabeth of Poplin 1772 Doc 1407
KIMBALL Harriet of Atkinson 1846 Doc 22356
KIMBALL Jonathan (c) of Poplin 1772 Doc 1407
KIMBALL Joseph of Manchester 1827 Doc 8077
KIMBALL Olive of Exeter 1853 Doc 2371
KIMBALL Olive of Exeter 1850 Doc 311
KIMBALL Olive of Exeter 1853 Doc 2085
KIMBALL Olive of Exeter 1852 Doc 1554
KIMBALL Olive of Exeter 1851 Doc 931
KIMBALL Polly of Hampstead 1850 Doc 311
KIMBALL Polly of Hampstead 1851 Doc 931

KIMBALL Polly of Hampstead 1854 Doc 2371
KIMBALL Polly of Hampstead 1852 Doc 1554
KIMBALL Samuel (Mrs) of Exeter 1812 Doc 34232
KIMBALL Sarah of Concord 1819 Doc 47427
KIMBALL Sarah of Manchester 1827 Doc 8077
KIMBALL Sarah of Manchester 1828 Doc 9201
KIMBALL Scipo of Exeter 1787 Doc 9740
KIMBALL William H (c) of Atkinson 1846 Doc 22356
KINCADE Isaac of Poplin 1792 Doc 12882
KINCADE Mary of Poplin 1792 Doc 12882
KINESTON Jenney of Northwood 1787 Doc 9898
KINESTON Jonathan of Northwood 1787 Doc 9898
KING John of Portsmouth 1846 Doc 22356
KING John of Portsmouth 1851 Doc 311
KING John of Portsmouth 1852 Doc 1554
KING John of Portsmouth 1851 Doc 931
KINGSTON Thomas of Brentwood 1788 Doc 10229
KINGSTONE Abigail of Poplin 1801 Doc 20206
KINGSTONE Martha of Raymond 1794 Doc 14018
KINKAID William of Hampstead 1769 Doc 1612
KINNEY James of Portsmouth 1827 Doc 8073
KINNEY Keziah of Newmarket 1850 Doc 931
KINNISON Aaron of Newmarket 1789 Doc 10229
KINNISON Ebenezer of Newmarket 1789 Doc 10229
KINNISON Elizabeth of Newmarket 1789 Doc 10229
KINNISON Elizabeth of Newmarket 1789 Doc 10754
KINNISON Eunice of Northwood 1846 Doc 22356
KINNISON Jane of Newmarket 1788 Doc 10229
KINNISON Love of Newmarket 1789 Doc 10754
KINNISON Polly (c) of Newmarket 1789 Doc 10229
KINNISON Samuel of Newmarket 1789 Doc 10754
KINNISON Thomas of Newmarket 1789 Doc 10229
KINNISTON Abigail of Exeter 1790 Doc 11310
KINNISTON Jeremiah of Exeter 1790 Doc 11310
KINNISTON Thomas of Exeter 1790 Doc 11310
KISLY Patrick of Portsmouth 1842 Doc 20107
KITTREDGE D Rufus of Portsmouth 1832 Doc 13754
KITTREDGE Dorothy of Newmarket 1850 Doc 931
KNIGHT Abigail of Nottingham 1804 Doc 23419
KNIGHT Abraham of Nottingham 1804 Doc 23419
KNIGHT Martha of Hampstead 1795 Doc 14648
KNIGHT Mary of Greenland 1797 Doc 16897
KNIGHT Rhoda of Deerfield 1807 Doc 28434
KNIGHT Sally of Deerfield 1801 Doc 19665
KNIGHT Samuel of Portsmouth 1842 Doc 20107
KNIGHT Sarah of Nottingham 1804 Doc 23419
KNOSE Margaret of Portsmouth 1843 Doc 20629
KNOSE Margaret of Portsmouth 1846 Doc 22356
KNOSE Samuel of Portsmouth 1843 Doc 20629
KNOWLES Fanny of Concord 1812 Doc 34232
KNOWLES Jonathan of Stratham 1812 Doc 34232
KNOWLES Smith of Epping 1849 Doc 24261

KNOX Margaret of Portsmouth 1851 Doc 311
KYNASTON Abigail of Newmarket 1783 Doc 5630
KYNASTON Abraham (c) of Newmarket 1783 Doc 5630
KYNASTON Samuel of Newmarket 1783 Doc 5630
KYNASTON Samuel (c) of Newmarket 1783 Doc 5630
LACY Charlotte of Exeter 1817 Doc 45992
LACY Charlotte of ? 1817 Doc 44178
LADD John of Deerfield 1852 Doc 1554
LADEN John (Negro) of Deerfield 1793 Doc 14018
LAIGHTON William of Greenland 1851 Doc 931
LALINN Lolan of Exeter 1831 Doc 13399
LAMPREY Jeremiah of Hampton 1850 Doc 311
LAMPSON Rachel (w) of Hampton Falls 1795 Doc 15359
LAMPSON Rufus of Hampton Falls 1795 Doc 15359
LANAHAN Andrew of Portsmouth 1836 Doc 16214
LANAHAN Andrew of Portsmouth 1836 Doc 16216
LANAHAN Andrew of Portsmouth 1837 Doc 16931
LANAKAUM Andrew of Portsmouth 1836 Doc 16216
LANCASTER Mary of Kingston 1778 Doc 4111
LAND Abigail of Epping 1800 Doc 19247
LAND Abigail (c) of Epping 1800 Doc 19247
LAND Eliphalet of Epping 1800 Doc 19247
LAND Lucy (c) of Epping 1800 Doc 19247
LAND Molly (c) of Epping 1800 Doc 19247
LAND Nancy (c) of Epping 1800 Doc 19247
LAND Rebeccah (c) of Epping 1800 Doc 19247
LANDER Hans of Portsmouth 1841 Doc 19510
LANDNER Hans of Portsmouth 1842 Doc 20107
LANE Charles of Portsmouth 1834 Doc 14818
LANE Dinah of Stratham 1842 Doc 20424
LANE Dinah of Newmarket 1800 Doc 20206
LANE Dinah of Stratham 1843 Doc 20629 S
LANE Jacob of Raymond 1843 Doc 20629 A
LANE Jacob of Raymond 1843 Doc 20928
LANE Olive of Greenland 1795 Doc 15018
LANE Rebekah of Poplin 1808 Doc 29235
LANE Robert of Portsmouth 1852 Doc 1555
LANE Robert of Rye 1853 Doc 2085
LANG Dinah of Stratham 1795 Doc 15359
LANG John (c) of Hampton 1772 Doc 731
LANG Theodate of Portsmouth 1834 Doc 14818
LANG Thomas G of Exeter 1846 Doc 22356
LANG William of Hampton 1772 Doc 731
LANGDON John (c) of Kingston 1791 Doc 12531
LANGLEY Benjamin of Newmarket 1842 Doc 20424
LANGLEY Betty of Newmarket 1842 Doc 20424
LANGLEY Lavinia C of Newmarket 1838 Doc 17575
LANGLEY Lovey (c) of Newmarket 1842 Doc 20424
LANGMAID Jonathan of Deerfield 1852 Doc 1842
LANKFORD Joseph of Derry 1850 Doc 311
LARGRAVES Jabez of N Hampton 1826 Doc 7524
LARY Mary of Greenland 1780 Doc 4406

LAVENING Abial of Andover 1823 Doc 3965
LAVIDEON Sarah of Derry 1836 Doc 16214
LAWLEY Elizabeth of Stratham 1808 Doc 29235
LAWRENCE Nancy of Poplin 1804 Doc 23419
LAWRENCE William of Portsmouth 1841 Doc 19510
LAWRENCE William of Portsmouth 1840 Doc 18856
LAWRENCE William of Portsmouth 1839 Doc 18856
LAWSON Mary of Portsmouth 1851 Doc 311
LAWSON Mary of Portsmouth 1851 Doc 931
LAWSON Mary of Portsmouth 1852 Doc 1554
LAWSON William of Portsmouth 1831 Doc 13081
LEACH Comfort of Hampton 1851 Doc 931
LEACH Comfort of Hampton 1846 Doc 22356
LEACH Comfort of Hampton 1842 Doc 20424
LEACH Comfort of Hampton 1843 Doc 20629
LEACH Comfort of Hampton 1850 Doc 311
LEACH Comfort of Kensington 1853 Doc 2085
LEACH Comfort of Hampton 1845 Doc 21835
LEACH Comfort of Hampton 1844 Doc 21216
LEACH Hannah of Hampstead 1771 Doc 1612
LEACH John of Hampton Falls 1851 Doc 931
LEACH John of Hampton Falls 1850 Doc 311
LEACH John of Hampton Falls 1846 Doc 22356
LEACH John of Raymond 1843 Doc 20928
LEACH John of Hampton Falls 1845 Doc 21835
LEACH Joseph of Hampton 1842 Doc 20424
LEAFFAN Jean of Portsmouth 1851 Doc 311
LEARY (w) of Exeter 1795 Doc 14648
LEARY Peter O of Portsmouth 1837 Doc 16931
LEATHERS Joseph (c) of Stratham 1846 Doc 22356
LEATHERS Anna of Northwood 1798 Doc 17408
LEATHERS Anna of Nottingham 1794 Doc 14339
LEATHERS Benajmin of Nottingham 1791 Doc 12228
LEATHERS Benjamin (c) of Nottingham 1791 Doc 12228
LEATHERS Eleanor of Barrington 1791 Doc 12228
LEATHERS Elizabeth (c) of Nottingham 1791 Doc 12228
LEATHERS Elnor of Nottingham 1791 Doc 12228
LEATHERS Hannah of Newmarket 1812 Doc 34232
LEATHERS Joseph of Stratham 1845 Doc 21835
LEATHERS Marjoria of Nottingham 1791 Doc 12228
LEATHERS Thomas of Northfield 1796 Doc 15598
LEATHERS William of Northwood 1798 Doc 17408
LEATHERS William of Nottingham 1794 Doc 14339
LEAVIT Catherine of Portsmouth 1851 Doc 311
LEAVITT Daniel of Bow 1834 Doc 15899
LEAVITT Deborah of Bow 1834 Doc 15899
LEAVITT Deborah of Bow 1831 Doc 12683
LEAVITT Deborah (c) of Concord 1819 Doc 47427
LEAVITT Fanny of Concord 1819 Doc 47427
LEAVITT Fanny of Concord 1813 Doc 36435
LEAVITT Fanny of Concord 1811 Doc 32876
LEAVITT Fanny of Stratham 1812 Doc 34232

LEAVITT John of Greenland 1786 Doc 9151
LEAVITT Josiah (c) of Concord 1819 Doc 47427
LEAVITT Mary (c) of Concord 1819 Doc 47427
LEAVITT Meribah of Exeter 1772 Doc 1880
LEAVITT William (Negro) of Exeter 1850 Doc 311
LEAVITT William of Exeter 1851 Doc 931
LECOMB Lois of Newmarket 1850 Doc 931
LECOMB Louis of Newmarket 1853 Doc 2085
LECOMB of Newmarket 1853 Doc 2371
LEE Edward of Brentwood 1801 Doc 20206
LEE Martha of Brentwood 1801 Doc 20206
LEIGH Joseph of ? 1803 Doc 2352
LEIGHTON William of Greenland 1843 Doc 21216
LEIGHTON William of Greenland 1845 Doc 21835
LEIGHTON William of Greenland 1846 Doc 22356
LEIGHTON William of Portsmouth 1852 Doc 1555
LEIGHTON William of Greenland 1843 Doc 20629 A
LEIGHTON William of Greenland 1850 Doc 311
LEIGHTON William of Exeter 1840 Doc 18856
LEIGHTON William of Greenland 1853 Doc 2085
LEIGHTON Wm of Greenland 1852 Doc 1554
LENCH John of Hampton Falls 1843 Doc 20928
LEVEY John of ? 1786 Doc 9366
LEVINGSTON Jeremiah of Plaistow 1797 Doc 16546
LEWIS Jacob of Portsmouth 1846 Doc 22356
LEWIS Jacob of Portsmouth 1842 Doc 20629
LEWIS John of Portsmouth 1827 Doc 9200
LEWIS Joshua of Portsmouth 1845 Doc 21835
LEWIS Lydia of Portsmouth 1845 Doc 21835
LEWIS Lydia of Portsmouth 1842 Doc 20107
LEWIS Lydia of Portsmouth 1842 Doc 20107
LEWIS William of Londonderry 1838 Doc 17575
LIANCE Nanna of Plaistow 1796 Doc 15733
LIBBEY Abraham of Raymond 1790 Doc 11611
LIBBEY Hannah of Kingston 1790 Doc 11310
LIFORD Judith of Poplin 1795 Doc 15018
LIGHT Lucy of Nottingham 1850 Doc 311
LIGHT Lucy of Nottingham 1850 Doc 931
LIGHT Prince (Negro) of Kingston 1798 Doc 17408
LIGHTS Lucy of Nottingham 1854 Doc 2371
LIGHTS Lucy of Nottingham 1852 Doc 1554
LILLIS Sally of Hollis 1826 Doc 6965
LINCH Abigail of Windham 1789 Doc 11183
LINCH Benjamin of Windham 1788 Doc 10640
LINCH Patrick of Raymond 1851 Doc 931
LINCH Polly of Windham 1792 Doc 13587
LINCH Sarah of Windham 1791 Doc 12531
LINCH Sarah of Windham 1788 Doc 10640
LINCH Sarah of Nottingham 1818 Doc 45992
LINDEN Hans of Portsmouth 1851 Doc 931
LINENER Hans of Portsmouth 1841 Doc 19511
LINSEY Mathew of Windham 1779 Doc 4241

LISKCUM Samuel of Epping 1794 Doc 14339
LISKCUM Samuel of Deerfield 1796 Doc 16050
LISKCUM Samule of Raymond 1798 Doc 17408
LISKCUM Sarah of Raymond 1798 Doc 17408
LISKCUM Sarah of Deerfield 1796 Doc 16050
LITTLE Elizabeth of Chester 1853 Doc 2371
LITTLE Elizabeth M of Chester 1852 Doc 1554
LITTLE Joshua of Chester 1852 Doc 1554
LITTLE Joshua of Chester 1851 Doc 931
LITTLE Joshua of Chester 1853 Doc 2085
LITTLE Joshua of Auburn 1843 Doc 311
LITTLE Sarah of Atkinson 1795 Doc 15018
LITTLE Walter of Atkinson 1795 Doc 15018
LITTLEFIELD Elizabeth of Portsmouth 1839 Doc 18267
LIVINGSTON George of Portsmouth 1844 Doc 21503
LOAN John of Portsmouth 1842 Doc 20107
LOCK Becky (c) of Kingston 1798 Doc 17408
LOCK Joshua of Pembroke 1790 Doc 11910
LOCK Lydia (c) of Kingston 1798 Doc 17408
LOCK Lydia (c) of Poplin 1793 Doc 13587
LOCK Mary of Poplin 1793 Doc 13587
LOCK Mary (c) of Kingston 1798 Doc 17408
LOCK Mirian of Poplin 1799 Doc 18299
LOCK Patience (c) of Kingston 1798 Doc 17408
LOCK Rebeckah (c) of Poplin 1793 Doc 13587
LOCK Ruth of Nottingham 1792 Doc 12882
LOCK Simon of Poplin 1793 Doc 13587
LOCK Simon of Kingston 1798 Doc 17408
LOCKE Patience of Rye 1846 Doc 22356
LOCKE William of Rye 1829 Doc 10409
LOINS Daniel of Derry 1851 Doc 931
LONG David of Portsmouth 1841 Doc 19511
LONG John of Portsmouth 1841 Doc 19511
LONG John of Portsmouth 1841 Doc 19510
LORD Anna of Poplin 1816 Doc 40757
LORD Anna of Poplin 1808 Doc 29235
LORD Isaac (c) of Poplin 1808 Doc 29235
LORD Jefferson of Rockingham County 1831 Doc 13399
LORD John of Poplin 1808 Doc 29235
LORD Mary of Dover 1825 Doc 6505
LORD Rebekah (c) of Poplin 1808 Doc 29235
LOUD Mehitable of Rye 1798 Doc 16897
LOW Nathan of Plaistow 1772 Doc 731
LOWELL Lydia of S Hampton 1780 Doc 4331
LOWELL Moses of Kingston 1777 Doc 3797
LOWERBEG Thomas of Windham 1836 Doc 16214
LOWERBY Thomas of Portsmouth 1835 Doc 16214
LOWERBY Thomas of Derry 1841 Doc 19510
LUCAS Betsey of Stratham 1846 Doc 22356
LUCAS Elizabeth of Wolfeborough 1846 Doc 22592
LUCY Benjamin of Nottingham 1843 Doc 20629
LUCY Lydia of Nottingham 1843 Doc 20629

LULFKIN Eleanor of Weare 1821 Doc 1592
LULL Hannah of Pembroke 1780 Doc 4331
LULL John of Plaistow 1784 Doc 7181
LULL Samuel (c) of Pembroke 1780 Doc 4331
LULL Simon of Pembroke 1780 Doc 4331
LULL Simon (c) of Pembroke 1780 Doc 4331
LYNCH Cornelius of Portsmouth 1850 Doc 932
LYNCH Cornelus of Portsmouth 1851 Doc 931
LYNCH Ellen of Portsmouth 1851 Doc 311
LYNEK Daniel of Portsmouth 1851 Doc 311
LYON William of Loudon 1815 Doc 39186
LYONS Betty of Acworth 1827 Doc 8077
MACCARIS Rachael of Hampton Falls 1774 Doc 3061
MACCARIS Rachael of Keningston 1776 Doc 3714
MACCOY Samuel of Kensington 1843 Doc 3714
MACE Ithanar of Rye 1846 Doc 22356
MACE Joshua of Greenland 1828 Doc 10409
MACE Rachael of Rye 1846 Doc 22356
MACE Sarah of Rye 1846 Doc 22356
MACE Sarah of Rye 1844 Doc 21503
MACE Sarah of Rye 1845 Doc 21835
MACE Sarah of Greenland 1796 Doc 15359
MACE William of Portsmouth 1832 Doc 13754
MACE William of Portsmouth 1836 Doc 16214
MACE William of Portsmouth 1836 Doc 16214
MACE William of Portsmouth 1832 Doc 13755
MACE William of Portsmouth 1837 Doc 16931
MACE William of Portsmouth 1839 Doc 18856
MACKAY Joseph of Rochester 1816 Doc 40757
MACWELL Desire of Portsmouth 1851 Doc 311
MAHON Roseann of Portsmouth 1839 Doc 18856
MAHONEY Michael of Raymond 1851 Doc 931
MAHONEY Michael of Portsmouth 1851 Doc 932
MAHONY Michael of Portsmouth 1851 Doc 311
MAHOONEY Michael of Portsmouth 1851 Doc 931
MAINFOLD John of Derry 1844 Doc 21216
MAINFOLD John of Derry 1851 Doc 931
MAKENNA Michael of Raymond 1852 Doc 1554
MALCON Bathesba of Salem 1827 Doc 8655
MALLAY Patrick of Portsmouth 1851 Doc 931
MALLEY Patrick of Portsmouth 1851 Doc 931
MALLEY Patrick of Portsmouth 1850 Doc 932
MALLEY Patrick of Portsmouth 1851 Doc 311
MALLY Patrick of Portsmouth 1852 Doc 1554
MALOON Jas of Portsmouth 1851 Doc 311
MALOONEY Mary of Portsmouth 1850 Doc 932
MALOONEY Timothy of Portsmouth 1851 Doc 932
MALOONY Mary of Portsmouth 1851 Doc 931
MALOY Lois of Kingston 1861 Doc 7306
MALOY Lois of Plaistow 1862 Doc 7016
MALOY William of Kingston 1861 Doc 7306
MALOY William A of Plaistown 1861 Doc 7016

MALOY William J (c) of ? 1862 Doc 7016
MANAFOLD Susanna of Atkinson 1819 Doc 47427
MAND James of Exeter 1795 Doc 14648
MAND James (c) of Exeter 1795 Doc 14648
MANIFOLD John of Derry 1853 Doc 2371
MANIFOLD John of Derry 1842 Doc 20424
MANIFOLD John of Derry 1845 Doc 21835
MANIFOLD John of Derry 1850 Doc 311
MANIFOLD John of Derry 1853 Doc 2085
MANIFOLDS John of Derry 1852 Doc 1554
MANIFOLDS John of Derry 1843 Doc 20629 S
MANN Dorothy of Hampton Falls 1789 Doc 11025
MANN Roseann of Portsmouth 1846 Doc 22592
MANNER Betsey of Windham 1790 Doc 11611
MANNING Harriet of Portsmouth 1822 Doc 3416
MANOY Alphonso of Nottingham 1823 Doc 3965
MANOY Harrison of Nottingham 1823 Doc 3965
MANOY Israel Jr of Nottingham 1823 Doc 3965
MANOY Patty of Conway 1823 Doc 3965
MANS Abigail (c) of Seabrook 1786 Doc 9151
MANS Dolley (c) of Seabrook 1786 Doc 9151
MANS Dolly of Seabrook 1786 Doc 9151
MANS John of Seabrook 1786 Doc 9151
MANSFIELD Susannah of New Boston 1816 Doc 40757
MANSUR Mary of Hampstead 1853 Doc 2085
MARBLE Sam of ? 1782 Doc 5272
MARCH Daniel (c) of Chester 1817 Doc 44178
MARCH George (Capt) of Stratham 1846 Doc 22356
MARCH Hannah (c) of Chester 1817 Doc 44178
MARCH John (c) of Chester 1817 Doc 44178
MARCH Martha of Greenland 1854 Doc 2371
MARCH Martha of Greenland 1851 Doc 931
MARCH Martha of Stratham 1846 Doc 22356
MARCH Martha of Greenland 1853 Doc 2085
MARCH Martha of Sandown 1846 Doc 22356
MARCH Martha of Greenland 1850 Doc 311
MARCH Martha of Greenland 1852 Doc 1554
MARCH Miriam of Chester 1817 Doc 44178
MARCH Nancy of Stratham 1794 Doc 14018
MARCH Paul of Deerfield 1794 Doc 14339
MARCH Sarah (c) of Chester 1817 Doc 44178
MARCH Stephen of Chester 1817 Doc 44178
MARCH Stephen (c) of Chester 1817 Doc 44178
MARDA Michael of Portsmouth 1852 Doc 1554
MARHAE Catherine (c) of S Hampton 1838 Doc 17575
MARLEY Jonathan of Exeter 1773 Doc 2472
MARSH Gilman (Negro) of Exeter 1845 Doc 20629 A
MARSH Mary of Stratham 1800 Doc 19247
MARSH Salley of Windham 1792 Doc 13587
MARSH Susanna of Epping 1788 Doc 10754
MARSH Trueworth of Raymond 1785 Doc 8644
MARSH Zebulon of Portsmouth 1791 Doc 11910

MARSH Zebulon of Epping 1775 Doc 3514
MARSHALL Mary (c) of Brentwood 1772 Doc 1407
MARSHALL Nancy of Hampton Falls 1842 Doc 20424
MARSHALL Nancy (w) of Hampton Falls 1843 Doc 20928
MARSHALL Robert G of Portsmouth 1851 Doc 311
MARSHALL Sarah of Brentwood 1772 Doc 1407
MARSHALL Sarah (c) of Brentwood 1772 Doc 1407
MARSHALL William Cantin of Brentwood 1772 Doc 1407
MARSTON Hannah of Seabrook 1779 Doc 4241
MARSTON Jacob of N Hampton 1817 Doc 44178
MARSTON Josiah of Seabrook 1779 Doc 4241
MARSTON Luce (c) of Seabrook 1779 Doc 4241
MARSTON Nathaniel of Northwood 1842 Doc 20424
MARSTON Patricia of Northwood 1842 Doc 20424
MARSTON Philis of Exeter 1830 Doc 11710
MARSTON Sarah (c) of Seabrook 1779 Doc 4241
MARTIN Aiken of Londonderry 1854 Doc 2371
MARTIN Andrew of Portsmouth 1836 Doc 16214
MARTIN Archelus of Exeter 1852 Doc 2086
MARTIN Archelus of Exeter 1853 Doc 2371
MARTIN Daniel of ? 1770 Doc 1612
MARTIN Ebenezer of Nottingham 1789 Doc 10229
MARTIN Elizabeth (c) of Kingston 1792 Doc 12531
MARTIN George (c) of Windham 1790 Doc 11611
MARTIN James of Poplin 1804 Doc 23419
MARTIN James (c) of Londonderry 1854 Doc 2371
MARTIN John of Londonderry 1854 Doc 2371
MARTIN Margaret of Londonderry 1854 Doc 2371
MARTIN Martha (c) of Kingston 1792 Doc 12531
MARTIN Mary/Molly of Hampton Falls 1788 Doc 10397
MARTIN Mary (c) of Kingston 1792 Doc 12531
MARTIN Mehitibel of Poplin 1804 Doc 23419
MARTIN Miriam of Kingston 1792 Doc 12531
MARTIN Miriam (c) of Kingston 1792 Doc 12531
MARTIN Nancy of Poplin 1804 Doc 23419
MARTIN Nathaniel (c) of Windham 1790 Doc 11611
MARTIN Nathaniel of Windham 1790 Doc 11611
MARTIN Peter of Londonderry 1854 Doc 2371
MARTIN Peter (c) of Londonderry 1854 Doc 2371
MARTIN Sarah of Windham 1790 Doc 11611
MARTIN Sarah (c) of Kingston 1792 Doc 12531
MARTIN Thomas (c) of Kingston 1792 Doc 12531
MARTIN William of Portsmouth 1836 Doc 16216
MARTIN William of Portsmouth 1837 Doc 16931
MARTIN William R P of Salem 1837 Doc 17575
MARY (w) of Hampton Falls 1783 Doc 5630
MARY (w) of Kensington 1781 Doc 4574
MASON Abel of Portsmouth 1851 Doc 311
MASON Abel of Portsmouth 1841 Doc 19136
MASON Abel of Portsmouth 1851 Doc 1554
MASON Abel of Portsmouth 1842 Doc 20107
MASON Abel of Portsmouth 1851 Doc 931

MASON Abel of Portsmouth 1841 Doc 19510
MASON Abel of Portsmouth 1852 Doc 1554
MASON Abel of Portsmouth 1839 Doc 18856
MASON Abel of Portsmouth 1839 Doc 18542
MASON Ann of Portsmouth 1851 Doc 1554
MASON Anna of Portsmouth 1852 Doc 1554
MASON Hannah of Newmarket 1804 Doc 23419
MASON Jeremiah of Salem 1792 Doc 13051
MASON Jeremy of ? 1803 Doc 2352
MASON Mary of N Hampton 1777 Doc 3797
MASON Nathaniel of Tamworth 1824 Doc 5045
MASON Omri (c) of Loudon 1812 Doc 34232
MASON Rachael of Loudon 1812 Doc 34232
MASON Sally of Salem 1792 Doc 13051
MASSEY Beverly of Salem 1845 Doc 21835
MASSEY Deborah of Salem 1845 Doc 21835
MATES Thomas of Portsmouth 1839 Doc 18267
MATHES Ann B of Portsmouth 1851 Doc 931
MATHES Ann B of Portsmouth 1851 Doc 311
MATHES George of Portsmouth 1851 Doc 311
MATHES George of Portsmouth 1851 Doc 931
MATHES John of Portsmouth 1835 Doc 15900
MATHES Joseph of Portsmouth 1851 Doc 931
MATHES Joseph of Portsmouth 1851 Doc 311
MATHES Thomas of Portsmouth 1839 Doc 18856
MATHEWS Sally of Stratham 1794 Doc 14648
MATHEWS Samuel of Candia 1845 Doc 21835
MATHIS John of Portsmouth 1836 Doc 16214
MATTHEW Molly of Hampton 1791 Doc 11910
MATTHEWS Ellen of Portsmouth 1828 Doc 9200
MATTHEWS Owen of Portsmouth 1828 Doc 9200
MAXWELL Harriet (c) of Rye 1853 Doc 2086
MAYBECOME Patrick of Nottingham 1794 Doc 14339
MAYBECOME Sarah of Nottingham 1791 Doc 13587
MCCARTY Ann of Portsmouth 1851 Doc 311
MCDANIEL Betsy of Nottingham 1842 Doc 20424
MCDANIEL Daniel of Nottingham 1840 Doc 18856
MCGOWAN Felix of Exeter 1845 Doc 21835
MCGOWAN Lettice of Exeter 1845 Doc 21835
MCKEEN Catharian of Derry 1840 Doc 18856
MCKEEN James of Derry 1840 Doc 18856
MCKIM Esther of Exeter 1784 Doc 7181
MEACH Anna of Exeter 1772 Doc 1880
MEAD John of Portsmouth 1852 Doc 1554
MEAD John of Portsmouth 1852 Doc 1555
MEAD Sarah of Newmarket 1831 Doc 12683
MEADE John of Portsmouth 1852 Doc 1554
MEADER Abigail of Epping 1799 Doc 18299
MEADER Hannah of Pittsfield 1792 Doc 13051
MEADER John of Exeter 1852 Doc 2086
MEADER John of Exeter 1853 Doc 2085
MEADER Nicholas of Epping 1799 Doc 18299

MEDAR Mary of Newmarket 1816 Doc 40757
MEDER Abigail of Poplin 1797 Doc 16546
MEEKER Thaddeus of Windham 1846 Doc 22356
MEEKER Thaddeus of Windham 1845 Doc 21835
MEEKER Thaddeus of Windham 1843 Doc 21503
MEGEOND Phylis of Northwood 1780 Doc 4331
MEGOON Hannah of Deerfield 1779 Doc 4293
MELANA Anna of Exeter 1844 Doc 21216
MELBURN Thomas of Derry 1831 Doc 12682
MELELPIN (alias) of Poplin 1792 Doc 12882
MELLEN Charles of Exeter 1821 Doc 2912
MELLEN Elizabeth of Exeter 1821 Doc 2912
MELONA Anna of Exeter 1843 Doc 20629 S
MELONA Anna of Exeter 1845 Doc 21835
MELONA Anna of Exeter 1846 Doc 22356
MELONEY Hannah of Exeter 1779 Doc 4293
MELONY Abel of Exeter 1842 Doc 20107
MELONY Anna of Exeter 1842 Doc 20107
MELONY Anna of Exeter 1842 Doc 20107
MELONY Mary of Greenland 1786 Doc 9151
MELVIN Elizabeth of Portsmouth 1846 Doc 22356
MELVIN Michael of Portsmouth 1846 Doc 22356
MELVIN George of Nottingham 1791 Doc 12531
MELVIN George (c) of Nottingham 1791 Doc 12531
MELVIN Mehitable (c) of Nottingham 1791 Doc 12531
MELVIN Molly (c) of Nottingham 1791 Doc 12531
MELVIN Nancy (c) of Nottingham 1791 Doc 12531
MELVIN Susannah of Nottingham 1791 Doc 12531
MELVIN Susannah (c) of Nottingham 1791 Doc 12531
MENDUNA Hannah of Greenland 1798 Doc 16897
MENDURN Sarah of Portsmouth 1852 Doc 1554
MENDURN Sarah of Portsmouth 1851 Doc 931
MENGOAND Ebenezer of Northwood 1780 Doc 4331
MERREL David of Bow 1792 Doc 13587
MERREL Nathan (c) of Bow 1792 Doc 13587
MERRELL Nathan (c) of Bow 1792 Doc 13587
MERRETT Rachael of Portsmouth 1841 Doc 19510
MERRETT Samuel of Portsmouth 1841 Doc 19510
MERRILL Daniel of Kingston 1794 Doc 14339
MERRILL Polly of Kingston 1794 Doc 14339
MERRILL Washington of Sandown 1846 Doc 22356
MERRILL Abiathah of Pittsfield 1816 Doc 40757
MERRILL Deliverace of Atkinson 1784 Doc 7804
MERRILL Hannah of Atkinson 1784 Doc 7804
MERRILL Molly of Hampstead 1831 Doc 12683
MERRILL Moses of Atkinson 1784 Doc 7804
MERRILL Moses of Exeter 1773 Doc 2801
MERRILL Nancy of Kingston 1807 Doc 27572
MERRILL Rebeccane of Salem 1846 Doc 22356
MERRILL Samuel of Hawke 1789 Doc 10229
MERRILL Samuel of Portsmouth 1840 Doc 18857
MERRILL Sandra of Atkinson 1784 Doc 7804

MERRILL Susanna of Kingston 1795 Doc 14648
MERRILL William of Atkinson 1784 Doc 7804
MERRITT Samuel of Portsmouth 1840 Doc 18857
MESERVE Deborah (c) of Greenland 1806 Doc 27572
MESERVE Sally (c) of Greenland 1806 Doc 27572
MESERVE Samuel (c) of Greenland 1806 Doc 27572
MESERVE Sarah (w) of Greenland 1806 Doc 27572
MESSER Cyrus of Londonderry 1838 Doc 17575
MESSER Hannah of Hawke 1789 Doc 10229
MESSER Mary of Londonderry 1838 Doc 17575
MEWMAN Mary of Seabrook 1853 Doc 2085
MIALS Thomas of Exeter 1810 Doc 32876
MICHIMON John of Portsmouth 1833 Doc 14122
MIDDLETON Richard of Windham 1787 Doc 10229
MILES (Mrs) of Meredith 1818 Doc 45992
MILES Andrew of Brentwood 1859 Doc 5505
MILES Lucy of Meredith 1821 Doc 1592
MILES Thomas of Exeter 1827 Doc 8073
MILES Thomas of Exeter 1810 Doc 31571
MILES Thomas of Exeter 1810 Doc 33660
MILIS Thomas of Exeter 1810 Doc 31571
MILLER Iannis of Portsmouth 1835 Doc 15900
MILLER James of Portsmouth 1836 Doc 16214
MILLER James of Portsmouth 1836 Doc 16214
MILLER Martha of Newington 1799 Doc 18692
MILLER Mary of Hampton 1817 Doc 44178
MILLER William of Northfield 1835 Doc 15899
MILLES Thomas of Exeter 1825 Doc 6965
MILLS Althea of Portsmouth 1852 Doc 1554
MILLS Arabella of Portsmouth 1852 Doc 1554
MILLS Elizabeth of Brentwood 1788 Doc 10229
MILLS Jacob of Brentwood 1788 Doc 10229
MILLS Washing of Portsmouth 1852 Doc 1554
MILS Mary Ann of Portsmouth 1852 Doc 1554
MINERD Joseph of Kensington 1789 Doc 11183
MINGOE Ebenezer of Hampton Falls 1774 Doc 3061
MITCHELL Arthur of Portsmouth 1833 Doc 14122
MITCHELL Peter of Newington 1805 Doc 24720
MOFFEY John of Exeter 1840 Doc 19510
MONTAGUS William of N Hampton 1839 Doc 19136
MONTGOMERY Hugh of Windham 1842 Doc 20424
MONTGOMERY John of Windham 1789 Doc 11183
MONTGOMERY Nathaniel (c) of Windham 1789 Doc 11183
MONTGOMERY Polley of Windham 1789 Doc 11183
MONTGOMERY Rebbecca of Windham 1846 Doc 22356
MONTGOMERY Rebecca of Windham 1842 Doc 20424
MONTGOMERY Rebecca of Windham 1845 Doc 21835
MONTGOMERY Rebecca of Windham 1842 Doc 20629
MONTGOMERY Rebecca of Windham 1843 Doc 21503
MONTGOMERY Rebeckah of Windham 1843 Doc 20928
MONTGOMERY William of Manchester 1840 Doc 18857
MOODY Benjamin of Nottingham 1854 Doc 2371

MOOR Mary Ann of Chester 1853 Doc 2085
MOOR Betty (c) of Windham 1787 Doc 10142
MOOR Enoch of Pembroke 1797 Doc 16546
MOOR Enoch (c) of Pembroke 1797 Doc 16546
MOOR Joseph (c) of Pembroke 1797 Doc 16546
MOOR Juda of Pembroke 1797 Doc 16546
MOOR Margaret of Windham 1787 Doc 10142
MOOR Mary Ann of Auburn 1843 Doc 311
MOOR Mary Ann of Chester 1852 Doc 1554
MOOR Mary Ann of Chester 1851 Doc 931
MOOR Nancy (c) of Windham 1787 Doc 10142
MOOR Peter of Windham 1787 Doc 10142
MOOR Polly (c) of Windham 1787 Doc 10142
MOORE George of Auburn 1851 Doc 931
MOORE George of Auburn 1851 Doc 932
MOORE George of Auburn 1852 Doc 1554
MOORE George of Auburn 1853 Doc 2085
MOORE James of Rockingham County 1825 Doc 6505
MOORE Katharine of Exeter 1791 Doc 12531
MOORE Nancy of Portsmouth 1830 Doc 12197
MOORE Nancy of Portsmouth 1830 Doc 12197
MOORE Rachael of Exeter 1791 Doc 12531
MOORE Richard of Portsmouth 1851 Doc 311
MOORS Davis of Exeter 1813 Doc 36435
MORAN Andrew of Rockingham County 1831 Doc 13399
MORAN Martha of Brentwood 1836 Doc 16931
MOREY Abigail of Atkinson 1795 Doc 15018
MOREY James of Atkinson 1795 Doc 15018
MORGAN Abigail (w) of Poplin 1797 Doc 16546
MORGAN Abigail of Chichester 1821 Doc 2397
MORGAN Abigail of Brentwood 1821 Doc 1592
MORGAN Abigail of Bridgewater 1822 Doc 2912
MORGAN Archibald of Portsmouth 1832 Doc 13755
MORGAN Joseph of Portsmouth 1828 Doc 9200
MORGAN Joseph of Portsmouth 1827 Doc 8073
MORGAN Joseph of Portsmouth 1832 Doc 13754
MORGAN Joseph of Portsmouth 1830 Doc 12197
MORGAN Joseph of Portsmouth 1846 Doc 22356
MORGAN Joseph of Portsmouth 1841 Doc 19510
MORGAN Joseph of Portsmouth 1837 Doc 16931
MORGAN Joseph of Portsmouth 1839 Doc 18856
MORGAN Joseph of Portsmouth 1851 Doc 931
MORGAN Joseph of Portsmouth 1830 Doc 12197
MORGAN Joseph of Portsmouth 1851 Doc 311
MORGAN Joseph of Portsmouth 1852 Doc 1554
MORGAN Joseph of Portsmouth 1831 Doc 13081
MORGAN Joseph of Portsmouth 1832 Doc 13755
MORGAN Joseph of Portsmouth 1836 Doc 16214
MORGAN Joseph of Portsmouth 1842 Doc 20107
MORGAN Lucy of Portsmouth 1827 Doc 8073
MORGAN Lucy of Portsmouth 1825 Doc 6965
MORLAND Elizabeth (c) of Windham 1791 Doc 11910

MORLAND James of Windham 1791 Doc 11910
MORLAND James (c) of Windham 1791 Doc 11910
MORLAND John of Windham 1791 Doc 11910
MORLAND Mary (c) of Windham 1791 Doc 11910
MORLAND Susana of Windham 1791 Doc 11910
MORLAND Thomas (c) of Windham 1791 Doc 11910
MORLAND William (c) of Windham 1791 Doc 11910
MORLEY Alexander of Portsmouth 1839 Doc 18267
MORLEY Catherine of Portsmouth 1852 Doc 1555
MORLEY Catherine of Portsmouth 1852 Doc 1554
MORLEY William of Portsmouth 1852 Doc 1554
MORRILL Danel W of Kingston 1795 Doc 14648
MORRILL Ezekiel of Canterbury 1812 Doc 34232
MORRILL Hannah of Northfield 1794 Doc 14018
MORRILL Sarah of Merrideth 1836 Doc 16215
MORRILL Sarah of Meredith 1836 Doc 16215
MORRILL Stephen of Exeter 1853 Doc 2371
MORRILL Stephen of Exeter 1851 Doc 931
MORRILL Stephen (Negro) of Exeter 1850 Doc 311
MORRISON William of Portsmouth 1842 Doc 20107
MORSE Ambrose of Portsmouth 1851 Doc 311
MORSE Betsey of Chester 1852 Doc 1554
MORSE Calef of Portsmouth 1833 Doc 14119
MORSE Cristina (c) of Hawke 1806 Doc 26134
MORSE Edna of Chester 1852 Doc 1554
MORSE Edna of Chester 1853 Doc 2371
MORSE Eliphalet of Candia 1854 Doc 2371
MORSE Elizabeth of Newmarket 1789 Doc 10911
MORSE Ephram of Hawke 1806 Doc 26134
MORSE Henry (c) of Hawke 1806 Doc 26134
MORSE Jacob (c) of Pembroke 1797 Doc 16546
MORSE Mary Ann of Chester 1853 Doc 2371
MORSE Nancy of Candia 1854 Doc 2371
MORSE Nancy of Candia 1855 Doc 3620
MORSE Richard of Pembroke 1797 Doc 16546
MORSE Sally of Pembroke 1797 Doc 16546
MORSE Sarah of Chester 1852 Doc 1554
MORSE Sarah of Hawke 1806 Doc 26134
MORSE Stephen (c) of Pembroke 1797 Doc 16546
MORSE Supply (c) of Hawke 1806 Doc 26134
MORSE Timothy (c) of Hawke 1806 Doc 26134
MORSE Waity (c) of Hawke 1806 Doc 26134
MORSI Benajmin of Exeter 1794 Doc 14018
MOSEK Abigail (c) of Loudon 1794 Doc 14339
MOSEK Elizabeth (c) of Loudon 1794 Doc 14339
MOSEK Jacob of Loudon 1794 Doc 14339
MOSEK Judith of Loudon 1794 Doc 14339
MOSEK Mary (c) of Loudon 1794 Doc 14339
MOSEK Mary (w) of Loudon 1794 Doc 14339
MOSEK Olive (c) of Loudon 1794 Doc 14339
MOSEK Timothy (c) of Loudon 1794 Doc 14339
MOSES Abial of Salem 1845 Doc 21835

MOSES Abigail of Loudon 1795 Doc 15018
MOSES Betsey of Newmarket 1846 Doc 22356
MOSES Betsey of Greenland 1797 Doc 16897
MOSES Betsey of Newmarket 1844 Doc 21209
MOSES Betsey of Newmarket 1843 Doc 20928
MOSES Betsey (c) of Deerfield 1803 Doc 22285
MOSES Betsy of Nottingham 1842 Doc 20424
MOSES Betsy of Newmarket 1850 Doc 311
MOSES Betsy of Newmarket 1850 Doc 931
MOSES Betsy of Newmarket 1844 Doc 21216
MOSES Betsy of Newmarket 1852 Doc 1554
MOSES Betty (c) of Loudon 1795 Doc 15018
MOSES Charlotte (c) of Deerfield 1803 Doc 22285
MOSES Elizabeth of Exeter 1781 Doc 4574
MOSES Elizabeth of Newmarket 1843 Doc 20629
MOSES Elizabeth (w) of Kingston 1795 Doc 15018
MOSES John (c) of Deerfield 1803 Doc 22285
MOSES Leonard of Nottingham 1842 Doc 20424
MOSES Molly of Salem 1845 Doc 21835
MOSES Nabby of Deerfield 1803 Doc 22285
MOSES Nancy (c) of Deerfield 1803 Doc 22285
MOSES Patty (c) of Deerfield 1803 Doc 22285
MOSES Phinchas of Nottingham 1842 Doc 20424
MOSES Samuel of Deerfield 1803 Doc 22285
MOSES Samuel of Loudon 1795 Doc 15018
MOSES Samuel of Allenstown 1796 Doc 15598
MOSES Susanna (c) of Deerfield 1803 Doc 22285
MOSES Susannah of Atkinson 1780 Doc 4331
MOSLEY Keziah of Nottingham 1794 Doc 14339
MOSLEY Mary of Nottingham 1794 Doc 14339
MOSS Mary of Kingston 1779 Doc 4293
MOSS Sussanah of Northwood 1780 Doc 4331
MOULTIN Asa of Poplin 1808 Doc 29235
MOULTIN Polly of Poplin 1808 Doc 29235
MOULTON Atnna of Poplin 1816 Doc 40757
MOULTON Bettey of Deerfield 1800 Doc 19247
MOULTON Doreas Jane of Portsmouth 1851 Doc 311
MOULTON Doreas Jane (c) of Portsmouth 1851 Doc 931
MOULTON Emily of Portsmouth 1851 Doc 931
MOULTON Emily of Portsmouth 1852 Doc 1554
MOULTON Emily of Portsmouth 1851 Doc 311
MOULTON Margaret of Portsmouth 1851 Doc 931
MOULTON Mary of Epping 1828 Doc 9201
MOULTON Peter of Exeter 1787 Doc 9740
MOULTON Sherborn (c) of Deerfield 1800 Doc 19247
MOULTON Stephen of Deerfield 1843 Doc 20629 S
MOULTON Stephen of Deerfield 1844 Doc 21216
MOULTON Stephen of Plaistow 1839 Doc 17185
MOULTON Stephen of Loudon 1839 Doc 17185
MOULTON Stephen (c) of Deerfield 1800 Doc 19247
MOULTON Thomas of Portsmouth 1851 Doc 931
MOULTON Thomas of Portsmouth 1851 Doc 311

MOULTON Thomas of Portsmouth 1852 Doc 1554
MUFFLIN Anne of Newmarket 1788 Doc 10229
MUFFLIN James H of Newmarket 1788 Doc 10229
MULLEN (Mrs) of Portsmouth 1840 Doc 19137
MULLEN James of Portsmouth 1830 Doc 12197
MULLEN James of Portsmouth 1832 Doc 13754
MULLEN James of Portsmouth 1831 Doc 13081
MULLEN James of Portsmouth 1836 Doc 16214
MULLEN James of Portsmouth 1834 Doc 14818
MULLEN James of Portsmouth 1846 Doc 22356
MULLEN James of Portsmouth 1842 Doc 20107
MULLEN James of Portsmouth 1842 Doc 20107
MULLEN James of Portsmouth 1841 Doc 19510
MULLEN James of Portsmouth 1837 Doc 16931
MULLEN James (Mrs) of Portsmouth 1836 Doc 16214
MULLEN Mary of Portsmouth 1834 Doc 14818
MULLER James of Portsmouth 1830 Doc 12197
MULLIAN James of Portsmouth 1840 Doc 19137
MULLIN James of Portsmouth 1841 Doc 19510
MULLINS (widow of) Izak of Portsmouth 1840 Doc 18856
MULLINS James of Portsmouth 1840 Doc 18856
MULLINS James of Portsmouth 1841 Doc 19511
MUNSON Mary of Hampstead 1854 Doc 2371
MURDOCK Jane of Portsmouth 1838 Doc 18267
MURDOCK William of Portsmouth 1851 Doc 311
MURDOCK William W of Portsmouth 1851 Doc 931
MURDOCK William W of Portsmouth 1846 Doc 22356
MURDOCK William W of Portsmouth 1852 Doc 1554
MURPHY Jeremiah of Portsmouth 1839 Doc 18542
MURPHY Jeremiah of Portsmouth 1839 Doc 18856
MURPHY Jeremiah of ? 1839 Doc 19136
MURPHY Jeremiah of Portsmouth 1841 Doc 19510
MURPHY Jeremiah of Portsmouth 1841 Doc 19511
MURPHY Jeremiah of Portsmouth 1852 Doc 1842
MURPHY Julia of Portsmouth 1852 Doc 1554
MURPHY Mary of Greenland 1777 Doc 4164
MURPHY Mary of Kingston 1792 Doc 12531
MURPHY Nancy of Portsmouth 1841 Doc 19511
MURPHY Nancy of Portsmouth 1842 Doc 20107
MURPHY Nancy of Portsmouth 1841 Doc 19511
MURRAY Catharine of Portsmouth 1852 Doc 1842
MURRAY John of Portsmouth 1827 Doc 8073
MURRAY John of Portsmouth 1826 Doc 6965
MURRAY Margaret of Portsmouth 1851 Doc 311
MURRAY Margaret of Portsmouth 1851 Doc 931
MURRAY Samuel of Greenland 1821 Doc 2397
MURRAY Samuel of Stratham 1823 Doc 3965
MURRAY Samuel of Stratham 1822 Doc 3416
MURRY Catherine of Portsmouth 1852 Doc 1554
MURRY Keziah of Newmarket 1850 Doc 311
MacCOY James of Kenington 1776 Doc 3714
MacMURPHY Elizabeth of Alexandria 1826 Doc 7524

MacMURPHY John of Alexandria 1826 Doc 7524
McCALLAUGH Roger of Portsmouth 1851 Doc 931
McCALLEY Caroline M of Stratham 1853 Doc 2085
McCANN Betsy Robinson of Stratham 1846 Doc 22356
McCANN George (c) of Stratham 1846 Doc 22356
McCANN John (c) of Stratham 1846 Doc 22356
McCANN Sarah (c) of Stratham 1846 Doc 22356
McCANN Sophronia (c) of Stratham 1846 Doc 22356
McCANN Thomas of Stratham 1846 Doc 22356
McCARTEE Eleanor of Atkinson 1774 Doc 2656
McCARTHY Anna of Portsmouth 1851 Doc 931
McCARTHY Orvin of Windham 1849 Doc 311
McCARTY Elizabeth of Portsmouth 1841 Doc 19510
McCARTY Elizabeth of Portsmouth 1840 Doc 18857
McCARTY John of Portsmouth 1839 Doc 18856
McCARTY John of Portsmouth 1839 Doc 18267
McCARTY Mary Elizabeth of Portsmouth 1840 Doc 18857
McCLARY Samuel of Windham 1784 Doc 7804
McCLEARY Samuel of Windham 1780 Doc 4574
McCLERY Samuel of Windham 1780 Doc 4574
McCOLLISTER Mary of Epping 1783 Doc 5630
McCOY Betsy of Windham 1843 Doc 20928
McCOY Betsy of Windham 1843 Doc 21503
McCOY Betsy of Windham 1845 Doc 21835
McCOY Betsy of Windham 1846 Doc 22356
McCOY Betty of Goffstown 1822 Doc 2912
McCOY Elizabeth of Windham 1842 Doc 20424
McCOY Elizabeth of Windham 1842 Doc 20629 S
McCOY Jan of Windham 1851 Doc 931
McCOY Jenny of Windham 1850 Doc 311
McCOY Jenny of Windham 1842 Doc 20424
McCOY Jermy of Windham 1845 Doc 21835
McCOY Jimmy of Windham 1843 Doc 20928
McCOY Jimmy of Windham 1843 Doc 21503
McCOY John of Nottingham 1843 Doc 20629
McCOY John of Windham 1842 Doc 20424
McCOY Larry of Windham 1846 Doc 22356
McCOY Nancy of Nothingham 1844 Doc 21216
McCOY Nancy of Nottingham 1853 Doc 2085
McCOY Nancy of Nottingham 1843 Doc 20629
McCOY Nancy of Nottingham 1845 Doc 21835
McCOY Nancy of Nottingham 1854 Doc 2371
McCOY Nancy of Deerfield 1801 Doc 20206
McCOY Salley of Nottingham 1843 Doc 20629
McCRAIGHEN Samuel of Derry 1841 Doc 19510
McDANIEL Betsy of Nottingham 1846 Doc 22356
McDANIEL Betty of Epping 1790 Doc 11310
McDANIEL Daniel of Nottingham 1840 Doc 18856
McDANIEL David of Nottingham 1795 Doc 14879
McDANIEL Eunice of Nottingham 1795 Doc 14879
McDANIEL Hannah of Epping 1790 Doc 11310
McDANIEL Hannah M of Nottingham 1795 Doc 14879

McDANIEL John of Nottingham 1795 Doc 14879
McDANIEL Miles of Portsmouth 1830 Doc 12197
McDANIEL Molly of Nottingham 1795 Doc 14879
McDANIEL Nancy of Epsom 1801 Doc 19665
McDANIEL Robert of Epsom 1801 Doc 19665
McDANIEL Whitcher John of Epping 1790 Doc 11310
McDANIEL William of Nottingham 1795 Doc 14879
McDANIELS Miles of Derry 1833 Doc 14122
McDANIELS Edward of Portsmouth 1830 Doc 12197
McDANIELS Edward of Portsmouth 1830 Doc 12197
McDANIELS Eleanor of Portsmouth 1830 Doc 12197
McDANIELS James of Portsmouth 1832 Doc 13399
McDANIELS Miles of Derry 1832 Doc 13754
McDANIELS Miles of Portsmouth 1830 Doc 12197
McDANIELS Nancy of Portsmouth 1832 Doc 13754
McDANIELS Phebe of Portsmouth 1830 Doc 12197
McDANOLD David of Nottingham 1838 Doc 17575
McDEVIT Francis M of Portsmouth 1843 Doc 20629
McDONALD (Mrs) Betsy of Nothingham 1844 Doc 21216
McDONALD Betsey of Nottingham 1850 Doc 311
McDONALD Betsy of Nottingham 1845 Doc 21835
McDONALD Daniel of Nottingham 1839 Doc 18267
McDONALD Donald of Portsmouth 1828 Doc 9200
McDONALD Eleanor of Derry 1836 Doc 16214
McDONALD Eleanor of Derry 1836 Doc 16214
McDONALD Lawrence of Nottingham 1842 Doc 20424
McDUFFE Frances of Derry 1839 Doc 18267
McDUFFY Francis of Derry 1838 Doc 17575
McFINN (Mrs) Michael of Portsmouth 1841 Doc 19511
McFINN Michael of Portsmouth 1841 Doc 19510
McFINN Michael of Portsmouth 1841 Doc 19511
McGINESS Margaret of Portsmouth 1840 Doc 18857
McGINNESS Margaret of Portsmouth 1840 Doc 18857
McGINNESS Margaret of Portsmouth 1841 Doc 19510
McGINNESS Patrick of Portsmouth 1840 Doc 18857
McGINNESS Patrick W of Portsmouth 1841 Doc 19510
McGINNIS Patrick of Portsmouth 1839 Doc 18856
McGINNIS Patrick of Portsmouth 1839 Doc 18542
McGIVEN John of Portsmouth 1852 Doc 1554
McGUIRE John of Portsmouth 1852 Doc 1554
McGWINE John of Portsmouth 1851 Doc 931
McINTOSH of ? 1812 Doc 35625
McKINLEY Margaret of Exeter 1837 Doc 17575
McKINLEY William of Exeter 1837 Doc 17575
McLARY Nancy Jenne of Windham 1784 Doc 7804
McLEAN Margaret of Portsmouth 1840 Doc 18856
McLEARY Agnes of Windham 1792 Doc 12531
McLEARY David (c) of Windham 1792 Doc 12531
McLEARY John of Windham 1792 Doc 12531
McLELAN Margaret of Portsmouth 1839 Doc 18542
McLELLAN Margaret of Portsmouth 1839 Doc 18856
McMULLIN Mary Ann of Portsmouth 1817 Doc 44178

McMURPHY James of Dover 1824 Doc 50452
McMURPHY Mary of Poplin 1797 Doc 16546
McNARD Harriet of Portsmouth 1822 Doc 3416
NAHAR John of Portsmouth 1837 Doc 16931
NANIS Levi of Epping 1792 Doc 12531
NASON Charles of Hampton Falls 1851 Doc 931
NAUGHA Mary of Portsmouth 1851 Doc 931
NAUGHAN Mary of Portsmouth 1852 Doc 1554
NAUGHAN Mary of Portsmouth 1851 Doc 311
NAUGHAN Michael of Portsmouth 1851 Doc 311
NAUGHAN Michael of Portsmouth 1851 Doc 931
NAUGHAN Michael (c) of Portsmouth 1852 Doc 1554
NAUGHAN Thomas of Portsmouth 1851 Doc 311
NAUGHAN Thomas of Portsmouth 1851 Doc 931
NAY Daghet of Sandown 1812 Doc 34232
NAY Patience of Sandown 1812 Doc 34232
NEAL Andrew of Sandown 1842 Doc 20424
NEAL Daniel of Portsmouth 1832 Doc 13399
NEAL David of Portsmouth 1832 Doc 13754
NEAL Eleanor of Sandown 1842 Doc 20424
NEAL Eleanor of Sandown 1844 Doc 21503
NEAL Eleanor of Sandown 1843 Doc 20629 S
NEAL Eleanor of Sandown 1843 Doc 20928
NEAL Eleanor of Sandown 1845 Doc 21835
NEAL Eliphalet of Newmarket 1775 Doc 3695
NEAL James of Deerfield 1783 Doc 5630
NEAL John of Raymond 1800 Doc 18692
NEAL John of Deerfield 1804 Doc 22771
NEAL Lester of Deerfield 1804 Doc 22771
NEAL Levi of Deerfield 1804 Doc 22771
NEAL Levi of Deerfield 1804 Doc 22771
NEAL Levi (gc) of Raymond 1800 Doc 18692
NEAL Mary of Newmarket 1775 Doc 3695
NEAL Rhoda of Raymond 1851 Doc 1554
NEAL Witham of Deerfield 1804 Doc 22771
NEEDER Mehitable of Brentwood 1849 Doc 24261
NEEDHORN Catherine of Portsmouth 1837 Doc 16931
NELSON Hannah of Deerfield 1787 Doc 10016
NELSON James of Deerfield 1787 Doc 10016
NELSON John of Portsmouth 1842 Doc 20424
NELSON John of Greenland 1806 Doc 27572
NELSON John of Rye 1802 Doc 21391
NELSON Mary (c) of Greenland 1806 Doc 27572
NELSON Ruth of Greenland 1806 Doc 27572
NELSON Sarah of Rye 1802 Doc 21391
NELSON Thomas (c) of Greenland 1806 Doc 27572
NELSON Wm of Portsmouth 1852 Doc 1554
NEMIRO John of Newmarket 1850 Doc 311
NENDENAN Hannah of Epping 1800 Doc 19247
NERRY Mary M of Windham 1852 Doc 1554
NEVAN Andrew of Portsmouth 1830 Doc 12197
NEVAN Andrew of Portsmouth 1830 Doc 12197

NEVAN Clarisa of Portsmouth 1830 Doc 12197
NEWELL Clarisa of Portsmouth 1830 Doc 12197
NEWHALL Clarisa of Portsmouth 1830 Doc 12197
NEWICK (Mrs) of Portsmouth 1852 Doc 1554
NEWICK Elizabeth of Portsmouth 1852 Doc 1554
NEWICK Elizabeth of Portsmouth 1852 Doc 1554
NEWING Mary of Portsmouth 1852 Doc 1554
NEWMAN Mary of Seabrook 1853 Doc 2085
NEWMAN Sally of Exeter 1794 Doc 14018
NEWMARCH Grace of Exeter 1784 Doc 7181
NEWNING Dennis of Portsmouth 1852 Doc 1555
NEWNING Dennis of Portsmouth 1852 Doc 1554
NEWNING Dennis of Portsmouth 1852 Doc 1554
NEWTON David of Chesterfield 1806 Doc 35625
NICHOLAS Elizabeth of Kingston 1792 Doc 12531
NICHOLAS Eather of Brentwood 1792 Doc 12882
NICHOLAS John of Brentwood 1792 Doc 12882
NICHOLAS Rufus (c) of Kingston 1792 Doc 12531
NICHOLS Betty (c) of Plaistow 1791 Doc 12228
NICHOLS Daniel (c) of Plaistow 1791 Doc 12228
NICHOLS David of Plaistow 1791 Doc 12228
NICHOLS Hattie of Plaistow 1791 Doc 12228
NICHOLS Nathl of Epsom 1801 Doc 20738
NICHOLS Phebe of Epsom 1801 Doc 20738
NICHOLS Rebeckah of Hawke 1798 Doc 17408
NICHOLS Samuel (c) of Plaistow 1791 Doc 12228
NICHOLS Stephen (c) of Plaistow 1791 Doc 12228
NICHOLS Unice (c) of Plaistow 1791 Doc 12228
NICKSON John H of Pembroke 1795 Doc 15359
NIGHT Elizabeth of Windham 1795 Doc 15359
NIGHT Joseph of Windham 1795 Doc 15359
NIGHT Polley of Windham 1795 Doc 15359
NIGHT Stephen of Windham 1795 Doc 15359
NIGHT Susanna of Windham 1795 Doc 15359
NILES Betsy of Brentwood 1859 Doc 5505
NIMRO John of Newmarket 1850 Doc 931
NOAKES Timothy of Kensington 1774 Doc 3061
NOBEY Cynthia of Nottingham 1850 Doc 931
NOBLE Lydia of Portsmouth 1832 Doc 13755
NOBLE Moses of Portsmouth 1843 Doc 20629
NOBLE Robert of Portsmouth 1843 Doc 20629
NOBLE Robert of Portsmouth 1851 Doc 931
NOBLE Robert of Portsmouth 1851 Doc 311
NOBLE Robert of Portsmouth 1852 Doc 1554
NOBLE Robert of Portsmouth 1846 Doc 22356
NOIS Cynthia of Nottingham 1854 Doc 2371
NOLEN John of Portsmouth 1839 Doc 18267
NOROLAN James of Portsmouth 1791 Doc 12228
NORRIS David of Deerfield 1795 Doc 14879
NORRIS Deborah of Deerfield 1795 Doc 14879
NORRIS Elizabeth of Stratham 1774 Doc 2656
NORRIS Mary of Deerfield 1795 Doc 14879

NORTON William of Windham 1831 Doc 15123
NORTON William of Windham 1834 Doc 15123
NOWICK Elizabeth of Portsmouth 1852 Doc 1555
NOYES Abigail of Plaistow 1794 Doc 14339
NOYES Cynthia of Nottingham 1846 Doc 22356
NOYES Cynthia of Nottingham 1852 Doc 1554
NOYES Cynthia of Nothingham 1844 Doc 21216
NOYES Cynthia of Nottingham 1851 Doc 932
NOYES Cynthia of Nottingham 1850 Doc 311
NOYES Cynthia of Nottingham 1845 Doc 21835
NOYES Jane of Epsom 1794 Doc 14339
NOYES John E of Portsmouth 1852 Doc 1554
NOYES John E of Portsmouth 1851 Doc 311
NOYES John E of Portsmouth 1851 Doc 931
NOYES John E of Portsmouth 1851 Doc 1554
NOYES John Harvey (c) of Nottingham 1850 Doc 311
NOYES Ruth of Nottingham 1843 Doc 20629
NOYES Ruth of Nottingham 1842 Doc 20424
NUDD John of North Hampton 1794 Doc 14018
NUDD John of Greenland 1792 Doc 12882
NUDD Levi of Northfield 1823 Doc 3965
NUDD Patty of Greenland 1792 Doc 12882
NUDD Patty of North Hampton 1794 Doc 14018
NUTTER Lear of Pittsfield 1802 Doc 20738
NUTTER Betsey of Deerfield 1805 Doc 23965
NUTTER Betsy of Newington 1796 Doc 15359
NUTTER Caroline of Portsmouth 1821 Doc 1592
NUTTER Christopher of Newmarket 1800 Doc 18692
NUTTER Daniel of Newington 1796 Doc 15359
NUTTER Hannah of Newington 1796 Doc 15359
NUTTER James (c) of Newington 1794 Doc 14648
NUTTER Lear of Northwood 1793 Doc 13190
NUTTER Marsha (c) of Deerfield 1805 Doc 23965
NUTTER Mary of Newington 1792 Doc 12882
NUTTER Miriam of Newington 1794 Doc 14648
NUTTER Nabby (c) of Newington 1792 Doc 12882
NUTTER Nancy of Newmarket 1800 Doc 18692
NUTTER Nathan of Deerfield 1805 Doc 23965
NUTTER Polly (c) of Newington 1792 Doc 12882
NUTTER Samuel of Newington 1792 Doc 12882
NUTTER Samuel of Newington 1800 Doc 18692
NUTTER Susy (c) of Newington 1792 Doc 12882
O'BRIANT John of Exeter 1840 Doc 19510
O'BRIEN James of Portsmouth 1840 Doc 18857
O'BRIEN James of Portsmouth 1840 Doc 19137
O'BRIEN Mary of New Market 1853 Doc 2086
O'BRIEN Mary of Newmarket 1853 Doc 2371
O'BRIEN Thomas of Derry 1829 Doc 12682
O'BRIEN Thomas of Derry 1831 Doc 12682
O'BRIEN Thomas of Derry 1831 Doc 13081
O'BRIWN James of Portsmouth 1841 Doc 19510
O'BRIWN Mary of Epping 1782 Doc 5186

O'CONNELL Thomas of Derry 1841 Doc 19510
ODDIORN Betty of Newmarket 1773 Doc 2472
ODDIORN Ebenezer of Newmarket 1773 Doc 2472
ODDIORN William of Newmarket 1773 Doc 2472
ODELL E of Greenland 1851 Doc 931
ODIONE Abigail of Portsmouth 1852 Doc 1554
ODIONE Abigail of Portsmouth 1851 Doc 931
ODIONER Abigail of Portsmouth 1853 Doc 2086
ODIONNE Benjamin of Portsmouth 1834 Doc 14817
ODIONNE Sarah of Newmarket 1844 Doc 21216
ODIORE Sarah of Newmarket 1850 Doc 311
ODIORNE Abigail of Portsmouth 1851 Doc 311
ODIORNE Abigail of Portsmouth 1843 Doc 20629
ODIORNE Abigail of Portsmouth 1846 Doc 22356
ODIORNE Samuel (Capt) of Portsmouth 1791 Doc 12228
ODIORNE Sarah of Newmarket 1843 Doc 20928
ODIORNE Sarah of Newmarket 1843 Doc 20629
ODIORNE Sarah of Newmarket 1850 Doc 931
ODIORNE Sarah of Newmarket 1846 Doc 22356
OMAR Mary of Portsmouth 1830 Doc 12197
OMAR Mary of Portsmouth 1830 Doc 12197
ORDWAY Betty (c) of Poplin 1801 Doc 20738
ORDWAY John of Atkinson 1773 Doc 2656
ORDWAY Nehemiah of Poplin 1801 Doc 20738
ORDWAY Sarah of Poplin 1801 Doc 20738
ORKINS Hannah of Canterbury 1816 Doc 40757
OSBORNE William of Portsmouth 1827 Doc 8073
OSBORNE William of Portsmouth 1826 Doc 7524
OWEN Ann M (c) of Portsmouth 1846 Doc 22356
OWEN George E (c) of Portsmouth 1846 Doc 22356
OWEN John J (c) of Portsmouth 1846 Doc 22356
OWEN Patrick of Portsmouth 1851 Doc 931
OWEN Patrick of Portsmouth 1851 Doc 932
OWEN Patrick of Portsmouth 1853 Doc 2086
OWEN Patrick of Portsmouth 1852 Doc 1554
OWEN T of Portsmouth 1852 Doc 1554
OWENS John of Portsmouth 1837 Doc 16931
OWENS Patrick of Portsmouth 1851 Doc 932
OWN Elizabeth of Portsmouth 1851 Doc 311
PACKARD Susan of Candia 1842 Doc 20424
PAGE Aaron of Hampton 1770 Doc 1612
PAGE Abigail of Hampton Falls 1790 Doc 11310
PAGE Abigail of Salem 1843 Doc 20629
PAGE Abraham of Hampton 1770 Doc 1612
PAGE Betty of Hampton Falls 1788 Doc 10640
PAGE Charles of Hampton Falls 1790 Doc 11310
PAGE David of ? 1772 Doc 731
PAGE Dexter of Raymond 1851 Doc 931
PAGE Dolly (c) of Hampton Falls 1788 Doc 10640
PAGE Ebenezer of Salem 1777 Doc 3981
PAGE Elizabeth of Hampton 1770 Doc 1612
PAGE Emily P of Gilford 1861 Doc 6710

PAGE Ensley of Hampton Falls 1788 Doc 10640
PAGE Hannah of Hampton 1770 Doc 1612
PAGE Jose of Northwood 1787 Doc 9898
PAGE Joseph of Salem 1843 Doc 20629 A
PAGE Joseph of Seabrook 1843 Doc 20928
PAGE Joseph (c) of Hampton Falls 1788 Doc 10640
PAGE Joseph (c) of Hampton Falls 1788 Doc 10640
PAGE Miriam of Hampton 1770 Doc 1612
PAGE Moses of Gilford 1861 Doc 6710
PAGE Persis (c) of Salem 1843 Doc 20629
PAGE Persis of Portsmouth 1845 Doc 21835
PAGE Persis of Salem 1846 Doc 22356
PAGE Persis of Salem 1854 Doc 2371
PAGE Persis of Stratham 1851 Doc 931
PAGE Persis of Salem 1843 Doc 20928
PAGE Persis of Salem 1853 Doc 2085
PAGE Robert of Seabrook 1843 Doc 20928
PAGE Samuel of Rockingham County 1825 Doc 6505
PAGE Tabithy of Hampton 1816 Doc 40757
PAGE William of Hampton 1770 Doc 1612
PAIN John of Raymond 1784 Doc 7459
PAIN John of Raymond 1788 Doc 10397
PALMER Hannah of Pembroke 1787 Doc 9898
PALMER Hannah of Exeter 1784 Doc 7181
PALMER Hannah of Exeter 1791 Doc 12531
PALMER Hannah of Pembroke 1817 Doc 44178
PALMER Isaac (Negro) of Portsmouth 1851 Doc 311
PALMER Isaac of Portsmouth 1843 Doc 20629
PALMER Joseph of Pembroke 1787 Doc 9898
PALMER Joseph (c) of Exeter 1784 Doc 7181
PALMER Thomas of Portsmouth 1852 Doc 1842
PARK Nancy (Negro) of Salem 1845 Doc 21835
PARKER Elery of Derry 1839 Doc 18267
PARKER John of Derry 1839 Doc 18267
PARKER John of Northwood 1812 Doc 35052
PARKER John of Portsmouth 1851 Doc 931
PARKER John of Portsmouth 1850 Doc 932
PARKER Mary J of Portsmouth 1845 Doc 21835
PARKER Mary J of Kingston 1826 Doc 8077
PARKER Nancy of Portsmouth 1845 Doc 21835
PARKER Nancy of Salem 1850 Doc 311
PARKER Nancy of Stratham 1851 Doc 931
PARKER Nancy of Salem 1846 Doc 22356
PARKER Nancy (Negro) of Salem 1843 Doc 20928
PARKER Nancy of Salem 1853 Doc 2085
PARKER Nancy of Salem 1843 Doc 20629
PARKER Nancy of Salem 1854 Doc 2371
PARKER Samuel Burrell of Hawke 1804 Doc 23419
PARKER William of Sanbornton 1772 Doc 731
PARKER William of E Kingston 1838 Doc 17909
PARKS Mary of Portsmouth 1851 Doc 311
PARSON Daniel of Portsmouth 1828 Doc 9200

PARSON Daniel of Portsmouth 1827 Doc 8073
PARSON Daniel (c) of Portsmouth 1826 Doc 6965
PARSON Harriet of Portsmouth 1837 Doc 16931
PARSON Harriet Newall of Portsmouth 1836 Doc 16216
PARSON Harriett of Portsmouth 1839 Doc 18856
PARSON Harriett of Portsmouth 1841 Doc 19510
PARSON John of Portsmouth 1851 Doc 311
PARSON John of Portsmouth 1851 Doc 931
PARSON John of Portsmouth 1846 Doc 22356
PARSON John of Portsmouth 1836 Doc 16216
PARSON John of Portsmouth 1826 Doc 6965
PARSON John of Portsmouth 1827 Doc 8073
PARSON Josephine of Portsmouth 1827 Doc 8073
PARSON Joseph M of Portsmouth 1828 Doc 9200
PARSON Joseph M (c) of Portsmouth 1826 Doc 6965
PARSON Sally of Portsmouth 1826 Doc 6965
PARSON Sally of Portsmouth 1827 Doc 8073
PARSON Sarah of Portsmouth 1837 Doc 16931
PARSON Sarah of ? 1836 Doc 16214
PARSON Sarah of Portsmouth 1836 Doc 16216
PARSON Sarah Ann of Portsmouth 1827 Doc 8073
PARSON Sarah Ann (c) of Portsmouth 1826 Doc 6965
PARSONS Harriett of Portsmouth 1840 Doc 18856
PARSONS John of Portsmouth 1852 Doc 1554
PASON Ebenezer of Strafford 1822 Doc 2912
PATIENCE (Mulatto) of Poplin 1793 Doc 13587
PATIENCE (Mulatto) of Exeter 1796 Doc 15359
PATIENCE (Mulatto) of ? 1792 Doc 13587
PATRIDGE Polly of Stratham 1851 Doc 931
PATTE Abigail of Salem 1777 Doc 3981
PATTE John of Salem 1777 Doc 3981
PATTE Mary of Salem 1777 Doc 3981
PATTEN Sarah of Candia 1842 Doc 20424
PATTERSON Phebe of Exeter 1785 Doc 8391
PATTIN James of Kensington 1795 Doc 15018
PATTIN Polly (c) of Kensington 1795 Doc 15018
PATTIN Sally (c) of Kensington 1795 Doc 15018
PATTIN Sarah of Kensington 1795 Doc 15018
PAUL Amos of Portsmouth 1852 Doc 1554
PAUL Benjamin of Exeter 1844 Doc 21216
PAUL Benjamin of Portsmouth 1843 Doc 20629 A
PAUL Benjamin of Exeter 1843 Doc 20629 S
PAUL Benjamin of Exeter 1845 Doc 21835
PAUL Benjamin of Exeter 1846 Doc 22356
PAUL Benjamin (s) of Portsmouth 1843 Doc 20629 A
PAUL Danias of Exeter 1792 Doc 12882
PAUL Dolly (Negro) of Exeter 1842 Doc 20107
PAUL Ephraim of Portsmouth 1845 Doc 21835
PAUL Jacob of Portsmouth 1843 Doc 20629 A
PAUL Jane of Portsmouth 1845 Doc 21835
PAUL Jane of Portsmouth 1851 Doc 311
PAUL Jane of Portsmouth 1851 Doc 931

PAUL Jane of Portsmouth 1852 Doc 1554
PAUL John of Portsmouth 1838 Doc 18267
PAUL John of Portsmouth 1839 Doc 18856
PAUL Joseph of Portsmouth 1843 Doc 20629
PAUL Keziah of Portsmouth 1843 Doc 20629
PAUL Shadreck of Portsmouth 1827 Doc 9201
PAULS Sarah Phelps of Exeter 1842 Doc 20107
PAYSON Aurelia of Kingston 1792 Doc 12531
PAYSON John of Kingston 1792 Doc 12531
PEAR Levis of Portsmouth 1827 Doc 8073
PEARCY William of Brentwood 1790 Doc 11310
PEARS William of Pelham 1813 Doc 36435
PEARSON Rachel of Hampstead 1852 Doc 1554
PEARSON Rachel of Hampstead 1854 Doc 2371
PEARSON Rachel of Hampstead 1853 Doc 2085
PEASE William of Greenland 1829 Doc 10409
PEASLEY Mark of Newtown 1805 Doc 24720
PEASLEY (Mrs) H of Portsmouth 1841 Doc 19511
PEASLEY Hiram of Portsmouth 1841 Doc 20107
PEASLY Katherine of Newmarket 1784 Doc 7181
PEAVEY Elizabeth of Newmarket 1782 Doc 4997
PEAVEY King (Negro woman) of Portsmouth 1798 Doc 17408
PEAVY Hopley of Portsmouth 1833 Doc 14119
PEAVY John of Deerfield 1800 Doc 18692
PEAVY John (c) of Deerfield 1800 Doc 18692
PEAVY Sally of Deerfield 1800 Doc 18692
PEAVY Stephen (c) of Deerfield 1800 Doc 18692
PEEVEY Alice of Poplin 1806 Doc 25429
PEEVEY Benjamin (c) of Poplin 1806 Doc 25429
PEEVEY Doreas (w) of Poplin 1806 Doc 25429
PEEVEY Joseph (c) of Poplin 1806 Doc 25429
PEEVEY Polly (c) of Poplin 1806 Doc 25429
PEEVEY Samuel of Poplin 1806 Doc 25429
PEEVEY Samuel (c) of Poplin 1806 Doc 25429
PEEVEY Stephen (c) of Poplin 1806 Doc 25429
PEEVEY William (c) of Poplin 1806 Doc 25429
PEEVY Martha of Greenland 1780 Doc 4406
PERCELL Robert of Portsmouth 1840 Doc 19137
PERKINS Abigail B of Portsmouth 1842 Doc 20107
PERKINS Abram W of Seabrook 1846 Doc 22356
PERKINS Betty/Salley of Hampton Falls 1792 Doc 12882
PERKINS Daniel of Pittsfield 1789 Doc 11611
PERKINS David of Seabrook 1852 Doc 1554
PERKINS David of Seabrook 1853 Doc 2085
PERKINS David of Seabrook 1846 Doc 22356
PERKINS David of Seabrook 1850 Doc 311
PERKINS David of Seabrook 1851 Doc 931
PERKINS Davis of Seabrook 1852 Doc 2371
PERKINS George of Seabrook 1852 Doc 1554
PERKINS George H of Seabrook 1846 Doc 22356
PERKINS John W of Seabrook 1852 Doc 1554
PERKINS Joseph of Newmarket 1843 Doc 20629

PERKINS Merriam (w) of Seabrook 1846 Doc 22356
PERKINS William of Exeter 1792 Doc 12531
PERKS William of Portsmouth 1851 Doc 931
PERO Lois (Negro) of Pittsfield 1805 Doc 23965
PERRY Benjamin of Windham 1852 Doc 1554
PERRY Doit of Exeter 1853 Doc 2371
PERRY Mary of Portsmouth 1830 Doc 12197
PERRY Mary of Portsmouth 1834 Doc 14818
PERRY Mary of Portsmouth 1830 Doc 12197
PERRY Mary of Portsmouth 1836 Doc 16214
PERRY Patrick of Portsmouth 1834 Doc 14818
PERRY Patrick of Portsmouth 1838 Doc 18267
PERRY Thomas of Windham 1849 Doc 311
PERSON Benjamin of Brentwood 1801 Doc 20206
PETEGROW Ephraim of Portsmouth 1837 Doc 16931
PETEGROW Lydia (c) of Portsmouth 1837 Doc 16931
PETERS Fanney (Negro) of Sandown 1812 Doc 34232
PETERS Margaret of Exeter 1783 Doc 5923
PETERS Pomp of Brentwood 1743 Doc 14339
PETERS Robert of Exeter 1779 Doc 4199
PETERS Robinson of Dunbarton 1834 Doc 14817
PETERS Robinson of Exeter 1842 Doc 20107
PETERS Sarah of Loudon 1790 Doc 11611
PETERS Sarah (c) of Loudon 1790 Doc 11611
PETERS Trueworth of Dunbarton 1834 Doc 14817
PETERSON John of Portsmouth 1840 Doc 19137
PETERSON John of Portsmouth 1842 Doc 20107
PETERSON John of Portsmouth 1841 Doc 19510
PETERSON John (c) of Newmarket 1775 Doc 3695
PETERSON Mary of Newmarket 1775 Doc 3695
PETERSON Sarah of Portsmouth 1830 Doc 12197
PETGROW Adaline (c) of Portsmouth 1837 Doc 16931
PETGROW Lydia of Portsmouth 1837 Doc 16931
PETGROW William of Portsmouth 1837 Doc 16931
PETIGREW Lydia of Portsmouth 1838 Doc 18267
PETINGILL Asa of Salem 1793 Doc 14018
PETTIGREW Adeline (c) of Portsmouth 1840 Doc 18856
PETTIGREW Ephraim of Portsmouth 1839 Doc 18856
PETTIGREW Lydia of Portsmouth 1840 Doc 18856
PETTIGREW Sarah Ann (c) of Portsmouth 1840 Doc 18856
PETTIGREW Susan (c) of Portsmouth 1840 Doc 18856
PETTIGREW William of Portsmouth 1840 Doc 18856
PETTINGILL Deborah of Salem 1793 Doc 14018
PETTINGILL Enoch of Salem 1793 Doc 14018
PETTINGILL Hannah of S Hampton 1800 Doc 19247
PETTINGILL Jacob of Exeter 1774 Doc 2656
PETTINGILL Joseph of Portsmouth 1841 Doc 19510
PETTINGILL Joseph of Portsmouth 1840 Doc 18857
PHASET Betsy of Brentwood 1794 Doc 14339
PHEBE (Mulatto) of Exeter 1773 Doc 2801
PHELPS Sarah of Exeter 1790 Doc 11310
PHILBRICK Abigail (w) of Deerfield 1817 Doc 44178

PHILBRICK Hanah of Brentwood 1787 Doc 10016
PHILBRICK Hannah of Kingston 1794 Doc 14339
PHILBRICK Hannah of E Kingston 1805 Doc 24720
PHILBRICK Hannah of Windham 1788 Doc 10525
PHILBRICK John of Exeter 1795 Doc 14648
PHILBRICK Mary of Exeter 1846 Doc 22356
PHILBRICK Mary of Exeter 1850 Doc 311
PHILBRICK Mehitabel of Epping 1792 Doc 12882
PHILBRICK Sarah of Raymond 1798 Doc 17408
PHILBROK Benjam of Stratham 1852 Doc 1554
PHILBROOK John of Brentwood 1785 Doc 9466
PHILIP Benjamin of Stratham 1853 Doc 2371
PHILIPS Mary of Pembroke 1796 Doc 15733
PHILLIPS Hannah of Northwood 1796 Doc 15359
PHILLIPS Nathaniel of Portsmouth 1840 Doc 19137
PHILLIPS Nathaniel of Portsmouth 1841 Doc 19510
PHILLIPS Wm G of Portsmouth 1851 Doc 311
PHILPIT Benjam of Stratham 1807 Doc 27572
PHILPIT Benjamin of Stratham 1851 Doc 931
PHILPIT Sarah of Stratham 1851 Doc 931
PHILPIT Sarah Sr of Stratham 1851 Doc 931
PHILPIT Sarah of Stratham 1850 Doc 311
PICKERING Beckey of Gilford 1826 Doc 7524
PICKERING Betsey of Newmarket 1832 Doc 13399
PICKERING Betsy (c) of Pittsfield 1806 Doc 26134
PICKERING Hitty (c) of Pittsfield 1806 Doc 26134
PICKERING James of Pittsfield 1806 Doc 26134
PICKERING Jane of Newmarket 1832 Doc 13399
PICKERING Jeremiah (c) of Pittsfield 1806 Doc 26134
PICKERING John of Newmarket 1832 Doc 13399
PICKERING Jonathan (c) of Pittsfield 1806 Doc 26134
PICKERING Mary of Pittsfield 1806 Doc 26134
PICKERING Nancy (c) of Pittsfield 1806 Doc 26134
PICKERING Nathan of Newmarket 1832 Doc 13399
PICKERING Sally (c) of Pittsfield 1806 Doc 26134
PICKERING Saloma of Newmarket 1832 Doc 13399
PICKERING Samuel of Gilford 1826 Doc 7524
PICKERING Samuel (c) of Pittsfield 1806 Doc 26134
PICKERING Sara Ann (c) of Newmarket 1832 Doc 13399
PICKERING Winthrop of Gilford 1826 Doc 7524
PIERCE Elizabeth of Newmarket 1782 Doc 4997
PIERCE Jonathan of Newmarket 1782 Doc 4997
PIERCE William of Greenland 1829 Doc 10409
PIERCE William of Greenland 1829 Doc 11709
PIKE E of Hampton Falls 1851 Doc 931
PILLAR Elizabeth of Exeter 1783 Doc 5923
PILLSBURY Elizabeth of Newmarket 1773 Doc 2095
PILLSBURY Polly of Plaistow 1794 Doc 14339
PITCHEY Sarah of Portsmouth 1852 Doc 1555
PLACE Abigail of Portsmouth 1842 Doc 20107
PLACE Abigail of Portsmouth 1841 Doc 19510
PLACE Abigail of Portsmouth 1841 Doc 19136

PLACE James (alias) of Barrington 1822 Doc 2912
PLACE Richard of Deerfield 1788 Doc 10229
PLEASANT James of Rockingham County 1831 Doc 13399
PLUMMER David of Chester 1832 Doc 13399
PLUMMER Ephraim Sr of Dover 1852 Doc 2086
POLARD Dollar of Raymond 1784 Doc 7459
POLEN Abigail of N Hampton 1789 Doc 10911
POMP Peters of Loudon 1790 Doc 11611
POOL William of Londonderry 1821 Doc 2382
POOL William of Rockingham County 1831 Doc 13399
POOR Hannah (w) of Kingston 1785 Doc 8391
POOR Lewis of Portsmouth 1828 Doc 9200
POPLIN Robert of Poplin 1830 Doc 11710
PORTER Alexander of Exeter 1795 Doc 14648
PORTER John of Hampstead 1769 Doc 1612
PORTER Molley of Exeter 1795 Doc 14648
POTTER Hugh of Plaistow 1787 Doc 10016
POTTER Hugh of Brentwood 1787 Doc 10016
POTTER Hugh of Plaistow 1791 Doc 12531
POTTER Martha of Plaistow 1787 Doc 10016
POTTER Sarah of Exeter 1831 Doc 13399
POTTLE Elanor of Stratham 1852 Doc 1554
POTTLE Eleanor of Stratham 1850 Doc 311
POTTLE Eleanor of Stratham 1851 Doc 931
POTTLE Elenor of Stratham 1853 Doc 2085
POWEL David of Windham 1792 Doc 12531
PRATT Feby of Deerfield 1779 Doc 4199
PRAY John D of Portsmouth 1831 Doc 13082
PREBLE Horace M (c) of Plaistow 1861 Doc 7174
PRESCOTT Betsy (c) of Deerfield 1805 Doc 23965
PRESCOTT Chase of Deerfield 1805 Doc 23965
PRESCOTT Eleanor (c) of Deerfield 1805 Doc 23965
PRESCOTT Jonathan (c) of Deerfield 1805 Doc 23965
PRESCOTT Joseph of Epping 1794 Doc 14339
PRESCOTT Polley of Deerfield 1805 Doc 23965
PRESCOTT Reuben of Epping 1794 Doc 14339
PRESCOTT Reuben Jr of Epping 1794 Doc 14339
PRESCOTT Samuel (c) of Deerfield 1805 Doc 23965
PRESCOTT Sarah of Loudon 1796 Doc 15359
PRESCUTT Bety of Raymond 1800 Doc 18692
PRICE Thomas of Portsmouth 1791 Doc 12228
PRINCE Mark (Negro) of Kingston 1797 Doc 16546
PROCTOR Abigail (c) of Atkinson 1797 Doc 16050
PROCTOR Betsey (c) of Atkinson 1797 Doc 16050
PROCTOR Ebenezer of Atkinson 1797 Doc 16050
PROCTOR Hannah (c) of Atkinson 1797 Doc 16050
PROCTOR John (c) of Atkinson 1797 Doc 16050
PROCTOR Judith (c) of Atkinson 1797 Doc 16050
PROCTOR Lydia (c) of Atkinson 1797 Doc 16050
PROCTOR Polley (c) of Atkinson 1797 Doc 16050
PROCTOR Salley (c) of Atkinson 1797 Doc 16050
PROCTOR Sarah of Atkinson 1797 Doc 16050

PUNCH (Mrs) of Exeter 1840 Doc 19510
PURCELL Robert of Portsmouth 1841 Doc 19510
PURCELL Robert of Portsmouth 1839 Doc 18856
PURCELL Robert of Portsmouth 1840 Doc 18856
PURINGTON Abner of Poplin 1804 Doc 23419
PURINGTON Joseph of Poplin 1804 Doc 23419
PURINGTON Mary of Poplin 1804 Doc 23419
PURINGTON Susanna (c) of Poplin 1804 Doc 23419
PURINTON Elijah of Poplin 1805 Doc 24720
PURRAY Mary of Portsmouth 1840 Doc 18856
PURRY Mary of Portsmouth 1836 Doc 16214
PURRY Mary of Portsmouth 1845 Doc 21835
PURRY Mary of Portsmouth 1837 Doc 16931
PURRY Mary of Portsmouth 1846 Doc 22356
PURRY Mary of Portsmouth 1842 Doc 20107
PUTNAM Joseph of Exeter 1827 Doc 8073
PUTNAM Thomas of Enfield 1835 Doc 15557
PUTNAM Thomas of Portsmouth 1839 Doc 18542
PUTNEY Elisa of Londonderry 1846 Doc 22358
QUACKLEY James of Epping 1778 Doc 4043
QUAKELEY Sarah of Epping 1772 Doc 1407
QUARLES John of Concord 1810 Doc 32876
QUENTON Robert of Windham 1789 Doc 11310
QUIMBY Anna of Danville 1844 Doc 21216
QUIMBY Anna of Danville 1846 Doc 22356
QUIMBY Anna of Danville 1843 Doc 20629 S
QUIMBY Anna of Danville 1852 Doc 1554
QUIMBY Anna of Danville 1853 Doc 2371
QUIMBY Anna of Danville 1850 Doc 311
QUIMBY Anna of Danville 1842 Doc 20424
QUIMBY Susanna of Kingston 1794 Doc 14339
QUINBEE Andrew of Exeter 1775 Doc 3703
QUINBEE Elizabeth of Exeter 1785 Doc 8391
QUINBY Avery of Danville 1851 Doc 931
QUINN Eunice of Exeter 1840 Doc 18856
QUINN George of Exeter 1839 Doc 18267
QUINN George of Exeter 1840 Doc 18856
QUINN George of Exeter 1843 Doc 20629 A
QUINT Benjamin (c) of Portsmouth 1807 Doc 27572
QUINT Benjamin R of Portsmouth 1807 Doc 27572
QUINT Betsey (c) of Portsmouth 1807 Doc 27572
QUINT John (c) of Portsmouth 1807 Doc 27572
QUINT Joseph (c) of Portsmouth 1807 Doc 27572
QUINT Lucy (c) of Portsmouth 1807 Doc 27572
QUINT Mary of Portsmouth 1807 Doc 27572
QUINT Mary (c) of Portsmouth 1807 Doc 27572
QUINT Peggy of Greenland 1796 Doc 15359
QUINT Samuel (c) of Portsmouth 1807 Doc 27572
QUINT Stephen (c) of Portsmouth 1807 Doc 27572
RACKCLIFF Andrew of Portsmouth 1852 Doc 1842
RADCLIFF John of Portsmouth 1838 Doc 18267
RALPS James of Pembroke 1796 Doc 15359

RALPS Libel (c) of Pembroke 1796 Doc 15359
RALPS Lucey of Pembroke 1796 Doc 15359
RALPS Lucey (c) of Pembroke 1796 Doc 15359
RAND Amanada (c) of New Durham 1849 Doc 24261
RAND Ann S (c) of New Durham 1849 Doc 24261
RAND Anna of Brentwood 1796 Doc 15359
RAND Calvin (c) of New Durham 1849 Doc 24261
RAND Edmund of Deerfield 1851 Doc 932
RAND Frances of New Durham 1849 Doc 24261
RAND George (c) of New Durham 1849 Doc 24261
RAND Hannah of Nothingham 1788 Doc 10397
RAND Hannah of Nottingham 1781 Doc 4605
RAND Joseph (c) of New Durham 1849 Doc 24261
RAND Joseph H of New Durham 1849 Doc 24261
RAND Olive of New Durham 1849 Doc 24261
RAND Susan (Negro) of Epsom 1825 Doc 6965
RAND William of Rye 1815 Doc 39186
RANDALL George of Portsmouth 1841 Doc 19510
RANDALL George of Portsmouth 1840 Doc 18857
RANDALL George of Portsmouth 1840 Doc 18856
RANDALL George of Portsmouth 1839 Doc 18856
RANDALL Hannah of Nottingham 1783 Doc 5630
RANDALL Joses of Stratham 1780 Doc 4406
RANDALL Sarah of Portsmouth 1840 Doc 18856
RANDALL Sarah Jane of Portsmouth 1839 Doc 18856
RANDALL Sarah Jane of Portsmouth 1840 Doc 18857
RANDALL Susanah of Exeter 1853 Doc 2085
RANDALL Susannah of Exeter 1853 Doc 2085
RANDALL Susannah of Exeter 1851 Doc 931
RANDALL William of Raymond 1786 Doc 9466
RANDALL William of Nothingham 1783 Doc 6644
RANDE Mercy of Rye 1846 Doc 22356
RANDEL Jon'n of Northwood 1796 Doc 15359
RANDEL Polle of Northwood 1796 Doc 15359
RANDELE Margaret of Portsmouth 1846 Doc 22356
RANDELL George of Portsmouth 1851 Doc 311
RANDELL George of Portsmouth 1840 Doc 18857
RANDELL Jane of Portsmouth 1840 Doc 18857
RANDELL Margaret of Portsmouth 1843 Doc 20629
RANDELL Susannah of Exeter 1852 Doc 1554
RANDELL Susannah of Exeter 1850 Doc 311
RANDLET Dolly of Stratham 1793 Doc 14018
RANERD Mary Ann of Exeter 1829 Doc 11709
RANKIN Thomas of Exeter 1784 Doc 7181
RANNELS Dolly of Portsmouth 1843 Doc 20629
RANNELS John of Portsmouth 1843 Doc 20629
RAWLIN Sarah of N Hampton 1773 Doc 2656
RAWLINGS Nancy of Epping 1793 Doc 13587
RAY Sarah of Londonderry 1844 Doc 21503
READ Abigal of Stratham 1798 Doc 16897
READ Ana of Rye 1804 Doc 23419
READ John of Rye 1804 Doc 23419

READ John S of Rye 1804 Doc 23419
READ Robert M of Nottingham 1819 Doc 47427
READ Sarah of N Hampton 1789 Doc 10911
READEY Michael of Portsmouth 1791 Doc 12228
RECKONS (alias) Nath'l of Loudon 1790 Doc 11611
REED Benjamin Clark of Exeter 1835 Doc 16214
REED Ruth of Farmington 1814 Doc 37727
REEGAN Nancy of Hampstead 1853 Doc 2085
REIMBATH Polly of Hampstead 1853 Doc 2085
REMICK Daniel (c) of Salem 1796 Doc 15598
REMICK David of Salem 1796 Doc 15598
REMICK David (c) of Salem 1796 Doc 15598
REMICK Lydia of Salem 1796 Doc 15598
REMICK Lydia (c) of Salem 1796 Doc 15598
REMINGTON Albert of Candia 1842 Doc 20424
REMINGTON Mary of Candia 1842 Doc 20424
REYNALDS Hugh of Portsmouth 1846 Doc 22356
REYNOLDS Wm of Rockingham County 1851 Doc 931
RIAN Nancy of Newmarket 1784 Doc 7181
RICE Thomas of Exeter 1790 Doc 11910
RICHARD Sarah M of Portsmouth 1836 Doc 16214
RICHARD Susana of Newmarket 1789 Doc 10229
RICHARDS Lucy of Poplin 1796 Doc 15733
RICHARDS Sarah M of Portsmouth 1835 Doc 15900
RICHARDSON Betsy J (c) of Springfield 1857 Doc 4985
RICHARDSON Charles of Portsmouth 1836 Doc 16216
RICHARDSON Charles of Portsmouth 1837 Doc 16931
RICHARDSON Charles of Portsmouth 1836 Doc 16214
RICHARDSON Charles T (c) of Springfield 1857 Doc 4985
RICHARDSON Dolley of Raymond 1792 Doc 12882
RICHARDSON Dolly of Newmarket 1791 Doc 12228
RICHARDSON Edman of Plaistow 1800 Doc 19247
RICHARDSON Elirebett (c) of Springfield 1857 Doc 4985
RICHARDSON Henry of Springfield 1857 Doc 4985
RICHARDSON James of Springfield 1857 Doc 4985
RICHARDSON James B (c) of Springfield 1857 Doc 4985
RICHARDSON John of Epping 1832 Doc 14119
RICHARDSON Jones of Springfield 1857 Doc 4985
RICHARDSON Madison (c) of Springfield 1857 Doc 4985
RICHARDSON Mary (c) of Springfield 1857 Doc 4985
RICHARDSON Sarah A of Springfield 1857 Doc 4985
RICHARSON Dolly of Kingston 1791 Doc 12531
RICHINSON Samuel of Loudon 1790 Doc 11611
RIED Lavinia of Kensington 1795 Doc 14648
RIESON Nat of Kingston 1785 Doc 8391
RILEY Bridget of Portsmouth 1831 Doc 13081
RILEY James of Portsmouth 1812 Doc 34232
RILEY Nancy of Portsmouth 1831 Doc 13081
RILEY Thomas of Portsmouth 1831 Doc 13081
RILEY Thomas L of Portsmouth 1830 Doc 12197
RILEY Thomas L of Portsmouth 1830 Doc 12197
RINES Josiah of Deerfield 1819 Doc 47427

RING Mary of Hampstead 1770 Doc 1612
ROACH John of Exeter 1839 Doc 18267
ROACH John of Portsmouth 1837 Doc 16931
ROACH John of Portsmouth 1839 Doc 18856
ROACH Mathew G of Exeter 1821 Doc 2381
ROACH Richard of Portsmouth 1840 Doc 18857
ROACH Richard of Portsmouth 1841 Doc 19510
ROBARD Priscilla of Poplin 1778 Doc 4011
ROBARDS Priscilla of Brentwood 1785 Doc 8644
ROBARDS Priscilla (c) of Brentwood 1785 Doc 8644
ROBBINS Margaret of Hampton Falls 1788 Doc 10397
ROBE Joseph of Portsmouth 1843 Doc 20629
ROBE Nancy of Portsmouth 1843 Doc 20629
ROBE Nancy of Portsmouth 1846 Doc 22356
ROBE Nancy of Portsmouth 1845 Doc 21835
ROBERSON Anna (c) of Newmarket 1777 Doc 3797
ROBERSON Anne of Newmarket 1777 Doc 3797
ROBERSON Deborah (c) of Newmarket 1777 Doc 3797
ROBERSON Elizabeth (c) of Newmarket 1777 Doc 3797
ROBERSON Joseph of Northwood 1789 Doc 11183
ROBERSON Josiah of Newmarket 1777 Doc 3797
ROBERSON Josiah of Raymond 1783 Doc 6232
ROBERSON Josiah (c) of Newmarket 1777 Doc 3797
ROBERSON Tristram (c) of Newmarket 1777 Doc 3797
ROBERSON Walter (c) of Newmarket 1777 Doc 3797
ROBERT Dyonicia (alias) of Portsmouth 1846 Doc 22356
ROBERTS Lydia of Northwood 1846 Doc 22356
ROBERTS Emiline (Negro) of Greenland 1851 Doc 931
ROBERTS James (c) of Seabrooke 1842 Doc 20424
ROBERTS Jesse of Hampton Falls 1846 Doc 22356
ROBERTS Jesse of Kensington 1855 Doc 3620
ROBERTS Jesse of Seabrook 1843 Doc 20629 S
ROBERTS Jessey of Seabrook 1846 Doc 22356
ROBERTS John of Danville 1846 Doc 22356
ROBERTS John of Danville 1844 Doc 21216
ROBERTS John of Danville 1845 Doc 21835
ROBERTS John of Danville 1843 Doc 20928
ROBERTS John of Raymond 1784 Doc 7459
ROBERTS John of Salem 1855 Doc 4985
ROBERTS John (c) of Salem 1855 Doc 4985
ROBERTS Jonathan of Seabrook 1842 Doc 20424
ROBERTS Lydia of Northwood 1853 Doc 2085
ROBERTS Lydia of Londonderry 1851 Doc 931
ROBERTS Lydia of Northwood 1842 Doc 20629
ROBERTS Lydia of Northwood 1842 Doc 20424
ROBERTS Lydia of Northwood 1844 Doc 21216
ROBERTS Lydia of Northwood 1850 Doc 311
ROBERTS Lydia of Norwood 1852 Doc 1554
ROBERTS Lydia of Northwood 1853 Doc 2371
ROBERTS Margaret of Seabrooke 1842 Doc 20424
ROBERTS Margaret of Seabrook 1843 Doc 20629 S
ROBERTS Mary of Newtown 1806 Doc 26134

ROBERTS Mary (c) of Seabrooke 1842 Doc 20424
ROBERTS Nancy (Mulatto) of Greenland 1798 Doc 16897
ROBERTS Phebe (c) of Seabrookc 1842 Doc 20424
ROBERTS Phillis of Deerfield 1796 Doc 15948
ROBERTS Phyllis of Newmarket 1800 Doc 21391
ROBERTS Reuben of Deerfeild 1800 Doc 21391
ROBERTS Ruben of Deerfield 1796 Doc 15948
ROBERTS Ruth of Danville 1843 Doc 20928
ROBERTS Ruth of Danville 1844 Doc 21216
ROBERTS Ruth of Danville 1850 Doc 311
ROBERTS Sally (c) of Seabrooke 1842 Doc 20424
ROBERTS Samuel of Northwood 1842 Doc 20424
ROBERTS Sarah J of Salem 1855 Doc 4985
ROBERTS Thomas of Seabrook 1784 Doc 7459
ROBERTS Tilpha of Epping 1800 Doc 19247
ROBERTS William of Portsmouth 1851 Doc 311
ROBERTS William of Seabrooke 1842 Doc 20424
ROBERTS Zaechus of Seabrook 1842 Doc 20424
ROBERTS Zaechus of Seabrook 1843 Doc 20629 S
ROBERTSON Benjamin of Wolfeborough 1846 Doc 22592
ROBERTSON David of Greenland 1786 Doc 9466
ROBERTSON Samuel of Portsmouth 1836 Doc 16214
ROBERTSON Samuel of Portsmouth 1837 Doc 16931
ROBERTSON Samuel of Portsmouth 1835 Doc 15900
ROBERTSON Susannah of Epsom 1801 Doc 20738
ROBIE Nathan of Poplin 1808 Doc 29235
ROBINGSON Mary of Portsmouth 1842 Doc 20107
ROBINS Nat of Exeter 1842 Doc 20107
ROBINSON Tamin of Rye 1852 Doc 1554
ROBINSON Sophia Moore of Exeter 1842 Doc 20107
ROBINSON Amy of Exeter 1842 Doc 20107
ROBINSON Andrew of Exeter 1843 Doc 20629 S
ROBINSON Andrew J (c) of Exeter 1842 Doc 20107
ROBINSON Benjamin of Stratham 1846 Doc 22356
ROBINSON David of Stratham 1846 Doc 22356
ROBINSON David of Greenland 1792 Doc 12882
ROBINSON Eliza Jane of Raymond 1853 Doc 2371
ROBINSON Elizabeth of Nottingham 1790 Doc 11310
ROBINSON Frances (c) of Exeter 1842 Doc 20107
ROBINSON Francis of Raymond 1855 Doc 3620
ROBINSON Francis M of Raymond 1853 Doc 2371
ROBINSON Gach of Exeter 1842 Doc 20107
ROBINSON Hitty of Portsmouth 1840 Doc 18856
ROBINSON James of Tamworth 1819 Doc 47427
ROBINSON James C of Seabrook 1807 Doc 28434
ROBINSON Jane (c) of Exeter 1842 Doc 20107
ROBINSON Jeremiah of Danville 1851 Doc 931
ROBINSON Jeremiah of Derry 1851 Doc 931
ROBINSON John H of Nottingham 1790 Doc 11310
ROBINSON Joseph of Deerfield 1853 Doc 2086
ROBINSON Joseph of Stratham 1817 Doc 44178
ROBINSON Julia Ann of Raymond 1853 Doc 2371

ROBINSON Julie of Raymond 1855 Doc 3620
ROBINSON Lydia of Portsmouth 1843 Doc 20629
ROBINSON Lydia of Portsmouth 1846 Doc 22356
ROBINSON Margaret of Portsmouth 1830 Doc 12197
ROBINSON Margaret of Portsmouth 1830 Doc 12197
ROBINSON Mary of Stratham 1799 Doc 18299
ROBINSON Mary Smith of Candia 1842 Doc 20424
ROBINSON Mary J of Poplin 1853 Doc 2085
ROBINSON Mary J (c) of Portsmouth 1852 Doc 1554
ROBINSON Mehitable of Rye 1841 Doc 19510
ROBINSON Miliage (c) of Exeter 1842 Doc 20107
ROBINSON Peter of Gosport 1846 Doc 22356
ROBINSON Prince (Negro) of Kingston 1797 Doc 16546
ROBINSON Sally G of Deerfield 1849 Doc 24261
ROBINSON Sarah of Nottingham 1790 Doc 11310
ROBINSON Sarah (c) of Nottingham 1790 Doc 11310
ROBINSON Sophie of Exeter 1834 Doc 14817
ROBINSON Susanna of Deerfield 1803 Doc 22285
ROBINSON Susannah (w) of Deerfield 1799 Doc 17750
ROBINSON Tamah of Rye 1851 Doc 932
ROBINSON Thomas of Portsmouth 1843 Doc 20629
ROBINSON William of ? 1842 Doc 20107
ROBINSON William of Exeter 1834 Doc 14817
ROBY Ruth of Kingston 1773 Doc 2095
RODMAN Dorothy of Portsmouth 1791 Doc 12228
ROGERS Arthur of Pembroke 1797 Doc 16546
ROGERS Arthur (c) of Pembroke 1797 Doc 16546
ROGERS John of Northfield 1819 Doc 47427
ROGERS Levi of Stratham 1780 Doc 4406
ROGERS Mary Jan of Seabrook 1852 Doc 1554
ROGERS Peggey of Pembroke 1797 Doc 16546
ROGERS Robert (c) of Pembroke 1797 Doc 16546
ROGERS Sarah of Portsmouth 1846 Doc 22356
ROGERS Sarah of Stratham 1780 Doc 4406
ROGERS Sarah (w) of Stratham 1801 Doc 20206
ROGERS William of Exeter 1773 Doc 2268
ROLF Margaret (c) of Londonderry 1851 Doc 931
ROLFE John of Londonderry 1851 Doc 931
ROLLINGS Polly of Pembroke 1794 Doc 14648
ROLLINS Abigail (c) of Kingston 1801 Doc 19665
ROLLINS Benjamin of Deerfield 1801 Doc 19665
ROLLINS Betsey M of Auburn 1850 Doc 311
ROLLINS Betsy of Nottingham 1842 Doc 20424
ROLLINS Daniel of Deerfield 1798 Doc 16897
ROLLINS Daniel of Kingston 1801 Doc 19665
ROLLINS Dinah of Portsmouth 1846 Doc 22356
ROLLINS Dolly (c) of Rye 1804 Doc 23419
ROLLINS Edward (c) of Exeter 1792 Doc 12882
ROLLINS Elezer (c) of Rye 1804 Doc 23419
ROLLINS Eliphet of Exeter 1792 Doc 12882
ROLLINS Elizabeth of Auburn 1851 Doc 931
ROLLINS Elizabeth of Auburn 1852 Doc 1554

ROLLINS Joseph of Epping 1799 Doc 18299
ROLLINS Kesiah of Hampton Falls 1827 Doc 9201
ROLLINS Mehitabel of Epping 1799 Doc 18299
ROLLINS Molly (c) of Epping 1799 Doc 18299
ROLLINS Phebe of Exeter 1792 Doc 12882
ROLLINS Sally of Deerfield 1801 Doc 19665
ROLLINS Sally (c) of Exeter 1792 Doc 12882
ROLLINS Stephen of Rye 1803 Doc 23419
ROLLINS Stephen Jr (c) of Rye 1804 Doc 23419
ROODY Charlotte (c) of Newmarket 1794 Doc 14339
ROSE (Negro) of Rye 1796 Doc 16050
ROSS Walter (c) of Portsmouth 1830 Doc 12197
ROSS William (c) of Portsmouth 1830 Doc 12197
ROSS Dolley of Epping 1793 Doc 14339
ROSS George of Portsmouth 1840 Doc 19137
ROSS George of Portsmouth 1841 Doc 19510
ROSS George of Exeter 1841 Doc 19510
ROSS George of Exeter 1840 Doc 18856
ROSS George of Portsmouth 1840 Doc 18857
ROSS John of Exeter 1840 Doc 19510
ROSS Rebecca of Portsmouth 1830 Doc 12197
ROSS Rebecca of Portsmouth 1830 Doc 12197
ROSS Rebecca of Portsmouth 1831 Doc 13081
ROSS Rebecca (c) of Portsmouth 1831 Doc 13081
ROSS Rebecca (c) of Portsmouth 1830 Doc 12197
ROSS Sarah of Atkinson 1795 Doc 15018
ROSS Walter of Portsmouth 1830 Doc 12197
ROSS Walter (c) of Portsmouth 1831 Doc 13081
ROSS William of Portsmouth 1831 Doc 13081
ROSS William of Portsmouth 1830 Doc 12197
ROWAN Charles of Portsmouth 1851 Doc 311
ROWE Peter of Auburn 1843 Doc 311
ROWEL Anna of Atkinson 1791 Doc 11910
ROWEL Jonathan of Atkinson 1791 Doc 11910
ROWEL Maryann of Atkinson 1791 Doc 11910
ROWEL Olive of Atkinson 1791 Doc 11910
ROWEL William of Sandown 1788 Doc 10397
ROWELL Betsey of Windham 1842 Doc 20424
ROWELL Daniel of Windham 1827 Doc 8077
ROWELL Jonathan of Poplin 1816 Doc 40757
RUAN Bryon (c) of Portsmouth 1832 Doc 13755
RUAN Ann of Portsmouth 1832 Doc 13755
RUAN Ann of Portsmouth 1832 Doc 13082
RUAN Bryan of Portsmouth 1832 Doc 13082
RUAN James of Portsmouth 1832 Doc 13755
RUAN James of Portsmouth 1832 Doc 13754
RUAN James (c) of Portsmouth 1832 Doc 13082
RUAN John of Portsmouth 1832 Doc 13754
RUAN John (c) of Portsmouth 1832 Doc 13755
RUAN Mary of Portsmouth 1832 Doc 13754
RUAN Mary (c) of Portsmouth 1832 Doc 13082
RUAN Mary (c) of Portsmouth 1832 Doc 13755

RUAN Michael (c) of Portsmouth 1832 Doc 13755
RUAN Patrick of Portsmouth 1832 Doc 13754
RUAN Patrick (c) of Portsmouth 1832 Doc 13082
RUAN Patrick (c) of Portsmouth 1832 Doc 13755
RUND Thomas of Rye 1816 Doc 40757
RUND Tobias of Rye 1816 Doc 40757
RUND William of Rye 1816 Doc 40757
RUNDELL George of Portsmouth 1842 Doc 20107
RUNDELL James of Kensington 1793 Doc 14018
RUNDELL Nancy of Kensington 1793 Doc 14018
RUNDLET Rachal of Stratham 1794 Doc 14018
RUNDLETT James of Exeter 1790 Doc 11910
RUNNELLS Love of Nothingham 1782 Doc 5186
RUNNELLS Elizabeth of Portsmouth 1836 Doc 16214
RUNNELLS Dotty of Portsmouth 1852 Doc 1554
RUNNELLS Joseph of Portsmouth 1836 Doc 16214
RUNNELLS Thomas of Portsmouth 1826 Doc 6965
RUNNELS Dolly of Portsmouth 1851 Doc 931
RUNNELS Elizabeth of Portsmouth 1836 Doc 16214
RUNNELS Elizabeth of Portsmouth 1831 Doc 13081
RUNNELS Joseph of Portsmouth 1836 Doc 16214
RUNNELS Maria of Portsmouth 1836 Doc 16214
RUNNELS Maria of Portsmouth 1830 Doc 12197
RUNNELS Thomas of Portsmouth 1831 Doc 13081
RUNNELS William Thomas of Portsmouth 1831 Doc 13081
RUSS Nathan of Windham 1795 Doc 15359
RUSS Sally of Windham 1795 Doc 15359
RUSSELL Dolly of Portsmouth 1851 Doc 311
RUSSELL Hannah of Derry 1841 Doc 19510
RUSSELL Thomas of Portsmouth 1851 Doc 311
RYAN Augustus of Portsmouth 1827 Doc 8073
RYAN Augustus of Portsmouth 1826 Doc 7634
RYAN John of Portsmouth 1839 Doc 18856
RYAN Margarett of Newmarket 1853 Doc 2371
RYONS John of Exeter 1835 Doc 16214
RYONS John of Portsmouth 1839 Doc 18267
RYONS John (c) of Exeter 1835 Doc 16214
SAISUN Solan (Indian) of Exeter 1831 Doc 12682
SALLEY Olive of Windham 1787 Doc 10142
SANBORN Anna of Kensington 1786 Doc 9151
SANBORN Anna of Pittsfield 1801 Doc 19665
SANBORN Benjamin of Loudon 1794 Doc 14339
SANBORN Benjamin of Gilford 1829 Doc 10410
SANBORN Confort of Epping 1841 Doc 19512
SANBORN Daniel of Portsmouth 1840 Doc 18857
SANBORN Dolley of Seabrook 1772 Doc 731
SANBORN Dolly of Hampton Falls 1779 Doc 4199
SANBORN Dorothy of Hawke 1802 Doc 21391
SANBORN Dorothy of Newmarket 1850 Doc 931
SANBORN Dudley of Seabrook 1772 Doc 731
SANBORN Elizabeth J (c) of Portsmouth 1840 Doc 18857
SANBORN Elizabeth Jane of Portsmouth 1841 Doc 19510

SANBORN Frances Ann of Portsmouth 1841 Doc 19510
SANBORN Frances Ann (c) of Portsmouth 1840 Doc 18857
SANBORN Francis H of Portsmouth 1839 Doc 18856
SANBORN James of Gilford 1829 Doc 10410
SANBORN James of Hawke 1812 Doc 34232
SANBORN Jane of Portsmouth 1840 Doc 18857
SANBORN Jane of Portsmouth 1840 Doc 18856
SANBORN Jane of Portsmouth 1839 Doc 18856
SANBORN Jane of Portsmouth 1841 Doc 19510
SANBORN John of Pittsfield 1801 Doc 19665
SANBORN John Smith of Kensington 1786 Doc 9151
SANBORN Joseph of Kingston 1796 Doc 15733
SANBORN Mary of Seabrook 1772 Doc 731
SANBORN Moses H of Poplin 1845 Doc 21835
SANBORN Polly of Hawke 1812 Doc 34232
SANBORN Polly of Gilford 1829 Doc 10410
SANBORN Polly (c) of Hawke 1812 Doc 34232
SANBORN Sally of Kingston 1796 Doc 15733
SANBORN Sally (c) of Hawke 1812 Doc 34232
SANBORN Sarah of Newmarket 1791 Doc 11910
SANBORN Tristram of Epping 1841 Doc 19512
SANDERS Almyra (c) of Kingston 1828 Doc 9201
SANDERS Andrew (c) of Kingston 1828 Doc 9201
SANDERS Margrett (w) of Kingston 1828 Doc 9201
SANDERS Mary of Rye 1846 Doc 22356
SANDERS Mary of Rye 1850 Doc 931
SANDERS Peter of Salem 1795 Doc 15018
SANDERSON David (c) of Epping 1818 Doc 45992
SANDERSON Elmira (c) of Epping 1818 Doc 45992
SANDERSON Mary of Epping 1818 Doc 45992
SAPSON John of Raymond 1790 Doc 11310
SARGENT Abby F (c) of Loudon 1851 Doc 932
SARGENT Bettey (c) of Poplin 1802 Doc 21796
SARGENT Charles H (c) of Loudon 1851 Doc 932
SARGENT Christopher (c) of Kingston 1793 Doc 14018
SARGENT Clarinda (c) of Loudon 1851 Doc 932
SARGENT Dorothy of Loudon 1851 Doc 932
SARGENT Dorothy (c) of Loudon 1851 Doc 932
SARGENT Eliza J (c) of Loudon 1851 Doc 932
SARGENT John (c) of Loudon 1851 Doc 932
SARGENT John L of Moultonborough 1840 Doc 18857
SARGENT John L of N Hampton 1840 Doc 18858
SARGENT Joseph (c) of Loudon 1851 Doc 932
SARGENT Joshua of Poplin 1802 Doc 21796
SARGENT Joshua (c) of Poplin 1802 Doc 21796
SARGENT Josiah of Kingston 1799 Doc 18299
SARGENT Meriah (c) of Poplin 1802 Doc 21796
SARGENT Moses (c) of Poplin 1802 Doc 21796
SARGENT Polly of Poplin 1802 Doc 21796
SARGENT Polly (c) of Poplin 1802 Doc 21796
SARGENT Richard of Loudon 1851 Doc 932
SARGENT Samuel of Kingston 1793 Doc 14018

SARGENT William of Kingston 1793 Doc 14018
SARGENT William of Kingston 1821 Doc 2397
SARGENT William of Hampstead 1820 Doc 1143
SARGENT William of Hampstead 1810 Doc 32331
SARGENT William of Hampstead 1821 Doc 1592
SARGENT William (c) of Kingston 1793 Doc 14018
SARGENT William (alias) of Hampstead 1822 Doc 2912
SARGENT Zebidiah of Plaistow 1772 Doc 1612
SAUL John of Exeter 1843 Doc 20629 D
SAUL John of Exeter 1844 Doc 21216
SAUNDERS Caleb of Windham 1846 Doc 22356
SAUNDERS Elijah of Rye 1846 Doc 22356
SAUNDERS John of Rye 1844 Doc 21503
SAUNDERS John of Rye 1845 Doc 21835
SAUNDERS Mary of Rye 1845 Doc 21835
SAUNDERS Mary of Rye 1844 Doc 21503
SAUNDERS Mercy (Mrs) of Rye 1846 Doc 22356
SAUNDERS Molly of Rye 1846 Doc 22356
SAUNDERS Patience of Rye 1844 Doc 21503
SAUNDERS Patience of Rye 1845 Doc 21835
SAUNDERS Samuel of Rye 1846 Doc 22356
SAUNDERS Sarah of Rye 1846 Doc 22356
SAVORY Daniel of Kingston 1842 Doc 20424
SAVORY Elizabeth of Kingston 1842 Doc 20424
SAVORY Elizabeth of Kingston 1844 Doc 21503
SAVORY Elizabeth of Kingston 1851 Doc 931
SAVORY Elizabeth of Kingston 1846 Doc 22356
SAVORY Elizabeth of Kingston 1850 Doc 311
SAVORY Sarah of Kingston 1842 Doc 20424
SAWEIGE Joseph of Brentwood 1796 Doc 15359
SAWER Thomas of Portsmouth 1839 Doc 18856
SAWESBY Thomas of Derry 1828 Doc 10409
SAWESBY Thomas of Derry 1829 Doc 12682
SAWYER Chesly of Northwood 1787 Doc 9740
SAWYER Leonard of Newtown 1840 Doc 18856
SAWYER Rachel of Newtown 1840 Doc 18856
SCHOOVE Richard of Portsmouth 1846 Doc 22356
SCOTT William of Portsmouth 1851 Doc 311
SCOTT William of North Hampton 1791 Doc 12228
SCOTT Wm (Mrs) of Portsmouth 1852 Doc 1554
SCRIBNER Daniel of Brentwood 1772 Doc 1880
SCRIBNER James of Pittsfield 1810 Doc 32331
SCRIBNER Susanna of Brentwood 1772 Doc 1880
SCRIGGIN John of Newmarket 1792 Doc 12882
SCRIGGIN Nancy of Newmarket 1792 Doc 12882
SEACO Phillis (Negro) of Exeter 1799 Doc 17750
SEAFER Jen of Portsmouth 1852 Doc 1554
SEAFFER Jean of Portsmouth 1851 Doc 931
SEANGMAUL Jonathan of Deerfield 1851 Doc 931
SEAVEY see also SEVEY
SEAVEY Anna of Stratham 1798 Doc 17408
SEAVEY Noah of Portsmouth 1829 Doc 10410

SEAVEY Noah of Barrington 1827 Doc 8077
SEAVEY Noah of Deerfield 1852 Doc 1554
SEAVEY Noah of Deerfield 1845 Doc 21835
SEAVEY Noah of Deerfield 1851 Doc 931
SEAVEY Noah of Deerfield 1846 Doc 22356
SEAVEY Rachael of Greenland 1786 Doc 9151
SEAVY Sarah of Greenland 1790 Doc 11611
SECO & Wife (Negro?) No Last Name of Kingston 430154 Doc 4406
SECOMB Lois of Newmarket 1852 Doc 1554
SEDRICK Bridget of Nottingham 1802 Doc 20738
SEDRICK Cate of Nottingham 1802 Doc 20738
SEDRICK Joseph of Nottingham 1802 Doc 20738
SEDRICK Micah of Nottingham 1802 Doc 20738
SEEVY Jonathan of Auburn 1850 Doc 311
SENTER Also of Londonderry 1828 Doc 9823
SENTER Hannah Jane of Londonderry 1828 Doc 9823
SENTER Joseph of Londonderry 1828 Doc 9823
SENTER Sally of Londonderry 1828 Doc 9823
SERGENT Sterling of Plaistow 1787 Doc 10016
SERGINS Dorothy of Exeter 1795 Doc 14648
SEVARY Elizabeth of Kingston 1852 Doc 1554
SEVEGGINS Deborah of Exeter 1844 Doc 21216
SEVERANCE Chip of Kingston 1853 Doc 2085
SEVERANCE Dorothy of Kingston 1773 Doc 2095
SEVERANCE Dorothy (w) of Raymond 1795 Doc 14648
SEVERANCE Ebenezer of Raymond 1783 Doc 6232
SEVERANCE Ebenezer of Kingston 1773 Doc 2095
SEVERANCE Jacob of Kingston 1842 Doc 20424
SEVERANCE Mary of Kingston 1842 Doc 20424
SEVERANCE Mary of Kingston 1843 Doc 20928
SEVERANCE Naomi of Kingston 1773 Doc 2095
SEVERANCE Phebe of Kingston 1852 Doc 1554
SEVERANCE Phebe of Kingston 1851 Doc 931
SEVEY John of Deerfield 1786 Doc 9466
SEVY Abigail (c) of Poplin 1777 Doc 3797
SEVY Joanna (c) of Poplin 1777 Doc 3797
SEVY Mary of Poplin 1777 Doc 3797
SEVY Solomon of Poplin 1777 Doc 3797
SEVY Mary (c) of Poplin 1777 Doc 3797
SEVY William (c) of Poplin 1777 Doc 3797
SHACKFORD Deliverance of Epping 1790 Doc 11310
SHACKFORD Samuel of Newmarket 1790 Doc 11910
SHANNEN John of Raymond 1795 Doc 14648
SHANNON Abigail of Deerfield 1801 Doc 20206
SHANNON Anna of Raymond 1793 Doc 13587
SHANNON Anna (c) of Deerfield 1801 Doc 20206
SHANNON James of Portsmouth 1841 Doc 19510
SHANNON James of Portsmouth 1839 Doc 18267
SHANNON James of Portsmouth 1839 Doc 18856
SHANNON John of Deerfield 1801 Doc 20206
SHANNON Lukey (c) of Deerfield 1801 Doc 20206
SHANNON Nabby (c) of Deerfield 1801 Doc 20206

SHANNON Polly (c) of Deerfield 1801 Doc 20206
SHANNON Sally (c) of Deerfield 1801 Doc 20206
SHANNON Thomas of Raymond 1793 Doc 13587
SHAPELY Betsy of Rye 1840 Doc 18856
SHAPELY James of Portsmouth 1840 Doc 18856
SHAPELY Mercy of Portsmouth 1840 Doc 18856
SHAPLE Reuben of Rye 1837 Doc 16931
SHAPLEY Benjamin of Rye 1826 Doc 6965
SHAPLEY Benjamin of Rye 1827 Doc 9200
SHAPLEY Benjamin of Rye 1829 Doc 10409
SHAPLEY Betsey of Rye 1850 Doc 311
SHAPLEY Betsey of Rye 1853 Doc 2371
SHAPLEY Betsey of Rye 1854 Doc 2371
SHAPLEY Betsey of Rye 1842 Doc 20424
SHAPLEY Betsy of Rye 1852 Doc 1554
SHAPLEY Betsy of Rye 1841 Doc 19510
SHAPLEY Betsy of Rye 1850 Doc 931
SHAPLEY Betsy of Rye 1853 Doc 2085
SHAPLEY Dolly of Rye 1830 Doc 12682
SHAPLEY Dorothy (w) of Rye 1829 Doc 11709
SHAPLEY George of Rye 1833 Doc 14122
SHAPLEY George (c) of Rye 1831 Doc 12682
SHAPLEY George R of Rye 1832 Doc 13399
SHAPLEY Juadith of Rye 1854 Doc 2371
SHAPLEY Judith of Rye 1853 Doc 2085
SHAPLEY Judith of Rye 1826 Doc 7524
SHAPLEY Judith of Rye 1827 Doc 8073
SHAPLEY Judith of Rye 1850 Doc 931
SHAPLEY Judith of Rye 1852 Doc 1554
SHAPLEY Mary of Rye 1829 Doc 11709
SHAPLEY Mary of Rye 1831 Doc 12682
SHAPLEY Mercy of Rye 1842 Doc 20424
SHAPLEY Mercy of Rye 1837 Doc 16931
SHAPLEY Mercy of Rye 1836 Doc 16214
SHAPLEY Mercy of Rye 1833 Doc 14122
SHAPLEY Mercy of Rye 1832 Doc 13399
SHAPLEY Mercy of Rye 1841 Doc 19510
SHAPLEY Reuben of Rye 1846 Doc 22356
SHAPLEY Reuben of Rye 1832 Doc 13399
SHAPLEY Reuben of Rye 1833 Doc 14122
SHAPLEY Rueben of Rye 1830 Doc 12682
SHAPLEY Rueben of Rye 1836 Doc 16214
SHAPLEY Sara Ann of Rye 1829 Doc 11709
SHAPLEY Sara Ann of Rye 1831 Doc 12682
SHAPLEY Sarann of Rye 1832 Doc 13399
SHAPLEY Susan of Rye 1829 Doc 10409
SHAPLEY William of Portsmouth 1779 Doc 4331
SHARP Titus (Negro) of Exeter 1791 Doc 12531
SHAW Abigail of Chester 1852 Doc 2086
SHAW Alvah E of Kingston 1851 Doc 931
SHAW Betty of Seabrook 1784 Doc 7459
SHAW David of Chester 1852 Doc 2086

SHAW Elizabeth of Stratham 1781 Doc 4749
SHAW Elizabeth of Stratham 1782 Doc 4882
SHAW Elizabeth Frances of Hampton 1828 Doc 9823
SHAW Henry of Portsmouth 1833 Doc 14119
SHAW James of Epping 1830 Doc 11981
SHAW James of Greenland 1830 Doc 11981
SHAW James N of Epping 1830 Doc 20107
SHAW Ruth of Kensington 1789 Doc 10911
SHAW Sally of Chester 1852 Doc 2086
SHAW Sarah of Kensington 1789 Doc 11183
SHAW Thomas of Stratham 1781 Doc 4749
SHAW Thomas of Pembroke 1788 Doc 10754
SHAW Thomas of Pembroke 1813 Doc 36435
SHAW Thomas of Pembroke 1810 Doc 33660
SHAY Mary of Portsmouth 1841 Doc 19510
SHEHAN Patrick of Portsmouth 1852 Doc 1554
SHEPARD Elizabeth of Hawke 1800 Doc 18692
SHEPARD Hannah (c) of Hawke 1800 Doc 18692
SHEPARD Hannah Fife (c) of Kingston 1798 Doc 17408
SHEPARD Jesse (c) of Hawke 1800 Doc 18692
SHEPARD John of Northfield 1796 Doc 15598
SHEPARD Jona of Kingston 1798 Doc 17408
SHEPARD Jonathan of Hawke 1800 Doc 18692
SHEPARD Julia Ann of Portsmouth 1832 Doc 13755
SHEPARD Samuel of Northfield 1785 Doc 8391
SHEPHARD Julian Ann of Portsmouth 1832 Doc 13754
SHERBERT Mitchel of Deerfield 1853 Doc 2086
SHERBERTE Mitchel of Deerfield 1853 Doc 2085
SHERBORN Elizabeth of Greenland 1789 Doc 11025
SHERBURNE Samuel of North Hampton 1791 Doc 12228
SHERRY Mary of Portsmouth 1840 Doc 19137
SHIRLEY Robert of Chester 1842 Doc 20424
SHIRLEY Robert of Chester 1844 Doc 21216
SHIRLEY Robert of Chester 1845 Doc 21835
SHIRLEY Robert of Chester 1843 Doc 20629 S
SHIRLEY Robert of Exeter 1843 Doc 20629 D
SHORT William of Portsmouth 1831 Doc 13081
SHROVE Richard of Portsmouth 1852 Doc 1554
SHROVE Richard of Portsmouth 1851 Doc 931
SHUTE James Albert (c) of Franklin 1861 Doc 6144
SHUTE Mary of Franklin 1861 Doc 6144
SIAS David (c) of Northwood 1794 Doc 14018
SIAS Jane of Pembroke 1821 Doc 2397
SIAS Jenne of Northwood 1794 Doc 14018
SIBLEY Sarah of Stratham 1771 Doc 731
SIBLEY William of Stratham 1771 Doc 731
SIGNEY Betty (c) of Atkinson 1791 Doc 11910
SIGNEY Nancy (c) of Atkinson 1791 Doc 11910
SIGNEY Peggey Jr (c) of Atkinson 1791 Doc 11910
SIGNEY Peggy of Atkinson 1791 Doc 11910
SIGNEY Peter of Atkinson 1791 Doc 11910
SIGNEY Polly (c) of Atkinson 1791 Doc 11910

SILVER Betty of Bow 1792 Doc 13587
SILVER Hills of Poplin 1803 Doc 21796
SILVER Mary of Chester 1846 Doc 22356
SILVER Mary of Chester 1845 Doc 21835
SILVER Mary of Chester 1842 Doc 20424
SILVERS Daniel of Salem 1779 Doc 4241
SILVERS Susannah of Salem 1779 Doc 4241
SIMEONS Bethial (c) of Salem 1792 Doc 13190
SIMEONS Elizabeth (c) of Salem 1792 Doc 13190
SIMEONS Hannah of Salem 1792 Doc 13190
SIMEONS John (c) of Salem 1792 Doc 13190
SIMEONS Jonathan of Salem 1792 Doc 13190
SIMONS Abigail of Plaistow 1784 Doc 7181
SIMONS Bettey (c) of Plaistow 1791 Doc 12228
SIMONS Hannah of Plaistow 1791 Doc 12228
SIMONS John (c) of Plaistow 1791 Doc 12228
SIMONS Jonathan of Plaistow 1791 Doc 12228
SIMONS Moses of Atkinson 1784 Doc 7804
SIMONS Sarah of Atkinson 1784 Doc 7804
SIMONS Thayer (c) of Plaistow 1791 Doc 12228
SIMPSON Agnes (c) of Windham 1799 Doc 17750
SIMPSON Alexander of Windham 1799 Doc 17750
SIMPSON Charles of Salem 1850 Doc 311
SIMPSON Diah of Exeter 1792 Doc 12882
SIMPSON Esther of Kingston 1773 Doc 2268
SIMPSON Hannah of Gilmanton 1827 Doc 8077
SIMPSON Jinnet (c) of Windham 1799 Doc 17750
SIMPSON Mary of Windham 1799 Doc 17750
SIMPSON Polly/Mary of Stratham 1801 Doc 20206
SIMPSON Rachel (w) of New Castle 1817 Doc 44178
SINCLERE Sarah of Newmarket 1788 Doc 10640
SINKLER Elizabeth of Newmarket 1795 Doc 14879
SINKLER John of Newmarket 1795 Doc 14879
SINKLER Miajah (c) of Newmarket 1795 Doc 14879
SINKLER Patty (c) of Newmarket 1795 Doc 14879
SKINNEY Cosiah of Newmarket 1852 Doc 1554
SLADE Betsey Williams of Portsmouth 1843 Doc 20629
SLEEPER Anna of Warner 1821 Doc 1592
SLEEPER Anna of Warner 1820 Doc 1143
SLEEPER Benjamin of Brentwood 1785 Doc 8644
SLEEPER Elizabeth of Poplin 1799 Doc 18299
SLEEPER Hannah of Brentwood 1845 Doc 21835
SLEEPER Hannah of Atkinson 1851 Doc 931
SLEEPER Hannah of Brentwood 1850 Doc 311
SLEEPER Hannah of Brentwood 1846 Doc 22356
SLEEPER Hannah of Brentwood 1844 Doc 21216
SLEEPER James (c) of Poplin 1799 Doc 18299
SLEEPER Molly of Raymond 1798 Doc 17408
SLEEPER Nathaniel of Raymond 1798 Doc 17408
SLEEPER Ruth of Brentwood 1785 Doc 8644
SLEETES Hannah of Brentwood 1853 Doc 2085
SLINGSBY John of Windham 1792 Doc 13587

SLIVER Mary of Chester 1844 Doc 21216
SMALL Abigail of Epping 1792 Doc 12531
SMALL Anna (c) of Epping 1792 Doc 12531
SMALL Betty (c) of Epping 1792 Doc 12531
SMALL Cezar of Hampton 1774 Doc 3061
SMALL Edward of Epping 1792 Doc 12531
SMALL Isaac of Newmarket 1853 Doc 2371
SMART Abigail of Deerfield 1862 Doc 7664
SMART Benjamin of Epping 1782 Doc 5186
SMART Betty of Raymond 1790 Doc 11611
SMART Elizabeth of Raymond 1798 Doc 17408
SMART Elizabeth of Epping 1782 Doc 5186
SMART Elizabeth (c) of Epping 1838 Doc 17575
SMART Eloisa (c) of Epping 1838 Doc 17575
SMART Isaac (c) of Epping 1782 Doc 5186
SMART Jeremiah of Deerfield 1801 Doc 20206
SMART Jeremiah of Epping 1838 Doc 17575
SMART John of Exeter 1835 Doc 15557
SMART John (c) of Epping 1838 Doc 17575
SMART Mary of Epsom 1784 Doc 7181
SMART Mary (c) of Epping 1838 Doc 17575
SMART Mehitable of Epping 1838 Doc 17575
SMART Nathaniel of Raymond 1798 Doc 17408
SMART Nathaniel (c) of Epping 1838 Doc 17575
SMART Sarah (c) of Epping 1782 Doc 5186
SMART William of Raymond 1785 Doc 8391
SMART William of Epsom 1784 Doc 7181
SMILEY Phyllis of Newmarket 1800 Doc 21391
SMITH Sarah of Portsmouth 1851 Doc 931
SMITH Adin of Portsmouth 1852 Doc 1554
SMITH Alexander of Brentwood 1854 Doc 2371
SMITH Alice of Newmarket 1850 Doc 931
SMITH Almira of Portsmouth 1837 Doc 16931
SMITH Anna of Londonderry 1842 Doc 20107
SMITH Betty of Epping 1774 Doc 2656
SMITH Biley of Candia 1842 Doc 20424
SMITH Charles of Portsmouth 1831 Doc 13082
SMITH Charles of Rockingham County 1831 Doc 13399
SMITH Charles of Portsmouth 1832 Doc 13082
SMITH Daniel of Newmarket 1829 Doc 10410
SMITH Daniel (c) of Meredith 1831 Doc 12683
SMITH Donald of Derry 1846 Doc 22356
SMITH Dorothy of Stratham 1780 Doc 4406
SMITH Edward of Nothingham 1785 Doc 9466
SMITH Eleanor of Brentwood 1854 Doc 2371
SMITH Elisa of Sanbornton 1821 Doc 1592
SMITH Elizabeth of Chester 1823 Doc 3965
SMITH Elizabeth (c) of Brentwood 1854 Doc 2371
SMITH Elizabeth of Chester 1824 Doc 5045
SMITH Eunice of Portsmouth 1841 Doc 19510
SMITH Eunice of Portsmouth 1840 Doc 18857
SMITH Eunice of Portsmouth 1839 Doc 18856

SMITH Hannah of Deerfield 1846 Doc 22356
SMITH Hannah of Deerfield 1845 Doc 21835
SMITH Hannah of Deerfield 1851 Doc 931
SMITH Hannah of Deerfield 1843 Doc 20629 S
SMITH Hannah of Deerfield 1850 Doc 311
SMITH Hannah of Brentwood 1786 Doc 9151
SMITH India A H of Portsmouth 1837 Doc 16931
SMITH Jacob of Candia 1842 Doc 20424
SMITH James of ? 1782 Doc 5272
SMITH James N of Rockingham County 1825 Doc 6505
SMITH John of Portsmouth 1839 Doc 18267
SMITH John of Candia 1842 Doc 20424
SMITH John of Portsmouth 1852 Doc 1555
SMITH John of Portsmouth 1840 Doc 18857
SMITH John of Portsmouth 1839 Doc 18856
SMITH John of Portsmouth 1852 Doc 1554
SMITH John of Portsmouth 1841 Doc 19510
SMITH John of Portsmouth 1853 Doc 2086
SMITH John of Portsmouth 1840 Doc 19137
SMITH John of Portsmouth 1851 Doc 931
SMITH John of Seabrook 1850 Doc 311
SMITH John of Seabrook 1851 Doc 931
SMITH John of Portsmouth 1851 Doc 932
SMITH Joseph of Portsmouth 1836 Doc 16216
SMITH Luther of Portsmouth 1851 Doc 311
SMITH Mary of Kingston 1792 Doc 12531
SMITH Mary of Brentwood 1772 Doc 1880
SMITH Mary of Sanbornton 1821 Doc 1592
SMITH Molly of Candia 1850 Doc 311
SMITH Molly of Candia 1852 Doc 1554
SMITH Molly of Candia 1846 Doc 22356
SMITH Molly of Candia 1851 Doc 931
SMITH Molly of Candia 1854 Doc 2371
SMITH Molly of Candia 1845 Doc 21835
SMITH Molly of Candia 1855 Doc 3620
SMITH Molly of Candia 1853 Doc 2085
SMITH Molly of Brentwood 1844 Doc 21216
SMITH Morris of Sanbornton 1821 Doc 1592
SMITH Nancy of Newmarket 1829 Doc 10410
SMITH Nancy of Meredith 1831 Doc 12683
SMITH Nancy of Meredith 1836 Doc 16215
SMITH Nancy (c) of Merrideth 1836 Doc 16215
SMITH Nathaniel of Deerfield 1805 Doc 23965
SMITH Parnell of Brentwood 1772 Doc 1880
SMITH Phebe of Londonderry 1829 Doc 10410
SMITH Phebe of Londonderry 1828 Doc 9823
SMITH Plunna of Deerfield 1843 Doc 20629 S
SMITH Polly of Candia 1854 Doc 2371
SMITH Polly of Candia 1851 Doc 931
SMITH Polly of Candia 1852 Doc 1554
SMITH Polly of Candia 1842 Doc 20424
SMITH Polly of Portsmouth 1821 Doc 1592

SMITH Polly (w) of Candia 1846 Doc 22356
SMITH Polly (w) of Candia 1842 Doc 20107
SMITH Polly (w) of Candia 1850 Doc 311
SMITH Polly (w) of Candia 1843 Doc 20629 S
SMITH Polly (w) of Candia 1845 Doc 21835
SMITH Prudence of Greenland 1780 Doc 4574
SMITH Rachael of Hampton Falls 1774 Doc 3061
SMITH Rosanna of Portsmouth 1852 Doc 1554
SMITH Sally of Newmarket 1829 Doc 10410
SMITH Sally (c) of Meredith 1831 Doc 12683
SMITH Sarah of Portsmouth 1851 Doc 1554
SMITH Sarah of Portsmouth 1851 Doc 311
SMITH Sarah Maria of Portsmouth 1836 Doc 16214
SMITH Sarah Maria of Portsmouth 1836 Doc 16216
SMITH Sarah Mariah of Portsmouth 1837 Doc 16931
SMITH Susan of Portsmouth 1833 Doc 14122
SMITH T of Portsmouth 1852 Doc 1554
SMITH Tabythea of Deerfield 1805 Doc 23965
SMITH Theodate of Portsmouth 1832 Doc 13754
SMITH Theodate of Portsmouth 1837 Doc 16931
SMITH Theodate of Portsmouth 1832 Doc 13755
SMITH Theodate of Portsmouth 1836 Doc 16216
SMITH Theodate of Portsmouth 1836 Doc 16214
SMITH Thodate of Portsmouth 1836 Doc 16216
SMITH Timothy of Sanbornton 1821 Doc 1592
SMITH Widow Of Robert of Londonderry 1816 Doc 40757
SMITH William of Rockingham County 1826 Doc 6965
SMITH William of Rockingham County 1825 Doc 6505
SMITH William of Brentwood 1772 Doc 1880
SMITH William (Mrs) of Portsmouth 1851 Doc 311
SMITH Wm (Mrs) of Portsmouth 1851 Doc 931
SMITTY Hannah of Deerfield 1844 Doc 21216
SNELL Benjamin of Nothingham 1788 Doc 10397
SNELL George of Nothingham 1788 Doc 10397
SNELL Ginge of Portsmouth 1779 Doc 4331
SNELL John of Rockingham County 1831 Doc 13399
SNELL Lucy of Stratham 1794 Doc 14648
SOLUM Jane of Newmarket 1787 Doc 10016
SOMBERY Thomas of Derry 1831 Doc 13081
SOULE Betsey of Chester 1832 Doc 13754
SOUTER Benjamin (c) of Seabrook 1784 Doc 7459
SOUTER John of Seabrook 1784 Doc 7459
SOUTER John Jr (c) of Seabrook 1784 Doc 7459
SOUTER Jonathan (c) of Seabrook 1784 Doc 7459
SOUTER Susannah of Seabrook 1784 Doc 7459
SOUTHER John of Seabrook 1850 Doc 311
SOUTHER John of Seabrook 1846 Doc 22356
SOUTHER Thomas of Seabrook 1850 Doc 311
SOUTHER Thomas of Seabrook 1852 Doc 2371
SOUTHER Thomas of Seabrook 1852 Doc 1554
SOWARDS William of Hampstead 1770 Doc 1612
SOWBERY Thomas of Candia 1838 Doc 17575

SOWERBY Thomas of Hampstead 1833 Doc 14414
SOWERBY Thomas of Londonderry 1840 Doc 18856
SOWERBY Thomas of Candia 1839 Doc 18267
SOWERBY Thomas of Londonderry 1839 Doc 18267
SOWERLY Thomas of Londonderry 1840 Doc 18856
SPAGUE Archibald of Portsmouth 1832 Doc 13755
SPALDING John of Rockingham County 1825 Doc 6965
SPARKMAN Peter of Portsmouth 1852 Doc 1554
SPEAR Mary of Newmarket 1773 Doc 2095
SPEED Mary of Stratham 1773 Doc 2472
SPEED Pegy of Kensington 1789 Doc 11183
SPEED Thomas of Stratham 1773 Doc 2472
SPEED Thomas of Stratham 1771 Doc 731
SPEND Mary of Newmarket 1774 Doc 2656
SPEND Thomas of Newmarket 1774 Doc 2656
SPENNER Nancey of Plaistow 1797 Doc 16546
SPINGER Henry of Atkinson 1772 Doc 2656
SPINNEY Ebenezer of Portsmouth 1832 Doc 13755
SPINNEY Keziah of Newmarket 1846 Doc 22356
SPINNEY Leonard of Portsmouth 1832 Doc 13755
SPINNEY Mary of Portsmouth 1832 Doc 13755
SPOLETT Mary of Londonderry 1821 Doc 2382
SPRAGUE Archibald of Portsmouth 1832 Doc 13754
SPRIMEY Keziah of Newmarket 1853 Doc 2085
SPRING Mary of Manchester 1826 Doc 4466
SPRINGER Joseph of Newtown 1772 Doc 731
SPRINGER Syda of Atkinson 1796 Doc 16050
SQUIRES Mary Ann of Portsmouth 1852 Doc 1554
SQUIRES William of Portsmouth 1852 Doc 1554
STAINER Ona M of Stratham 1845 Doc 21835
STANLEY Hannah of Exeter 1828 Doc 9200
STANLEY Hannah of Exeter 1827 Doc 8073
STANLEY Hannah of Exeter 1826 Doc 6965
STANLEY Hannah of Exeter 1826 Doc 7524
STANLEY Hannah of Exeter 1825 Doc 6505
STANWOOD Abel (c) of Loudon 1790 Doc 11611
STANWOOD Abigail (c) of Loudon 1790 Doc 11611
STANWOOD Betty of Loudon 1790 Doc 11611
STANWOOD Jonathan of Loudon 1790 Doc 11611
STANWOOD Jonathan (c) of Loudon 1790 Doc 11611
STAPLES A of Rockingham County 1831 Doc 13399
STAPLES Julia Ann of Portsmouth 1831 Doc 13081
STAPLES Mark of Newmarket 1791 Doc 12228
STAPLES Martha of Portsmouth 1851 Doc 931
STAPLES Martha of Portsmouth 1851 Doc 311
STAPLES Sarah of Newmarket 1791 Doc 12228
STAPLES Thomas (c) of Newmarket 1791 Doc 12228
STAPLEY John of Portsmouth 1846 Doc 22356
STAPLEY Martha of Portsmouth 1846 Doc 22356
STARBORD Betsy of Northwood 1807 Doc 27572
STARBORD Elizabeth (c) of Northwood 1807 Doc 27572
STARBORD John of Northwood 1807 Doc 27572

STARBORD Matilda (c) of Northwood 1807 Doc 27572
STARBORD Nathaniel (c) of Northwood 1807 Doc 27572
STEARNS Edward of Exeter 1845 Doc 20629 A
STEARNS Slyvanus of Hampton Falls 1854 Doc 2371
STEPHENS Catherine of Hampton Falls 1795 Doc 15359
STEPHENS Isaac of Hampton Falls 1795 Doc 15359
STEPHENS Sally of Seabrooke 1842 Doc 20424
STEPHENS Samuel of Raymond 1849 Doc 931
STEPHENS Sarah of Raymond 1849 Doc 931
STEPHENSON Abraham of Poplin 1798 Doc 17408
STEPHENSON Betty (c) of Poplin 1798 Doc 17408
STEPHENSON Joseph (c) of Poplin 1798 Doc 17408
STEPHENSON Molly of Poplin 1798 Doc 17408
STEPHENSON Samuel (c) of Poplin 1798 Doc 17408
STERLIN William of Exeter 1796 Doc 15359
STERNES Ona of Stratham 1843 Doc 20629 S
STERNES John of Stratham 1842 Doc 20424
STERNES Ona M of Stratham 1842 Doc 20424
STEVEN Charles of Epping 1846 Doc 22356
STEVEN John Jr of Kingston 1785 Doc 8391
STEVEN Maria of Portsmouth 1839 Doc 18856
STEVEN Mary (c) of Poplin 1796 Doc 15598
STEVEN William of Poplin 1796 Doc 15598
STEVENS Sarah of Epping 1844 Doc 21216
STEVENS Abigail (c) of New Chester 1827 Doc 8077
STEVENS Anna of Newmarket 1804 Doc 23419
STEVENS Aphia of Loudon 1817 Doc 44178
STEVENS Betty (c) of Plaistow 1790 Doc 11611
STEVENS Ceasar (Negro) of Kingston 1799 Doc 18299
STEVENS Charles of Epping 1843 Doc 20629 S
STEVENS Charles of Epping 1845 Doc 21835
STEVENS Charles of Epping 1851 Doc 931
STEVENS Charles of Epping 1844 Doc 21216
STEVENS Charles E of Epping 1852 Doc 1554
STEVENS Charles E of Epping 1853 Doc 2085
STEVENS Daniel of Epping 1846 Doc 22356
STEVENS Daniel of Epping 1851 Doc 931
STEVENS Daniel E of Epping 1852 Doc 1554
STEVENS David E of Epping 1853 Doc 2085
STEVENS Deborah of New Chester 1827 Doc 8077
STEVENS Ebenezer of Deerfield 1821 Doc 1592
STEVENS Edward of Exeter 1846 Doc 22356
STEVENS Edward of Exeter 1844 Doc 21216
STEVENS Edward of Kensington 1801 Doc 20206
STEVENS Edward of Exeter 1845 Doc 21835
STEVENS Edward of Exeter 1842 Doc 20107
STEVENS Edward (c) of Kingston 1795 Doc 14648
STEVENS Elisha (c) of New Chester 1827 Doc 8077
STEVENS Ephraim of Plaistow 1773 Doc 2268
STEVENS Ephraim of Exeter 1842 Doc 20107
STEVENS George (c) of New Chester 1827 Doc 8077
STEVENS George H of New Chester 1827 Doc 8077

STEVENS Hail (w) of Kingston 1795 Doc 14648
STEVENS Henry of Epping 1853 Doc 2085
STEVENS Josiah of Plaistow 1790 Doc 11611
STEVENS Josiah Jr (c) of Plaistow 1790 Doc 11611
STEVENS Levi of Portsmouth 1831 Doc 13081
STEVENS Levi of Epping 1845 Doc 21835
STEVENS Levi of Epping 1843 Doc 20629 S
STEVENS Levi (alias) of Epping 1842 Doc 20107
STEVENS Lucretia of Epping 1844 Doc 21216
STEVENS Lucretia of Epping 1853 Doc 2085
STEVENS Lucretia of Epping 1842 Doc 20424
STEVENS Lucretia of Epping 1845 Doc 21835
STEVENS Lucretia of Raymond 1849 Doc 931
STEVENS Lucretia of Epping 1852 Doc 1554
STEVENS Lucretia of Epping 1851 Doc 931
STEVENS Lydia of Kingston 1785 Doc 8391
STEVENS Lydia (c) of New Chester 1827 Doc 8077
STEVENS Margarett of Newmarket 1853 Doc 2085
STEVENS Margert of Epping 1853 Doc 2085
STEVENS Maria of Portsmouth 1841 Doc 19510
STEVENS Maria of Portsmouth 1839 Doc 18856
STEVENS Maria of Portsmouth 1839 Doc 18267
STEVENS Mariam of Epping 1852 Doc 1554
STEVENS Marion of Epping 1853 Doc 2085
STEVENS Mary of Brentwood 1827 Doc 8077
STEVENS Mary Ann (c) of New Chester 1827 Doc 8077
STEVENS Miriam of Epping 1851 Doc 931
STEVENS Patience of Kensington 1801 Doc 20206
STEVENS Patience (c) of Kingston 1795 Doc 14648
STEVENS Sally of Epping 1852 Doc 1554
STEVENS Sally of Epping 1851 Doc 931
STEVENS Sally of Chichester 1820 Doc 1143
STEVENS Sally of Epping 1853 Doc 2085
STEVENS Sarah of Epping 1845 Doc 21835
STEVENS Sarah of Epping 1843 Doc 20629 S
STEVENS Sarah of Plaistow 1790 Doc 11611
STEVENS Sarah of Newmarket 1776 Doc 3712
STEVENS Sarah of Newmarket 1773 Doc 1880
STEVENS Sarah of Epping 1846 Doc 22356
STEVENS Sarah of Epping 1842 Doc 20107
STEVENS Susanna of Concord 1813 Doc 36435
STEVENS Susanna of Concord 1812 Doc 35052
STEVENS Ursula (c) of New Chester 1827 Doc 8077
STEVENS William of Epping 1842 Doc 20107
STEVENSON Margaret of Newmarket 1846 Doc 22356
STEVENSON Margaret of Newmarket 1850 Doc 311
STEVENSON Margaret of Newmarket 1845 Doc 21835
STEVENSON Margaret of Newmarket 1852 Doc 1554
STEVENSON Margaret of Newmarket 1850 Doc 931
STEVESON Margaret of Newmarket 1850 Doc 311
STEWARD Charles of Portsmouth 1830 Doc 12197
STEWART Charles of Hampton 1770 Doc 1612

STEWART Charles of Portsmouth 1830 Doc 12197
STEWART David of Portsmouth 1835 Doc 15900
STEWART David of Portsmouth 1836 Doc 16214
STEWART Elizabeth of Portsmouth 1843 Doc 20629
STICKNEY Greenleaf K of Hampton 1843 Doc 20629
STICKNEY Henry of Exeter 1826 Doc 7524
STICKNEY Isaac of Auburn 1853 Doc 1842
STICKNEY Isaac of Auburn 1853 Doc 2085
STICKNEY Joseph (c) of Kingston 1798 Doc 17408
STICKNEY Levi of Kingston 1798 Doc 17408
STICKNEY Levi of Hampton 1843 Doc 20629
STICKNEY Lucy of Atkinson 1782 Doc 4997
STICKNEY Mary of Hampton Falls 1828 Doc 9823
STICKNEY Mary (c) of Kingston 1798 Doc 17408
STICKNEY Sarah (c) of Kingston 1798 Doc 17408
STILL Sally of Stratham 1781 Doc 4749
STILL Sarah of Stratham 1781 Doc 4749
STILLINS Molly of Rye 1800 Doc 19247
STIMPSON Joseph of Deerfield 1852 Doc 2086
STIMPSON Leanda of Salem 1827 Doc 9822
STIMSON Joseph of Portsmouth 1853 Doc 2086
STOCKBRIDGE B W of Stratham 1851 Doc 931
STOCKBRIDGE Bradstreet of Stratham 1850 Doc 311
STOCKBRIDGE Bradstreet of Stratham 1853 Doc 2085
STOCKBRIDGE Bradstreet of Stratham 1846 Doc 22356
STOCKBRIDGE Bradstreet of Stratham 1853 Doc 2371
STOCKBRIDGE Bradstreet of Stratham 1843 Doc 20629 A
STOCKBRIDGE Bradstreet of Stratham 1852 Doc 1554
STOCKBRIDGE John of Stratham 1852 Doc 1554
STOCKBRIDGE John of Hawke 1786 Doc 9631
STOCKBRIDGE Levi of Epping 1799 Doc 18299
STOCKBRIDGE Molly of Epping 1799 Doc 18299
STOCKBRIDGE Susannah of Epping 1799 Doc 18299
STOCKMAN Charles of Hampton 1853 Doc 2371
STOCKMAN Charlotte of Hampton 1853 Doc 2371
STOCKMAN David of Rockingham County 1851 Doc 931
STOCKMAN Freman of Deerfield 1861 Doc 6710
STOCKMAN Nancy of Deerfield 1861 Doc 6710
STOKES Betsy of Nottingham 1842 Doc 20424
STOODLY Mary of Hampstead 1770 Doc 1612
STRAN John of Loudon 1790 Doc 11611
STRAN Molle of Loudon 1790 Doc 11611
STRAW Anna (c) of Sandown 1788 Doc 10229
STRAW Benjamin C (c) of Sandown 1788 Doc 10229
STRAW Betty (c) of Sandown 1788 Doc 10229
STRAW Hannah of Sandown 1788 Doc 10229
STRAW John of Plaistow 1774 Doc 3061
STRAW Rachael F (c) of Sandown 1788 Doc 10229
STRINGER Catherine of Portsmouth 1851 Doc 931
STRINGER Catherine of Portsmouth 1852 Doc 1554
STRINGER Catherine of Portsmouth 1851 Doc 311
STRINGER Catherine of Portsmouth 1845 Doc 21835

STRINGER John of Portsmouth 1841 Doc 19510
STRINGER John of Portsmouth 1840 Doc 18857
STRINGER Joseph of Portsmouth 1845 Doc 21835
STRINGER William of Deerfield 1811 Doc 32876
STRONG James of Portsmouth 1840 Doc 18857
STRONG James of Portsmouth 1841 Doc 19510
STRONG James of Portsmouth 1839 Doc 18856
STRONG James of Portsmouth 1840 Doc 18857
SUCKO Cesar of Northwood 1787 Doc 9898
SULIVAN Andrew of Londonderry 1850 Doc 311
SULIVAN Daniel of Portsmouth 1851 Doc 311
SULIVAN Daniel of Portsmouth 1841 Doc 19510
SULIVAN Eugina of Portsmouth 1852 Doc 1555
SULIVAN John of Portsmouth 1832 Doc 13754
SULLIVAN Daniel of Portsmouth 1840 Doc 19137
SULLIVAN Daniel of Portsmouth 1846 Doc 22356
SULLIVAN Daniel of Portsmouth 1851 Doc 931
SULLIVAN David of Portsmouth 1842 Doc 20107
SULLIVAN David of Portsmouth 1852 Doc 1554
SULLIVAN Ellen of Portsmouth 1852 Doc 1555
SULLIVAN George of Exeter 1840 Doc 19510
SULLIVAN Jeremiah of Raymond 1855 Doc 3620
SULLIVAN John of Derry 1831 Doc 13081
SULLIVAN John of Portsmouth 1832 Doc 13755
SULLIVAN John of Portsmouth 1852 Doc 1554
SULLIVAN Margaret of Epping 1794 Doc 14339
SULLIVAN Mary of Portsmouth 1838 Doc 18267
SULLIVAN Mary of Portsmouth 1839 Doc 18267
SULLIVAN Matthew of Londonderry 1840 Doc 18856
SULLIVAN Matthew of Londonderry 1840 Doc 19510
SULLIVAN Matthew of Londonderry 1840 Doc 19136
SULLIVAN William of Hampton 1840 Doc 18856
SUTTON Solomon of Concord 1809 Doc 31571
SWAIN James of Newmarket 1784 Doc 7181
SWAIN John of Portsmouth 1843 Doc 20629
SWAIN Mary of Kensington 1786 Doc 9151
SWAN Betsy (c) of Windham 1813 Doc 36435
SWAN Elizabeth of Epsom 1806 Doc 25429
SWAN John of Windham 1813 Doc 36435
SWAN Joseph of Epsom 1806 Doc 25429
SWAN Joshua (c) of Windham 1813 Doc 36435
SWAN Ruth of Windham 1813 Doc 36435
SWASEY James of Exeter 1845 Doc 20629 A
SWASEY Jane of Exeter 1843 Doc 20629 S
SWASEY Jane of Exeter 1844 Doc 21216
SWASEY Jane of Exeter 1846 Doc 22356
SWASEY Jane of Exeter 1845 Doc 21835
SWASEY Jane of Exeter 1842 Doc 20107
SWASEY Jane of Boscawen 1838 Doc 17575
SWASEY June of Boscawen 1832 Doc 13399
SWASEY Sally of Exeter 1850 Doc 311
SWASEY Sally of Exeter 1851 Doc 931

SWASEY Sally of Exeter 1852 Doc 1554
SWASEY Sally of Exeter 1846 Doc 22356
SWEARS John of Portsmouth 1846 Doc 22356
SWEAT Benjamin of Exeter 1843 Doc 20629 S
SWEAT Elizabeth of Greenland 1786 Doc 9151
SWEAT John (c) of Kingston 1799 Doc 17750
SWEAT Joseph of Kingston 1799 Doc 17750
SWEAT Sarah of Kingston 1799 Doc 17750
SWEAT Stephen (c) of Kingston 1799 Doc 17750
SWEET Ann (c) of Pembroke 1795 Doc 15359
SWEET Benjamin (c) of Pembroke 1795 Doc 15359
SWEET Benjamin (c) of Exeter 1845 Doc 21835
SWEET Benjamin C of Exeter 1844 Doc 21216
SWEET Benjamin Calvin of Exeter 1842 Doc 20107
SWEET Betty of Pembroke 1795 Doc 15359
SWEET Eliphalett (gc) of Pembroke 1795 Doc 15359
SWEET John of Auburn 1846 Doc 22592
SWEET Joseph of Pembroke 1795 Doc 15359
SWEET Mary of Auburn 1846 Doc 22592
SWEET Polly of Exeter 1794 Doc 14018
SWIFT Ellen of Newmarket 1838 Doc 17575
SYLVESTER Elisha of Portsmouth 1831 Doc 13082
SYLVESTER Elisha of Portsmouth 1832 Doc 13754
SYLVESTER Elisha of Portsmouth 1832 Doc 13755
SYLVESTER Elisha of Portsmouth 1832 Doc 13082
SYMONDS Ruth of Portsmouth 1839 Doc 18856
SYMONDS Ruth of Portsmouth 1839 Doc 18267
SYMONDS Ruth of Portsmouth 1842 Doc 20107
SYMONDS Ruth of Portsmouth 1841 Doc 19511
SYMONDS Ruth of Portsmouth 1841 Doc 19510
TANDY David of Concord 1842 Doc 20107
TANDY Elizabeth of Deerfield 1787 Doc 10016
TANDY Esther (c) of Deerfield 1787 Doc 10016
TANDY Eunice (c) of Deerfield 1787 Doc 10016
TANDY John (c) of Deerfield 1787 Doc 10016
TANDY Rachael of Raymond 1817 Doc 44178
TANDY Richard of Deerfield 1787 Doc 10016
TANDY Richard of Brentwood 1783 Doc 5923
TANDY Richard of Sandown 1786 Doc 9151
TANDY Samuel of Raymond 1817 Doc 44178
TANDY Samuel (c) of Deerfield 1787 Doc 10016
TANDY Timothy of Brentwood 1783 Doc 5923
TANDY William (c) of Deerfield 1787 Doc 10016
TARLTON Hannah of Portsmouth 1845 Doc 21835
TARLTON Hannah of Portsmouth 1843 Doc 20629
TASKER Comfort of Northwood 1796 Doc 15359
TASKER Daniel of Northwood 1796 Doc 15359
TASKER John (c) of Northwood 1796 Doc 15359
TASKER Joseph (c) of Northwood 1796 Doc 15359
TASKER Ruth (c) of Northwood 1796 Doc 15359
TASKER Silas (c) of Northwood 1796 Doc 15359
TASKER Simon (c) of Northwood 1796 Doc 15359

TATE Daniel of Stratham 1801 Doc 20206
TAYLA Joseph of Candia 1851 Doc 931
TAYLOR James (c) of Newmarket 1791 Doc 12228
TAYLOR John of Exeter 1773 Doc 1880
TAYLOR John of Portsmouth 1841 Doc 20107
TAYLOR John of Portsmouth 1842 Doc 20107
TAYLOR Joseph of Candia 1850 Doc 311
TAYLOR Joseph of Epping 1773 Doc 2656
TAYLOR Joseph of Candia 1846 Doc 22356
TAYLOR Joseph of Candia 1843 Doc 20629 S
TAYLOR Joseph of Candia 1845 Doc 21835
TAYLOR Joseph of Candia 1852 Doc 1554
TAYLOR Juda (c) of Newmarket 1791 Doc 12228
TAYLOR Mary (w) of Exeter 1790 Doc 11910
TAYLOR Susannah of Newmarket 1791 Doc 12228
TAYLOR Thomas of Newmarket 1791 Doc 12228
TAYLOR Thomas (c) of Newmarket 1791 Doc 12228
TAYLOR William (c) of Newmarket 1791 Doc 12228
TEBBETTS Jonathan of Kensington 1851 Doc 931
TEBERNAL Lewis of Portsmouth 1851 Doc 311
TEMPLEMAN Levi of Portsmouth 1831 Doc 13081
TEMPLEMAN Levi of Portsmouth 1828 Doc 9200
TEMPLEMAN Levi of Portsmouth 1830 Doc 12197
TEMPLEMAN Levi of Portsmouth 1826 Doc 6965
TENNEY John F of N Hampton 1840 Doc 18858
TENNEY Patrick of Derry 1852 Doc 1554
TERRILL George of Windham 1850 Doc 311
TEWKSBERY Johnson of Deerfield 1803 Doc 21796
TEWKSBERY Joseph of Deerfield 1803 Doc 21796
TEWKSBERY Mary of Deerfield 1803 Doc 21796
TEWKSBERY Sally of Deerfield 1803 Doc 21796
TEWKSBERY Thomas of Deerfield 1803 Doc 21796
THERSON Nancy of Windham 1842 Doc 20629 S
THOMAS Abigail of Brentwood 1788 Doc 10229
THOMAS Elizha of Raymond 1786 Doc 9466
THOMAS Esther (Indian) of Windham 1772 Doc 1880
THOMAS James of Windham 1772 Doc 1880
THOMAS James of Nottingham 1850 Doc 931
THOMAS James of Nottingham 1840 Doc 19510
THOMAS James of Nottingham 1852 Doc 1554
THOMAS James of Nottingham 1843 Doc 20629
THOMAS James of Nothingham 1844 Doc 21216
THOMAS James of Nottingham 1846 Doc 22356
THOMAS James of Nottingham 1850 Doc 311
THOMAS John (Negro) of Portsmouth 1851 Doc 311
THOMAS John of Portsmouth 1846 Doc 22356
THOMAS John of Portsmouth 1842 Doc 20107
THOMAS John of Portsmouth 1844 Doc 21503
THOMAS John of Portsmouth 1840 Doc 19137
THOMAS John (Negro) of Portsmouth 1851 Doc 931
THOMAS John (Negro) of Portsmouth 1852 Doc 1554
THOMAS John of Portsmouth 1841 Doc 19510

THOMAS Lanies of Nottingham 1854 Doc 2371
THOMPSON Amos G of Center Harbor 1838 Doc 17575
THOMPSON Ann of Windham 1853 Doc 2371
THOMPSON George of Portsmouth 1840 Doc 18857
THOMPSON James of Windham 1842 Doc 20424
THOMPSON James of Farmington 1846 Doc 22592
THOMPSON John of Greenland 1795 Doc 15359
THOMPSON Margaret of Portsmouth 1840 Doc 18857
THOMPSON Nancy of Windham 1851 Doc 931
THOMPSON Nancy of Windham 1853 Doc 2085
THOMPSON Nancy of Windham 1852 Doc 1554
THOMPSON Nancy of Windham 1843 Doc 20928
THOMPSON Nancy of Windham 1843 Doc 21503
THOMPSON Nancy of Windham 1846 Doc 22356
THOMPSON Nancy of Windham 1845 Doc 21835
THOMPSON Samuel of Nottingham 1842 Doc 20424
THOMPSON Silias of Newmarket 1787 Doc 10016
THOMPSON Susana (Negro) of Rye 1798 Doc 16897
THOMPSON Thomas (Negro) of Rye 1798 Doc 16897
THOMPSON William H of Portsmouth 1842 Doc 20107
THOMPSON William H of Portsmouth 1842 Doc 20107
THOMPSON William Henry of Portsmouth 1840 Doc 18857
THOMPSON William Henry of Portsmouth 1846 Doc 22356
THOMPSON William Henry of Portsmouth 1845 Doc 21835
THOMPSON William Henry of Portsmouth 1841 Doc 19510
THOMSON Jacob of Newmarket 1773 Doc 2095
THOMSON Nanny of Windham 1842 Doc 20424
THOMSON Susannah of Epsom 1800 Doc 19247
THOMSON Thomas of Epsom 1800 Doc 19247
THORN Alfred of Poplin 1834 Doc 14817
THORN Betty of Poplin 1816 Doc 40757
THORN Elizabeth of Poplin 1834 Doc 14817
THORN Lydia of Poplin 1836 Doc 16215
THORN Lydia of Poplin 1834 Doc 14817
THORN Molly of Epping 1845 Doc 21835
THORN Moses of Danville 1845 Doc 21835
THORN Moses of Danville 1850 Doc 311
THORN Moses of Danville 1853 Doc 2085
THORN Moses of Poplin 1834 Doc 14817
THORN Moses of Poplin 1836 Doc 16215
THORN Moses of Danville 1843 Doc 20629 S
THORN Moses of Danville 1846 Doc 22356
THORN Moses of Danville 1844 Doc 21216
THORN Moses of Danville 1851 Doc 931
THORN Moses of Poplin 1842 Doc 20424
THORN Moses of Danville 1842 Doc 20424
THORN Sarah of N Hampton 1840 Doc 18857
THORN Sarah of N Hampton 1840 Doc 18858
THORNES John of Portsmouth 1844 Doc 21503
THOULDER Laura of Portsmouth 1852 Doc 1554
THURDIN Anna of Deerfield 1851 Doc 931
THURSTIAN Anna of Deerfield 1852 Doc 1554

THURSTON Abigail (c) of Deerfield 1805 Doc 23965
THURSTON Abigail (c) of Newmarket 1776 Doc 3712
THURSTON Anna of Deerfield 1845 Doc 21835
THURSTON Anna of Raymond 1830 Doc 11981
THURSTON Anna of Deerfield 1850 Doc 311
THURSTON Anna of Deerfield 1830 Doc 20107
THURSTON Anna of Deerfield 1846 Doc 22356
THURSTON Anna of Deerfield 1843 Doc 20629 S
THURSTON Anna of Deerfield 1844 Doc 21216
THURSTON Anna Jr of Deerfield 1844 Doc 21216
THURSTON Anna Jr of Deerfield 1846 Doc 22356
THURSTON Betsy of Pittsfield 1825 Doc 6505
THURSTON Betsy (c) of Deerfield 1805 Doc 23965
THURSTON Charles of Deerfield 1846 Doc 22356
THURSTON Deborah of Deerfield 1800 Doc 18692
THURSTON Deborah (c) of Newmarket 1776 Doc 3712
THURSTON Edward (c) of Deerfield 1800 Doc 18692
THURSTON Elizabeth of ? 1803 Doc 2352
THURSTON Ephriam of Newington 1804 Doc 22771
THURSTON Ezekiel of Epping 1789 Doc 10754
THURSTON James (c) of Deerfield 1805 Doc 23965
THURSTON James (c) of Deerfield 1800 Doc 18692
THURSTON Jesse of Deerfield 1800 Doc 18692
THURSTON Jesse of Allenstown 1789 Doc 11025
THURSTON John of Deerfield 1845 Doc 21835
THURSTON John of Deerfield 1843 Doc 20629 S
THURSTON John of Deerfield 1844 Doc 21216
THURSTON Mary of Newmarket 1776 Doc 3712
THURSTON Peter of Deerfield 1805 Doc 23965
THURSTON Polly of Epping 1789 Doc 10754
THURSTON Rachel of Deerfield 1805 Doc 23965
THURSTON Samuel (c) of Deerfield 1805 Doc 23965
THURSTON Stephen of Newmarket 1776 Doc 3712
THURSTON Susannah of Deerfield 1822 Doc 3416
TIBBETH Jonathan of Kensington 1850 Doc 311
TIBBETS John of Nottingham 1804 Doc 23419
TIBBETTS Jonathan of Kensington 1852 Doc 1554
TIBBETTS Joseph of Greenland 1797 Doc 16546
TIBBITS Elizabeth of Stratham 1798 Doc 16897
TILER David (c) of Hampton 1769 Doc 1612
TILER John (c) of Hampton 1769 Doc 1612
TILER Molly (c) of Hampton 1769 Doc 1612
TILER Samuel (c) of Hampton 1769 Doc 1612
TILER Sarah of Hampton 1769 Doc 1612
TILER William of Hampton 1769 Doc 1612
TILLETT Jonathan of Kensington 1853 Doc 2085
TILTON Samuel of Keningston 1785 Doc 9466
TILTON Beety of Brentwood 1796 Doc 15359
TILTON David of Brentwood 1803 Doc 22285
TILTON Ebenezer of Windham 1787 Doc 10142
TILTON Elizabeth of Brentwood 1800 Doc 18692
TILTON John of Exeter 1817 Doc 44178

TILTON John of Hampton 1817 Doc 44178
TILTON John Sullivan of Exeter 1819 Doc 47427
TILTON John Sullivan of Hampton Falls 1786 Doc 9151
TILTON Jonathan of Epping 1828 Doc 9823
TILTON Sarah of Keningston 1785 Doc 9466
TITUS (Negro) of Newington 1790 Doc 11310
TIVSTON Jonathan of Rockingham County 1831 Doc 13399
TOBEY Sarah of Hampton 1850 Doc 311
TOBEY Sarah of Hampton 1851 Doc 931
TOBEY Sarah (Mrs) of Hampton 1843 Doc 20629
TOBEY Sarah (Mrs) of Hampton 1846 Doc 22356
TOBY Sarah of Hampton 1852 Doc 1554
TOBY Sarah of Hampton 1845 Doc 21835
TOBY Sarah of Hampton 1843 Doc 21216
TODD Joanna of Portsmouth 1828 Doc 9200
TODD Joseph of Newmarket 1783 Doc 6644
TOMA Noal (Indian) of Exeter 1831 Doc 12682
TOMART Noal of Exeter 1831 Doc 13399
TOMSON Susananna of Newmarket 1773 Doc 2095
TOREY Samuel of Brentwood 1780 Doc 4406
TOREY William of Poplin 1790 Doc 11611
TORY Samuel of Raymond 1790 Doc 11310
TOWLE Anna (c) of Epping 1789 Doc 11611
TOWLE Elizabeth of Epping 1789 Doc 11611
TOWLE Jeremiah of Raymond 1783 Doc 6232
TOWLE Simeon of Epping 1789 Doc 11611
TOWLE Simeon Jr of Epping 1789 Doc 11611
TOWNSEND Aaron of Deerfield 1795 Doc 15018
TOWNSEND Hepzibah (c) of Deerfield 1795 Doc 15018
TOWNSEND Huldah of Hampstead 1769 Doc 1612
TOWNSEND Kimball (c) of Deerfield 1795 Doc 15018
TOWNSEND Phebe of Deerfield 1795 Doc 15018
TOWNSEND Phebe (c) of Deerfield 1795 Doc 15018
TOWNSEND Polly (c) of Deerfield 1795 Doc 15018
TOWNSEND Toppan (c) of Deerfield 1795 Doc 15018
TRACY Fortune of Exeter 1784 Doc 7181
TREFETHEN Abigail of Portsmouth 1851 Doc 931
TREFETHEN Abigail of Portsmouth 1846 Doc 22356
TREFETHERN Abigail of Portsmouth 1851 Doc 1554
TREFETHIN Abigail of Portsmouth 1852 Doc 1554
TREFTHIN Abigail of Portsmouth 1851 Doc 311
TRICKEY Betty of Exeter 1791 Doc 12531
TRICKEY Charles (c) of Epsom 1852 Doc 2086
TRICKEY Dorothy (c) of Epsom 1852 Doc 2086
TRICKEY Hannah of Epsom 1852 Doc 2086
TRICKEY Hannah (c) of Epsom 1852 Doc 2086
TRICKEY John (c) of Epsom 1852 Doc 2086
TRICKEY John S of Epsom 1852 Doc 20866
TRICKEY John S of Portsmouth 1852 Doc 1555
TRICKEY Mary of Newington 1843 Doc 20629
TRICKEY Mary (c) of Epsom 1852 Doc 2086
TRICKEY Mary/Molly of Newington 1817 Doc 44178

TRICKEY Molly of Londonderry 1842 Doc 20424
TRICKEY Molly of Newington 1842 Doc 20107
TRICKEY Samuel of Epsom 1853 Doc 20866
TRICKEY Scott of Pembroke 1830 Doc 11710
TRICKEY Scott C of Pembroke 1829 Doc 10610
TRIPE Sarah of Nottingham 1789 Doc 10754
TRIPPS W B of Londonderry 1840 Doc 18856
TROMBLEY Paula of Gilmanton 1835 Doc 15557
TROMBLY John of Gilmanton 1839 Doc 18543
TROMBLY Paul of Gilmington 1839 Doc 18543
TRUMAN Dianah of Derry 1836 Doc 16214
TRUMAN Dianah of Derry 1831 Doc 12682
TRUSDALE Anna of Stratham 1794 Doc 14648
TRYELL Rose of Portsmouth 1852 Doc 1554
TUCK Jeremiah of Hampton 1846 Doc 22356
TUCK Jeremiah of Hampton 1845 Doc 21835
TUCK Jeremiah of Hampton 1843 Doc 20928
TUCK Jeremiah of Hampton 1844 Doc 21216
TUCKER Charles of Portsmouth 1851 Doc 311
TUCKER Doras of Portsmouth 1846 Doc 22356
TUCKER Doreas & Wife of Portsmouth 1851 Doc 311
TUCKER Doreas (c) of Portsmouth 1851 Doc 931
TUCKER George of Portsmouth 1851 Doc 931
TUCKER George W of Portsmouth 1851 Doc 311
TUCKER Hannah of Brentwood 1794 Doc 14339
TUCKER Henry of Newmarket 1794 Doc 14339
TUCKER Henry (c) of Newmarket 1794 Doc 14339
TUCKER Jane (c) of Newmarket 1794 Doc 14339
TUCKER John E of Portsmouth 1851 Doc 311
TUCKER John E of Portsmouth 1851 Doc 931
TUCKER Julia of Portsmouth 1851 Doc 311
TUCKER June (c) of Newmarket 1794 Doc 14339
TUCKER Lydia Jane of Portsmouth 1851 Doc 311
TUCKER Mahittible of Loudon 1794 Doc 14339
TUCKER Mary of Newmarket 1794 Doc 14339
TUCKER Mary (c) of Newmarket 1794 Doc 14339
TUCKER Sally of Portsmouth 1851 Doc 931
TUCKER Sally H of Portsmouth 1851 Doc 311
TUCKER Sarah (c) of Newmarket 1794 Doc 14339
TUCKER Susanna of Poplin 1799 Doc 18299
TUCKER Thomas (c) of Newmarket 1794 Doc 14339
TUCKER William of Portsmouth 1851 Doc 311
TUCKER William of Portsmouth 1851 Doc 931
TUCKER William of Portsmouth 1846 Doc 22356
TUFTS Henry of ? 1782 Doc 5272
TUNSTS Abagil of Greenland 1796 Doc 15359
TUNSTS Mangoil of Greenland 1796 Doc 15359
TUNSTS Salomon of Greenland 1796 Doc 15359
TURNER Adam of Portsmouth 1828 Doc 9200
TURNER Mary Jane of Portsmouth 1842 Doc 20424
TUTLE Edwd of Portsmouth 1852 Doc 1554
TUTTLE Charles of Portsmouth 1839 Doc 18856

TUTTLE Charles of Portsmouth 1840 Doc 18856
TUTTLE Charles of Portsmouth 1839 Doc 18267
TUTTLE Issac of Epping 1793 Doc 13587
TUTTLE Levi of Epping 1793 Doc 13587
TUTTLE Miriam of Epping 1793 Doc 13587
TUTTLE Thomas of Londonderry 1851 Doc 931
TWOMBLEY John W of Greenland 1851 Doc 931
TWOMBLY Paul of Northwood 1823 Doc 3965
TYLER Belinda (c) of Atkinson 1796 Doc 16050
TYLER Isaac (c) of Atkinson 1796 Doc 16050
TYLER Jacob of Atkinson 1796 Doc 16050
TYLER Levina of Atkinson 1796 Doc 16050
TYNELL Rose of Portsmouth 1851 Doc 931
TYRELL Rose of Portsmouth 1851 Doc 311
UNDERHILL Moses of Chester 1850 Doc 5760
UPTON Christopher of Brentwood 1834 Doc 15123
UPTON Christopher of Brentwood 1836 Doc 16931
UPTON Christopher of ? 1831 Doc 15123
URIN Hannah of Epping 1801 Doc 20206
URIN John of Greenland 1778 Doc 4164
URIN Paul of Epping 1801 Doc 20206
URIN Paul of Newmarket 1783 Doc 6644
VARNERY Ezekiel of Exeter 1846 Doc 22356
VEASEY Esther of Stratham 1771 Doc 731
VEASEY Lydia of Epping 1789 Doc 11025
VEASEY Samuel of Epping 1789 Doc 11025
VEASEY Samuel of Tamworth 1823 Doc 3965
VEASEY Sarah of Epping 1772 Doc 1880
VEASEY Thomas of Stratham 1771 Doc 731
VEAZEY Mary of Epping 1775 Doc 3514
VEAZEY Mary (alias) of Seabrook 1782 Doc 5186
VERVEL Abigail (s) of Seabrook 1821 Doc 1592
VERVEL Betsey of Seabrook 1821 Doc 1592
VERVEL Clairissa (c) of Seabrook 1821 Doc 1592
VERVEL Daniel (c) of Seabrook 1821 Doc 1592
VERVEL Elizabeth of Seabrook 1821 Doc 1592
VERVEL John (c) of Seabrook 1821 Doc 1592
VERVEL June (c) of Seabrook 1821 Doc 1592
VERVEL Nancy (s) of Seabrook 1821 Doc 1592
VIZEY Choloc of Claremont 1851 Doc 932
WADDEL David of Poplin 1788 Doc 10640
WADE Joseph of Portsmouth 1851 Doc 931
WADE Joseph of Portsmouth 1852 Doc 1554
WADE Joseph of Portsmouth 1851 Doc 311
WADLEIGH Dean of Raymond 1790 Doc 11611
WADLEIGH Hannah of Hancock 1817 Doc 44178
WADLEIGH Henry of Hancock 1817 Doc 44178
WADLEIGH Judith of Deerfield 1781 Doc 4749
WADLEIGH Margaret of Raymond 1790 Doc 11611
WADLEIGH Peter of Northfield 1819 Doc 47427
WADLEIGH Sarah of Brentwood 1791 Doc 12228
WAINWRIGHT Hannah of Pittsfield 1790 Doc 11611

WAIT Dorothy of Brentwood 1852 Doc 1554
WAIT Bettey (c) of Epping 1794 Doc 14339
WAIT Dareby of Brentwood 1853 Doc 2085
WAIT Dolley of Brentwood 1843 Doc 20629 S
WAIT Dorothy of Brentwood 1842 Doc 20629 A
WAIT Dorothy of Brentwood 1842 Doc 20424
WAIT Rachel (c) of Epping 1794 Doc 14339
WAIT Rhoda of Epping 1794 Doc 14339
WAIT Richard of Pembroke 1810 Doc 33660
WAIT Ruth of Pembroke 1810 Doc 31571
WAIT Ruth of Pembroke 1810 Doc 32876
WAIT Samuel (c) of Epping 1794 Doc 14339
WAIT Susannah (c) of Epping 1794 Doc 14339
WAIT Thomas of Epping 1794 Doc 14339
WAITE Rhoda of Kensington 1778 Doc 4111
WAITE Thomas of Kensington 1778 Doc 4111
WALCH Betsy of Portsmouth 1852 Doc 1554
WALDRON George of Rye 1792 Doc 13587
WALING Johnathan (c) of Chester 1836 Doc 16214
WALKER (alias) Edward of Portsmouth 1791 Doc 12228
WALKER Abigail of Atkinson 1771 Doc 2656
WALKER George of Portsmouth 1851 Doc 931
WALKER George of Portsmouth 1851 Doc 932
WALKER George (c) of Atkinson 1771 Doc 2656
WALKER Goerge of Portsmouth 1851 Doc 932
WALKER Jane of Epping 1853 Doc 2085
WALKER John of Exeter 1840 Doc 18856
WALKER Leonard of Portsmouth 1831 Doc 13081
WALKER Margaret of Kingston 1780 Doc 4406
WALKER Margaret (c) of Atkinson 1771 Doc 2656
WALKER Pattey of Windham 1788 Doc 10525
WALKER Samuel of Portsmouth 1832 Doc 13754
WALKER Samuel of Portsmouth 1831 Doc 13081
WALKER Timothy of Sanbornton 1772 Doc 731
WALKINS John of Windham 1811 Doc 33660
WALL Simeon of Deerfield 1798 Doc 16897
WALLACE Simeon of Epping 1842 Doc 20107
WALLACE Alexander of Nottingham 1850 Doc 931
WALLACE Alexander of Nottingham 1852 Doc 1554
WALLACE Alexander of Nottingham 1850 Doc 311
WALLACE Betsey of Northwood 1850 Doc 311
WALLACE Betsey of Londonderry 1851 Doc 931
WALLACE Betsey of Northwood 1844 Doc 21216
WALLACE Betsey of Northwood 1846 Doc 22356
WALLACE Betsey of Norwood 1852 Doc 1554
WALLACE Betsey of Northwood 1842 Doc 20424
WALLACE Betsey of Northwood 1842 Doc 20424
WALLACE Betty of Northwood 1853 Doc 2371
WALLACE Betty of Northwood 1843 Doc 20629
WALLACE Catharine of Exeter 1784 Doc 7181
WALLACE Catharine (Negro) of Exeter 1845 Doc 20629 A
WALLACE Catharine of Exeter 1843 Doc 20629 S

WALLACE Catharine (c) of Exeter 1844 Doc 21216
WALLACE Catherine of Exeter 1853 Doc 2371
WALLACE Catherine of Exeter 1853 Doc 2085
WALLACE Catherine (c) of Exeter 1851 Doc 931
WALLACE Catherine (c) of Exeter 1850 Doc 311
WALLACE Ceasar of Exeter 1784 Doc 7181
WALLACE Charles of Epping 1842 Doc 20107
WALLACE Charles of Epping 1843 Doc 20629 S
WALLACE Charles of Epping 1844 Doc 21216
WALLACE Charles (c) of Epping 1842 Doc 20424
WALLACE Dolly of Exeter 1845 Doc 21835
WALLACE Dolly (Negro) of Exeter 1845 Doc 20629 A
WALLACE Dolly P of Exeter 1843 Doc 20629 S
WALLACE Dolly P of Exeter 1852 Doc 1554
WALLACE Dolly P of Exeter 1853 Doc 2085
WALLACE Dolly P of Exeter 1844 Doc 21216
WALLACE Dolly P of Exeter 1851 Doc 931
WALLACE Dolly P of Exeter 1850 Doc 311
WALLACE Dolly P of Exeter 1846 Doc 22356
WALLACE Florance of Northwood 1850 Doc 311
WALLACE Freeman (Negro) of Exeter 1845 Doc 20629 A
WALLACE Freeman (c) of Exeter 1843 Doc 20629 S
WALLACE Freeman (c) of Exeter 1846 Doc 22356
WALLACE Freeman (c) of Exeter 1844 Doc 21216
WALLACE Geor Henry (c) of Exeter 1852 Doc 1554
WALLACE George of Exeter 1843 Doc 20629 S
WALLACE George of Exeter 1844 Doc 21216
WALLACE James of Exeter 1853 Doc 2085
WALLACE James (Negro) of Exeter 1845 Doc 20629 A
WALLACE James of Exeter 1853 Doc 2371
WALLACE James (c) of Exeter 1850 Doc 311
WALLACE James (c) of Exeter 1844 Doc 21216
WALLACE James (c) of Exeter 1852 Doc 1554
WALLACE James (c) of Exeter 1843 Doc 20629 S
WALLACE James (c) of Exeter 1846 Doc 22356
WALLACE James (c) of Exeter 1851 Doc 931
WALLACE James (s) of Exeter 1843 Doc 20629 S
WALLACE Joseph of Epping 1842 Doc 20107
WALLACE Maria of Exeter 1853 Doc 2085
WALLACE Maria of Exeter 1850 Doc 311
WALLACE Mariah (c) of Exeter 1844 Doc 21216
WALLACE Marriah & Child of Exeter 1853 Doc 2371
WALLACE Moses (c) of Deerfield 1793 Doc 13587
WALLACE Nana of Exeter 1852 Doc 1554
WALLACE Plooma of Northwood 1846 Doc 22356
WALLACE Pluma of Northwood 1853 Doc 2371
WALLACE Pluma of Norwood 1852 Doc 1554
WALLACE Pluma of Northwood 1853 Doc 2085
WALLACE Polly of Kingston 1792 Doc 12531
WALLACE Salley of Nottingham 1854 Doc 2371
WALLACE Salley of Nottingham 1850 Doc 931
WALLACE Salley of Nottingham 1853 Doc 2085

WALLACE Salley of Nottingham 1851 Doc 932
WALLACE Sally of Nottingham 1852 Doc 1554
WALLACE Sarah of Epping 1852 Doc 1554
WALLACE Sarah of Epping 1842 Doc 20424
WALLACE Sarah of Epping 1846 Doc 22356
WALLACE Sarah of Epping 1842 Doc 20107
WALLACE Sarah of Epping 1844 Doc 21216
WALLACE Sarah of Epping 1843 Doc 20629 S
WALLACE Sarah of Epping 1851 Doc 931
WALLACE Susannah of Deerfield 1793 Doc 13587
WALLACE Thomas of Londonderry 1851 Doc 931
WALLACE William of Northwood 1842 Doc 20424
WALLAN Freeman of Exeter 1845 Doc 21835
WALLAN Catharine of Exeter 1845 Doc 21835
WALLAN James (c) of Exeter 1845 Doc 21835
WALLAS Rueben of Deerfield 1788 Doc 10397
WALLCE Sarah of Epping 1853 Doc 2085
WALLEY Elizabeth of Portsmouth 1851 Doc 311
WALLINGFORD Cato of Exeter 1784 Doc 7181
WALLIS Dolly Pauls of Exeter 1842 Doc 20107
WALLIS Anna of Kingston 1790 Doc 11310
WALLIS Catherine of Exeter 1842 Doc 20107
WALLIS Charles H of Epping 1845 Doc 21835
WALLIS Elizabeth of Portsmouth 1789 Doc 10754
WALLIS Freeman of Exeter 1842 Doc 20107
WALLIS George of Exeter 1842 Doc 20107
WALLIS James of Exeter 1842 Doc 20107
WALLIS James of Epping 1794 Doc 14339
WALLIS Jenney of Epping 1794 Doc 14339
WALLIS Rueben of Portsmouth 1789 Doc 10754
WALLIS Sarah of Epping 1845 Doc 21835
WALLIS Simeon of Nottingham 1792 Doc 12882
WALLS Sarah of Deerfield 1798 Doc 16897
WALLSI Caesar of Exeter 1842 Doc 20107
WALTERS Thomas of Raymond 1785 Doc 8391
WALTON Bathsheba of Salem 1827 Doc 9822
WALTON Susan of Seabrook 1853 Doc 2085
WALTON Susan of Seabrook 1852 Doc 1554
WALTON Susan of Seabrook 1852 Doc 2371
WALTON William of Seabrooke 1845 Doc 21835
WARD Maley of Allenstown 1789 Doc 11025
WARD Sarah of Pittsfield 1790 Doc 11611
WARREN Ira of Portsmouth 1839 Doc 18856
WARREN Ira of Portsmouth 1840 Doc 18857
WASHINGTON David of Deerfield 1822 Doc 3416
WASHINGTON George of Deerfield 1822 Doc 3416
WATE Dolly of Atkinson 1851 Doc 931
WATE Dolly of Brentwood 1845 Doc 21835
WATE Dolly of Brentwood 1844 Doc 21216
WATE Dolly of Brentwood 1846 Doc 22356
WATE Dorothy of Brentwood 1850 Doc 311
WATE Dorothy of Brentwood 1854 Doc 2371

WATER Deborah of Derry 1828 Doc 9823
WATERS Thomas of Londonderry 1828 Doc 9823
WATERS Thomas of Exeter 1784 Doc 7181
WATKINS Abner of Sandown 1809 Doc 30749
WATKINS Aderm of Windham 1812 Doc 34232
WATKINS John of Windham 1810 Doc 32331
WATKINS John of Exeter 1810 Doc 31571
WATKINS John of Windham 1810 Doc 31571
WATKINS Lydia (c) of Sandown 1809 Doc 30749
WATKINS Mariam of Sandown 1809 Doc 30749
WATKINS Ruth (c) of Sandown 1809 Doc 30749
WATKINS Thomas of Portsmouth 1851 Doc 311
WATSON Amy of Brentwood 1845 Doc 21835
WATSON Ann of Brentwood 1787 Doc 10016
WATSON Anna of Brentwood 1851 Doc 931
WATSON Anna of Brentwood 1843 Doc 20629 S
WATSON Anna of Brentwood 1842 Doc 20629 A
WATSON Anna of Brentwood 1842 Doc 20424
WATSON Anna of Brentwood 1844 Doc 21216
WATSON Anna of Brentwood 1853 Doc 2085
WATSON Anna of Brentwood 1846 Doc 22356
WATSON Anna of Brentwood 1850 Doc 311
WATSON Ebenezer of Hawke 1781 Doc 4574
WATSON John of Atkinson 1774 Doc 2656
WATSON Susanna of Epping 1792 Doc 12882
WATSON William of Epping 1792 Doc 12882
WATTS Edward of Portsmouth 1843 Doc 20629
WATTS Olive R of Portsmouth 1843 Doc 20629
WATTS Olive R of Portsmouth 1846 Doc 22356
WEAR Dianah of Portsmouth 1828 Doc 9200
WEAR Dianah of Portsmouth 1832 Doc 13755
WEAR Dianah of Portsmouth 1832 Doc 13754
WEARE Daniel of Hampton Falls 1783 Doc 5923
WEARE Dianah of Portsmouth 1830 Doc 12197
WEARE Dianah of Portsmouth 1830 Doc 12197
WEARE Dianah of Portsmouth 1825 Doc 6965
WEARE Dianah of Portsmouth 1827 Doc 8073
WEARE Dianah of Portsmouth 1831 Doc 13081
WEARE Ester of Hampton Falls 1783 Doc 5923
WEBBAR Stephen of Deerfield 1844 Doc 21216
WEBBER Abijah of Hillsboro 1818 Doc 45992
WEBBER Stephan of Deerfield 1843 Doc 20629 S
WEBSTER David of Portsmouth 1842 Doc 20424
WEBSTER Guiliam of Deerfield 1816 Doc 40757
WEBSTER Mary E of Portsmouth 1852 Doc 1554
WEBSTER Molly/Mary of Exeter 1799 Doc 17750
WEBSTER Poly of Kingston 1799 Doc 18299
WEBSTER Sarah of Deerfield 1850 Doc 311
WEED Elijah of Kingston 1790 Doc 11310
WEED John of Portsmouth 1840 Doc 18857
WEEKS Abigail of Exeter 1781 Doc 4574
WEEKS Elizabeth of Loudon 1789 Doc 10911

WEEKS Hannah of Loudon 1823 Doc 3965
WEEKS Leonard of Loudon 1789 Doc 10911
WEEKS Martha of Epping 1838 Doc 17910
WEEKS Martha of Gilford 1838 Doc 18543
WEEKS Rebecca of Portsmouth 1838 Doc 18267
WEEKS Thomas of Gilford 1838 Doc 18543
WEEKS Thomas of Epping 1838 Doc 17910
WEIGHT Dorothy of Brentwood 1844 Doc 21216
WELCH Betsey of Portsmouth 1853 Doc 2086
WELCH Betsey of Portsmouth 1837 Doc 16931
WELCH Betsey of Portsmouth 1836 Doc 16214
WELCH Betsey of Portsmouth 1851 Doc 932
WELCH Betsey of Portsmouth 1851 Doc 932
WELCH Betsey of Portsmouth 1851 Doc 931
WELCH Bridget of Portsmouth 1851 Doc 931
WELCH Bridgett of Portsmouth 1852 Doc 1554
WELCH Christianna of Portsmouth 1839 Doc 18856
WELCH Christinna of Portsmouth 1841 Doc 19510
WELCH Deborah of Bow 1792 Doc 13587
WELCH Deborah (c) of Bow 1792 Doc 13587
WELCH Elizabeth of Nottingham 1842 Doc 20424
WELCH Gilman of Northwood 1822 Doc 3416
WELCH James of Portsmouth 1830 Doc 12197
WELCH James of Portsmouth 1851 Doc 931
WELCH James of Portsmouth 1830 Doc 12197
WELCH James of Portsmouth 1834 Doc 14818
WELCH James of Portsmouth 1851 Doc 311
WELCH John of Bow 1792 Doc 13587
WELCH John of Deerfield 1883 Doc 2086
WELCH Lucretia (c) of Bow 1792 Doc 13587
WELCH Mary (alias) of Greenland 1777 Doc 4164
WELCH Mary Morfery of Newmarket 1774 Doc 2656
WELCH Nancy (c) of Bow 1792 Doc 13587
WELCH Olive of Rockingham County 1831 Doc 13399
WELCH Oliver of Rockingham County 1826 Doc 6965
WELCH Patrick of Portsmouth 1835 Doc 15900
WELCH Patrick of Rockingham County 1851 Doc 931
WELCH Patrick of Portsmouth 1836 Doc 16214
WELCH Patrick of Portsmouth 1837 Doc 16931
WELCH Rachal of ? 1816 Doc 40757
WELCH Rachel (c) of Bow 1792 Doc 13587
WELCH Sally (c) of Bow 1792 Doc 13587
WELLCH Bridget of Portsmouth 1851 Doc 311
WELLS Jane of Deerfield 1800 Doc 18692
WELLS John of Deerfield 1800 Doc 18692
WENTWORTH Isaac of Greenland 1851 Doc 931
WENTWORTH Jacob of Sandown 1846 Doc 22356
WENTWORTH Jacob of Greenland 1843 Doc 21216
WENTWORTH Jacob of Greenland 1843 Doc 20629 A
WENTWORTH Job of Portsmouth 1852 Doc 1554
WENTWORTH Job of Portsmouth 1852 Doc 1555
WENTWORTH Job of Portsmouth 1852 Doc 1555

WENTWORTH Luke of Newmarket 1845 Doc 21835
WENTWORTH Mary F of Portsmouth 1846 Doc 22356
WENTWORTH Mary F of Portsmouth 1851 Doc 311
WENTWORTH Mary F of Portsmouth 1852 Doc 1554
WENTWORTH Mary F of Portsmouth 1851 Doc 931
WESCOTT Jeremiah of Chester 1832 Doc 13754
WEST Betsey (c) of Poplin 1845 Doc 21835
WEST Betsey (c) of Poplin 1845 Doc 21835
WEST Betsey (c) of Poplin 1846 Doc 22356
WEST Betsy (c) of Poplin 1844 Doc 21216
WEST Betty of Deerfield 1804 Doc 22771
WEST Deborah of Deerfield 1804 Doc 22771
WEST Edward of Kingston 1797 Doc 16546
WEST Edward (c) of Poplin 1791 Doc 12531
WEST Elizabeth (c) of Poplin 1845 Doc 21835
WEST Elizabeth (c) of Poplin 1846 Doc 22356
WEST Elizabeth (c) of Poplin 1844 Doc 21216
WEST Hannah of Poplin 1791 Doc 12531
WEST Hannah of Nottingham 1854 Doc 2371
WEST Hannah of Nottingham 1852 Doc 1554
WEST Hannah of Deerfield 1804 Doc 22771
WEST Hannah (c) of Nottingham 1850 Doc 311
WEST Henry of Poplin 1846 Doc 22356
WEST Henry of Poplin 1845 Doc 21835
WEST Henry (c) of Poplin 1844 Doc 21216
WEST Henry M of Poplin 1843 Doc 20629
WEST Issac of Poplin 1791 Doc 12531
WEST Jeremiah (c) of Poplin 1844 Doc 21216
WEST Jonathan of Poplin 1844 Doc 21216
WEST Jonathan of Poplin 1845 Doc 21835
WEST Jonathan of Poplin 1846 Doc 22356
WEST Jonathan of Poplin 1798 Doc 17408
WEST Jonathan of Hawke 1803 Doc 21796
WEST Martha of Poplin 1846 Doc 22356
WEST Martha of Poplin 1845 Doc 21835
WEST Martha Mace of Poplin 1844 Doc 21216
WEST Mary of Hawke 1803 Doc 21796
WEST Molly (c) of Brentwood 1772 Doc 1880
WEST Nehemiah of Poplin 1791 Doc 12531
WEST Nehemiah of Brentwood 1843 Doc 20629 S
WEST Nehemiah of Brentwood 1842 Doc 20629 A
WEST Nehemiah of Brentwood 1842 Doc 20424
WEST Nehemiah of Deerfield 1817 Doc 44178
WEST Nehemiah of Kingston 1797 Doc 16546
WEST Nehemiah of Brentwood 1844 Doc 21216
WEST Nehemiah of Poplin 1793 Doc 13587
WEST Orin (c) of Poplin 1845 Doc 21835
WEST Orin (c) of Poplin 1844 Doc 21216
WEST Rebecker of Brentwood 1772 Doc 1880
WEST Rosanna of Poplin 1845 Doc 21835
WEST Rosanna (c) of Poplin 1844 Doc 21216
WEST Salley of Poplin 1845 Doc 21835

WEST Sally of Poplin 1846 Doc 22356
WEST Sally of Deerfield 1804 Doc 22771
WEST Sally (c) of Poplin 1844 Doc 21216
WEST Sarah of Poplin 1793 Doc 13587
WEST Sarah Ann (c) of Poplin 1844 Doc 21216
WEST Sarah Ann (c) of Poplin 1846 Doc 22356
WEST Sarah Ann (c) of Poplin 1845 Doc 21835
WEST Susan (c) of Poplin 1845 Doc 21835
WEST Susannah (c) of Hawke 1803 Doc 21796
WEST Wealtha of Greenfield 1831 Doc 12683
WESTON Ina of Derry 1852 Doc 1554
WGUTEKLOCK Mary of Portsmouth 1838 Doc 18267
WHAFFE Elizabeth Jane of Portsmouth 1828 Doc 9200
WHAFFE Hannah of Portsmouth 1828 Doc 9200
WHALING John of Chester 1836 Doc 16931
WHALING John of Chester 1839 Doc 18267
WHALING John of Chester 1844 Doc 21216
WHALING John of Chester 1835 Doc 16214
WHARF Sally of Auburn 1852 Doc 1554
WHARF Sally of Auburn 1853 Doc 2371
WHARFA Sally of Auburn 1851 Doc 931
WHARFFE Elizabeth of Portsmouth 1827 Doc 8073
WHARFFE Hannah of Portsmouth 1827 Doc 8073
WHEELER William (c) of Bow 1791 Doc 12228
WHEELER Clark of ? 1852 Doc 1555
WHEELER Clark of Portsmouth 1852 Doc 1554
WHEELER Jeremiah (c) of Bow 1791 Doc 12228
WHEELER Levina of Bow 1791 Doc 12228
WHEELER Levina (c) of Bow 1791 Doc 12228
WHEELER Nathan of Deerfield 1793 Doc 13587
WHEELER William of Bow 1791 Doc 12228
WHERREN Joseph of Rockingham County 1831 Doc 13399
WHIDDEN Rose of Exeter 1791 Doc 12531
WHIDDEN Samuel of Portsmouth 1791 Doc 12228
WHIDDEN Wilett of Greenland 1793 Doc 13190
WHITCHER Elle of Plaistow 1793 Doc 13587
WHITCHER Rueben of Nottingham 1789 Doc 11183
WHITCOMB Salome of Exeter 1796 Doc 15359
WHITE Catharine of Derry 1852 Doc 1554
WHITE Catharine of Derry 1845 Doc 21835
WHITE Catharine of Derry 1846 Doc 22356
WHITE Catharine of Derry 1844 Doc 21216
WHITE Catherine of Derry 1851 Doc 931
WHITE Catherine of Derry 1843 Doc 20629 S
WHITE Catherine of Derry 1850 Doc 311
WHITE Catherine of Derry 1842 Doc 20424
WHITE Catherine (Negro) of Derry 1842 Doc 20107
WHITE Cynthia of Portsmouth 1837 Doc 16931
WHITE Cynthia of Portsmouth 1839 Doc 18856
WHITE Cynthia of Portsmouth 1840 Doc 18856
WHITE Jane of Derry 1850 Doc 311
WHITE Jane of Derry 1841 Doc 19510

WHITE Jane (Negro) of Derry 1842 Doc 20107
WHITE Jane of Derry 1843 Doc 20629 S
WHITE Jane of Derry 1853 Doc 2371
WHITE Jane of Derry 1844 Doc 21216
WHITE Jane of Derry 1851 Doc 931
WHITE Jane of Derry 1832 Doc 13399
WHITE Jane of Derry 1830 Doc 12197
WHITE Jane of Derry 1829 Doc 11709
WHITE Jane of Derry 1837 Doc 16931
WHITE Jane of Derry 1846 Doc 22356
WHITE Jane of Derry 1853 Doc 2085
WHITE Jane of Derry 1840 Doc 18856
WHITE Jane of Derry 1845 Doc 21835
WHITE John of Londonderry 1826 Doc 7524
WHITE John of Salem 1826 Doc 7524
WHITE John of Chichester 1817 Doc 44178
WHITE John of Pittsfield 1817 Doc 44178
WHITE John of Salem 1827 Doc 8655
WHITE John of Derry 1829 Doc 10409
WHITE John of Derry 1829 Doc 11709
WHITE John of Salem 1827 Doc 9822
WHITE Joseph (Negro) of Exeter 1850 Doc 311
WHITE Joseph of Windham 1788 Doc 10525
WHITE June of Derry 1839 Doc 18267
WHITE Leonard of Exeter 1851 Doc 931
WHITE Levi (Negro) of Derry 1842 Doc 20107
WHITE Martha Jane (c) of Exeter 1830 Doc 11710
WHITE Mary of Newmarket 1795 Doc 14879
WHITE Nancy of Derry 1851 Doc 931
WHITE Nancy of Derry 1846 Doc 22356
WHITE Nancy of Derry 1853 Doc 2371
WHITE Nancy of Derry 1845 Doc 21835
WHITE Nancy (Negro) of ? 1842 Doc 20107
WHITE Nancy of Derry 1852 Doc 1554
WHITE Nancy of Derry 1842 Doc 20424
WHITE Nancy of Derry 1853 Doc 2085
WHITE Nathaniel of Rockingham County 1826 Doc 6965
WHITE Nicolas of Plaistow 1842 Doc 20424
WHITE Philis (alias) of Exeter 1830 Doc 11710
WHITE Sally of Plaistow 1845 Doc 21835
WHITE Sarah of Plaistow 1842 Doc 20424
WHITE Sarah W of Plaistow 1842 Doc 20424
WHITE Suskey/Susan (Negro) of Derry 1842 Doc 20107
WHITE William of Newmarket 1795 Doc 14879
WHITEFIELD Joseph (Negro) of Exeter 1799 Doc 17750
WHITLOCK Mary of Portsmouth 1839 Doc 18856
WHITLOCK Mary of Portsmouth 1836 Doc 16214
WHITMAN Charlotte of Raymond 1792 Doc 12882
WHITTIER James of Loudon 1790 Doc 11611
WHORF Sally of Auburn 1843 Doc 311
WIAT John of Portsmouth 1789 Doc 10754
WIDDEN Violet of Exeter 1792 Doc 12882

WIGGIN Aaron of Deerfield 1819 Doc 46680
WIGGIN Deborah of Stratham 1802 Doc 21391
WIGGIN Martha of Raymond 1790 Doc 11310
WIGGIN Winthrop of Greenland 1795 Doc 15018
WIGGINS Andrew of Newmarket 1783 Doc 6644
WIGGINS Caroline of Plymouth 1821 Doc 1592
WIGGINS Chase of Canterbury 1816 Doc 40757
WIGGINS James W of Stratham 1850 Doc 311
WIGGINS Martha of Brentwood 1789 Doc 11025
WIGGINS Mary of Newmarket 1783 Doc 6644
WIGGINS Molley of Exeter 1795 Doc 14648
WILEY Bridget of Portsmouth 1831 Doc 13081
WILEY James of Exeter 1842 Doc 20107
WILEY James of Exeter 1840 Doc 19510
WILEY Josiah of Nottingham 1845 Doc 21835
WILKINSON Allen of Epping 1794 Doc 14339
WILKINSON Betsey of Epping 1794 Doc 14339
WILKINSON David of Portsmouth 1828 Doc 9200
WILKISON Ellishar of Deerfield 1794 Doc 14339
WILKISON Samuel of Deerfield 1794 Doc 14339
WILLARD Joshua of Epsom 1819 Doc 47427
WILLET Polley of Chichester 1817 Doc 44178
WILLET Rhoda of Raymond 1790 Doc 11910
WILLEY Edwin of Gilford 1840 Doc 18857
WILLEY Jacob of Gilford 1840 Doc 18857
WILLEY Phebe of Gilford 1840 Doc 18857
WILLEY Bunea Lousa of Hampstead 1867 Doc 9409
WILLEY Charley of Nottingham 1842 Doc 20424
WILLEY Cynthia A of Hampstead 1867 Doc 9409
WILLEY Edwin of Gilford 1840 Doc 18858
WILLEY Fay (c) of Nothington 1777 Doc 3981
WILLEY Jacob of Gilford 1840 Doc 18858
WILLEY Jonathan of Nottingham 1842 Doc 20424
WILLEY Jonathan of Deerfield 1807 Doc 28434
WILLEY Jonathan (c) of Deerfield 1807 Doc 28434
WILLEY Mary of Nottingham 1777 Doc 3981
WILLEY Mary (c) of Nottingham 1777 Doc 3981
WILLEY Mary Felker of Nottingham 1842 Doc 20424
WILLEY Norah B (c) of Hampstead 1867 Doc 9409
WILLEY Phebe of Gilford 1840 Doc 18858
WILLEY Polly/Mary of Stratham 1801 Doc 20206
WILLEY Rhoda of Deerfield 1807 Doc 28434
WILLEY Rhoda (c) of Nottingham 1842 Doc 20424
WILLEY Robert of Nottingham 1777 Doc 3981
WILLEY Sally of Pittsfield 1801 Doc 19665
WILLEY Stephen of Rockingham County 1826 Doc 6965
WILLEY Vowel of Northwood 1836 Doc 16215
WILLIAM Benjamin of Portsmouth 1842 Doc 20424
WILLIAM John of Salem 1793 Doc 14018
WILLIAM Nancy of Portsmouth 1842 Doc 20424
WILLIAM Sarah of Salem 1793 Doc 14018
WILLIAMS Asa of Portsmouth 1837 Doc 16931

WILLIAMS John of Windham 1810 Doc 33660
WILLIAMS John of Portsmouth 1832 Doc 13082
WILLIAMS John of Windham 1795 Doc 15359
WILLIAMS John of Derry 1850 Doc 311
WILLIAMS John B of Portsmouth 1831 Doc 13082
WILLIAMS John B of Portsmouth 1832 Doc 13755
WILLIAMS John B of Portsmouth 1832 Doc 13754
WILLIAMS Lydia of Portsmouth 1842 Doc 20424
WILLIAMS Peter of ? 1782 Doc 5272
WILLIAMS Phebe of Portsmouth 1851 Doc 311
WILLIAMS Phebe of Portsmouth 1851 Doc 931
WILLIAMS Phebe of Portsmouth 1852 Doc 1554
WILLIAMS Phebe of Portsmouth 1846 Doc 22356
WILLIAMS Rebecca of Portsmouth 1846 Doc 22356
WILLIAMS Rebecca of Portsmouth 1851 Doc 311
WILLIAMS Rebecca of Portsmouth 1852 Doc 1554
WILLIAMS Rebecca of Portsmouth 1851 Doc 931
WILLIAMS Rebecca of Portsmouth 1843 Doc 20629
WILLIAMS Sarah of Windham 1795 Doc 15359
WILLIAMS Thomas of Portsmouth 1851 Doc 931
WILLIAMS Thomas of Portsmouth 1850 Doc 932
WILLIE Isaah of Nothingham 1785 Doc 9466
WILLIE John of Northwood 1788 Doc 10397
WILLIE Jona of Northwood 1805 Doc 24720
WILLIE Jona Jr of Northwood 1805 Doc 24720
WILLIE Roda of Northwood 1805 Doc 24720
WILLMOUTH Huldah of Rye 1800 Doc 19247
WILLOT Reuben of Weare 1817 Doc 44178
WILLY Robert of Portsmouth 1833 Doc 14119
WILS Eseral of Windham 1787 Doc 10142
WILS Mary of Windham 1787 Doc 10142
WILSON Aaron (Negro) of Portsmouth 1843 Doc 20629
WILSON Sally (Negro) of Portsmouth 1843 Doc 20629
WILSON Clem of E Kingston 1805 Doc 24720
WILSON Clement of Kingston 1797 Doc 16546
WILSON Hannah of E Kingston 1805 Doc 24720
WILSON Hannah of S Hampton 1845 Doc 21835
WILSON John of Londonderry 1846 Doc 22358
WILSON John of Windham 1819 Doc 47427
WILSON John of Sandown 1813 Doc 36435
WILSON John (c) of E Kingston 1805 Doc 24720
WILSON Mary of Stratham 1834 Doc 15123
WILSON Mary (c) of Stratham 1834 Doc 15123
WILSON Merry of Stratham 1835 Doc 15557
WILSON Nathaniel of Londonderry 1845 Doc 21835
WILSON Nathaniel of Londonderry 1851 Doc 931
WILSON Nathaniel of Londonderry 1852 Doc 1554
WILSON Nathaniel of Londonderry 1850 Doc 311
WILSON Nathaniel (c) of Epping 1799 Doc 18299
WILSON Nathaniel of Londonderry 1846 Doc 22356
WILSON Peggy of Londonderry 1850 Doc 311
WILSON Peggy of Londonderry 1854 Doc 2371

WILSON Peggy of Londonderry 1853 Doc 2085
WILSON Peggy of Londonderry 1852 Doc 1554
WILSON Peggy of Londonderry 1851 Doc 931
WILSON Peggy of Londonderry 1845 Doc 21835
WILSON Peggy (Illegitimate) of Londonderry 1846 Doc 22356
WILSON Rachel of Londonderry 1846 Doc 22358
WILSON W of Portsmouth 1852 Doc 1554
WINN Francis of Candia 1836 Doc 16214
WINN Francis of Candia 1836 Doc 16931
WINN Francis P of Exeter 1835 Doc 16214
WINN Samuel of Portsmouth 1830 Doc 12197
WINTHROP Kezia of Newington 1772 Doc 731
WITHAM Enoch of Candia 1851 Doc 931
WITHAM William of Portsmouth 1839 Doc 18267
WITHAM William of Portsmouth 1839 Doc 18856
WITTS Leonard D of Portsmouth 1853 Doc 2086
WIZWILL Joseph of Poplin 1804 Doc 23419
WODDEL Betty of Poplin 1788 Doc 10640
WOLINSFORD Cato of Brentwood 1799 Doc 17750
WOLINSFORD Pegg of Brentwood 1799 Doc 17750
WOOD Ann of Portsmouth 1839 Doc 18542
WOOD Ann of Portsmouth 1846 Doc 22356
WOOD Cord of Portsmouth 1851 Doc 931
WOOD Joseph of Portsmouth 1846 Doc 22356
WOOD Joseph (c) of Pembroke 1797 Doc 16546
WOOD Louis of S Hampton 1836 Doc 16215
WOOD Louis of S Hampton 1836 Doc 16215
WOOD Nancy of Pembroke 1797 Doc 16546
WOOD Nancy (c) of Pembroke 1797 Doc 16546
WOOD Ora of Portsmouth 1851 Doc 311
WOOD Poly (c) of Pembroke 1797 Doc 16546
WOOD Richard of Pembroke 1797 Doc 16546
WOOD Richard (c) of Pembroke 1797 Doc 16546
WOOD Tim of S Hampton 1836 Doc 16931
WOOD Timothy of S Hampton 1836 Doc 16215
WOOD Timothy of Portsmouth 1833 Doc 14119
WOODARD Samuel of Portsmouth 1832 Doc 13754
WOODARD Tanner of Hawke 1790 Doc 11310
WOODBURY John of Raymond 1785 Doc 8644
WOODMAN Charles of Exeter 1831 Doc 13399
WOODMAN Israel of S Hampton 1841 Doc 19510
WOODMAN Israel of Kingston 1842 Doc 20107
WOODMAN Loisa of Kingston 1842 Doc 20107
WOODMAN Mary of Poplin 1849 Doc 311
WOODMAN Moses of Poplin 1849 Doc 311
WOODMAN Nathan of S Hampton 1846 Doc 22356
WOODMAN Samuel of S Hampton 1841 Doc 19510
WOODMAN Susannah of S Hampton 1850 Doc 311
WOODMAN Susannah of S Hampton 1846 Doc 22356
WOODS Ann Maria Perry of Dover 1852 Doc 2086
WOODS Ann of Portsmouth 1840 Doc 18856
WOODS Ann of Portsmouth 1839 Doc 18856

WOODS Ann of Portsmouth 1840 Doc 18857
WOODS Eleanor of Portsmouth 1832 Doc 13755
WOODS George of Portsmouth 1851 Doc 311
WOODS George of Portsmouth 1843 Doc 20629
WOODS James of Dover 1852 Doc 2086
WOODS Margaret of Dover 1852 Doc 2086
WOODS Mary of Portsmouth 1843 Doc 20629
WOODS Michael of Portsmouth 1852 Doc 1554
WOODS Michael of Portsmouth 1851 Doc 931
WOODS Michael of Portsmouth 1851 Doc 932
WOODS Michael of Portsmouth 1850 Doc 932
WOODS Michal of Portsmouth 1852 Doc 1555
WOODWARD Samuel of Portsmouth 1832 Doc 13399
WOODWARD Tamar of Hampstead 1852 Doc 1554
WOODWARD Tamara of Hampstead 1850 Doc 311
WOODWARD Tanner of Hampstead 1851 Doc 931
WOOLMAN Sam of ? 1782 Doc 5272
WORMEWARD William of Raymond 1783 Doc 6232
WORMWOOD Mary of Raymond 1784 Doc 7459
WORTHEN Asa of Poplin 1844 Doc 21216
WORTHEN Asa of Poplin 1839 Doc 17185
WORTHEN Asa of Poplin 1845 Doc 21835
WORTHEN Asa of Poplin 1843 Doc 20629 A
WORTHEN Asa of Poplin 1853 Doc 2086
WORTHEN Asa of Poplin 1853 Doc 2085
WORTHEN Asa Jr (c) of Poplin 1853 Doc 2086
WORTHEN Charlet of Raymond 1850 Doc 931
WORTHEN Charlot of ? 1850 Doc 311
WORTHEN Charlot of Raymond 1844 Doc 21503
WORTHEN Charlott of Raymond 1843 Doc 20928
WORTHEN Charlott of Raymond 1850 Doc 1554
WORTHEN Charlott of Raymond 1846 Doc 22356
WORTHEN Charlotta of Raymond 1853 Doc 2371
WORTHEN Charlotte of Raymond 1853 Doc 2371
WORTHEN Charlotte of Raymond 1843 Doc 20629 A
WORTHEN Charlotte of Raymond 1843 Doc 20928
WORTHEN Charlotte of Raymond 1853 Doc 2085
WORTHEN Elizabeth of Kingston 1855 Doc 3620
WORTHEN Elizabeth Mary of Poplin 1849 Doc 24261
WORTHEN Enoch of Candia 1853 Doc 2085
WORTHEN Enoch of Candia 1855 Doc 3620
WORTHEN Enoch of Candia 1854 Doc 2371
WORTHEN Enoch of Candia 1850 Doc 311
WORTHEN Enoch of Candia 1842 Doc 20107
WORTHEN Enoch of Candia 1852 Doc 1554
WORTHEN Enoch of Candia 1843 Doc 20629 S
WORTHEN Enock of Candia 1845 Doc 21835
WORTHEN Ezekiel of Poplin 1797 Doc 16546
WORTHEN Jeremiah (c) of Poplin 1845 Doc 21835
WORTHEN John (c) of Poplin 1845 Doc 21835
WORTHEN John (c) of Poplin 1844 Doc 21216
WORTHEN John (c) of Poplin 1853 Doc 2086

WORTHEN Mary of Poplin 1853 Doc 2086
WORTHEN Mary of Poplin 1844 Doc 21216
WORTHEN Mary of Poplin 1843 Doc 20629 A
WORTHEN Mary of Poplin 1845 Doc 21835
WORTHEN Mary of Poplin 1843 Doc 20629
WORTHEN Mary of Poplin 1845 Doc 21835
WORTHEN Mary (c) of Poplin 1853 Doc 2086
WORTHEN Mehitable of Hampstead 1851 Doc 931
WORTHEN Mehitable of Hampstead 1850 Doc 311
WORTHEN Polly of Candia 1842 Doc 20424
WORTHEN Samuel of Candia 1842 Doc 20424
WORTHEN Samuel of Candia 1845 Doc 21835
WORTHEN Samuel of Candia 1843 Doc 20629 S
WORTHEN Samuel of Candia 1846 Doc 22356
WORTHEN Samuel of Candia 1842 Doc 20107
WORTHEN Sarah of Poplin 1797 Doc 16546
WORTHEN Seven of E Kingston 1838 Doc 17909
WORTHING Samuel of Poplin 1805 Doc 24720
WREAY Mary of Windham 1788 Doc 10525
WRIGHT Eunice of Londonderry 1812 Doc 35625
WYAM Luke of Londonderry 1839 Doc 18267
YEATON Ann of Portsmouth 1817 Doc 44178
YEATON Hannah of Portsmouth 1842 Doc 20424
YEATON Hannah of Portsmouth 1846 Doc 22356
YEATON Hannah of Portsmouth 1851 Doc 311
YEATON Hannah of Portsmouth 1851 Doc 931
YEATON Hannah of Portsmouth 1852 Doc 1554
YEATON Lydia of Hillsboro 1830 Doc 11981
YEATON Lydia of Newcastle 1830 Doc 11981
YEATON Lydia of Newcastle 1830 Doc 20107
YEATON Samuel of Portsmouth 1842 Doc 20424
YORK Alfred of Gilmanton 1826 Doc 6965
YORK Daniel of Allenstown 1819 Doc 47427
YORK Dolley of Strafford 1822 Doc 2912
YORK Dorothy of Exeter 1815 Doc 39186
YORK Dorothy of Brentwood 1815 Doc 39186
YORK Elizabeth of Exeter 1819 Doc 46680
YORK Elizabeth (c) of Epping 1819 Doc 47427
YORK Francis of Portsmouth 1831 Doc 13081
YORK Freeman of Portsmouth 1831 Doc 13081
YORK Jane (c) of Epping 1819 Doc 47427
YORK John of Brentwood 1800 Doc 19247
YORK Jonathan of Exeter 1843 Doc 20629 S
YORK Joseph of Epping 1785 Doc 9466
YORK Lucy of Deerfield 1818 Doc 45992
YORK Moley of Brentwood 1799 Doc 17750
YORK Moses (Negro) of Exeter 1850 Doc 311
YORK Polly of Epping 1819 Doc 47427
YORK Rachel of Exeter 1796 Doc 15359
YORK Richard of Exeter 1796 Doc 15359
YORK Sally of Newmarket 1843 Doc 20629
YORK Sally of Newmarket 1852 Doc 1554

YORK Sally of Newmarket 1845 Doc 21216
YORK Samuel of Newmarket 1845 Doc 21216
YORK Samuel of Newmarket 1843 Doc 20928
YORK Sarah of Exeter 1773 Doc 2472
YORK Thaxter of Epping 1819 Doc 47427
YORK Wife Of Robert of Epping 1799 Doc 18299
YORKE Sarah of Brentwood 1790 Doc 11910
YOUNG Daniel of Raymond 1846 Doc 22356
YOUNG Hannah of Hampstead 1772 Doc 1612
YOUNG Hannah of Pittsfield 1834 Doc 15123
YOUNG James of Raymond 1846 Doc 22356
YOUNG Louisa of Portsmouth 1837 Doc 16931
YOUNG Mary of Nottingham 1808 Doc 29235
YOUNG Moses (c) of Hampstead 1772 Doc 1612
YOUNG Nathaniel (servant) of Hampstead 1772 Doc 1612
YOUNG Reuben of Windham 1834 Doc 15123
YOUNG Rueben of Pittsfield 1835 Doc 15557
YOUNG Samuel of Hampstead 1772 Doc 1612
YOUNG Sarah of Atkinson 1774 Doc 2656
YOUNG Susannah of Stratham 1798 Doc 16897
ZACHEUS (Negro) of Exeter 1772 Doc 1880
ZANE Timothy H of Portsmouth 1845 Doc 21835
ZIMMERMAN Abby of Portsmouth 1827 Doc 8073
ZIMMERMAN Abby of Portsmouth 1828 Doc 9200
ZIMMERMAN John E of Portsmouth 1828 Doc 9200
ZIMMERMAN John E of Portsmouth 1827 Doc 8073
ZIMMERMAN John E of Portsmouth 1830 Doc 12197

www.ingramcontent.com/pod-product-compliance
Lightning Source LLC
Chambersburg PA
CBHW070450090426
42735CB00012B/2504